WHO PUT BELLA IN THE WYCH ELM?

Volume 2: A Crime Shrouded In Mystery

ALEX MERRILL

With

PETE MERRILL

APS PUBLICATIONS

APS Books,
4 Oakleigh Road,
Stourbridge,
West Midlands,
DY8 2JX

APS Books is a subsidiary of
the APS Publications imprint
www.andrewsparke.com

First published worldwide by APS Books in 2019

Front Cover: Rik Rawlings www.rickrawlings.co.uk
Illustrations: Alex & Pete Merrill
Other images reproduced by kind permission of the Library of Birmingham Archives & Collections (LBAC), West Mercia Police and Worcestershire Archive and Archaeology service (WAAS) and Black Country Bugle.
Research: Ann Swabey www.militaryandfamilyresearch.co.uk

ISBN 9781789960624

www.bellawychelm.com

CONTENTS

AUTHOR'S NOTE

Bella, the name attached to the mysterious body discovered in a hollow tree in Hagley Woods in 1943, remains both an unsolved murder and a source of obsession for so many people, both local to the Hagley, Stourbridge and Halesowen areas of the West Midlands of England and further afield.

Following on from 'Who Put Bella In The Wych Elm? Volume 1: The Crime Scene Revisited' which featured a facial reconstruction of Bella's face created by Professor Caroline Wilkinson's team at Liverpool University, the working title of this book was 'The Origins'. My plan was to try and fit both the official and unofficial elements of the mystery together like the pieces of a jigsaw puzzle in order to map out the origin of all the different elements of the story in chronological and themed order; the official version, in the form of the 2005 Police Closure Report, and the unofficial version, derived from scraps of conjecture, theory and gossip.

What I quickly discovered was that the Police Closure Report was less accurate than I had expected it to be. In too many places it is factually wrong and sometimes misleading and it fails to reflect or reference all the different inquiries that are housed in the Worcestershire archive. Being light in content when it comes to the scope and detail of the investigation, it is an unhelpful official overview. Hopefully, this volume addresses that shortfall and provides, for the first time, a detailed review of the case and the police investigation.

Not surprisingly, the unofficial elements of the mystery have, over time, constructed their own versions of what people believe is the truth, making it truly a crime shrouded in mystery. It's an undeniable fact that this murder holds an enduring fascination for many people hut much of what people believe to be based on historical and recorded facts in the case is in fact fiction? More importantly, does the reader know where the story or stories that they are familiar with originate?

Therefore, my aim is to present all the reported and unreported elements of the investigation, so that the reader can make an informed decision on which of the many versions and elements they choose to believe – or not.

Whilst this volume complements my first book, which shone a light on the first phase of the inquiry, revisiting the crime scene, I have updated and included within this volume two chapters from that book: one on the shoes thought to be the victim's and another on the chalked graffiti which the police took so seriously at the time, because of the extra information that I have uncovered, and because both topics are a common theme throughout this book and are referenced in numerous inquiries.

What this book promises is a 'big picture view' of the mystery with new revelations; a fresh perspective of all the different theories, thoroughly researched and referenced, and complemented by historical facsimiles, photographs, and bespoke maps and charts. Above all else it suggests the possibility that the identity of Bella was known to the police long ago and that the case was closed only because prosecutors deemed there to be insufficient evidence that the police had solved a mere gypsy murder. It also asks how much of the stories told by Wilfred Byford-Jones, Una Mossop, Donald McCormick and others was sheer fantasy, invented for personal gain and to sell newspapers and books and whether the shoes discovered at the scene of the crime pushed Professor Webster and his colleagues into misinterpretations of the evidence which set the police off on the wrong trail from the outset.

And surprisingly for some readers, the mystery now focuses more on the town of Halesowen and hardly at all on Hagley.

Alex Merrill

CHAPTER 1
THE SHOES

The skeleton and clothing arrived at the laboratory on the evening of 20th April, 1943, and the first line of inquiry was the shoes.

On 22nd, Dr LUND took the shoes to the England Shoes Shop[1] and was told by the manager, Arthur Charles ENGLAND, that they were of a type made about four years previously and no longer produced or in stock, but possibly made by the Waterfoot Company.

The crime scene shoes were photographed. Three photographs remain within the archive files at Worcester, together with another image of a similar shoe.

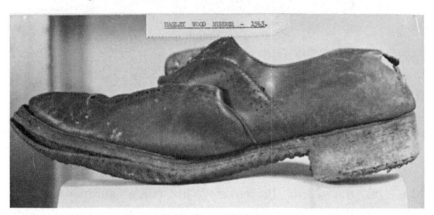

Detective Inspector WILLIAMS was tasked with investigating the source of manufacture and their distribution. At 9.30 a.m. on 23rd April, he attended the laboratory and took possession of the shoes from Professor WEBSTER. He was also in receipt of a letter of introduction from Mr Alan Gordon BARNES, the secretary of the Northampton Boot and Shoe Manufacturers Association.

By 11.30 a.m., DI WILLIAMS arrived in Northampton, meeting with Mr BARNES, who made several observations. He felt that

---

[1] England Shoes 40-42 Corporation Street, 66 New Street and 20 local stores.

the type of shoe was manufactured in an area in Lancashire—
known in the trade as the 'valley'— a Rossendale district called
Waterfront. The 'valley' would turn out to be a false lead.

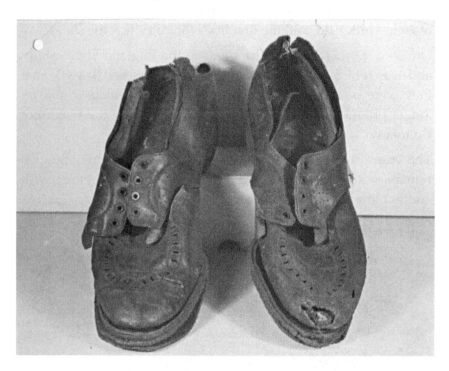

Also, on the 23rd, Professor WEBSTER's autopsy report
concluded that ...*It would appear probable that the pair of shoes
recovered one from the bole of the tree, and the other at some distance,
are connected with this body. These shoes are black shoes, size 5 ½, and
from the information which I obtained, are probably made by Waterfoot
Company, Lancashire. Inspector Williams, however, following his visit
to Northampton, has considerably more information. With regard to
these shoes, and this seems to me a likely line to follow up...*

Forming the opinion that the shoes belonged to the victim, and
the information already obtained about them could well have
influenced the laboratory findings—specifically his and Dr

LUND's opinions on the time (and season) of the murder—as well as the style and period of the clothing worn by the victim.

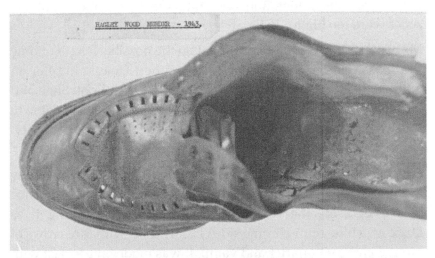

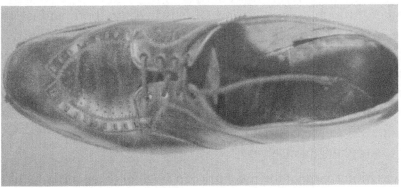

Additional photograph of similar shoe – possibly a prop.

There were also other observations. The shoes were not black but blue; it was felt that they had "seen six months' hard wear"; and the retail cost was somewhere between eight and 16 shillings, a figure which was later to be revised. Finally, DI WILLIAMS stated that "...the shoe size was 5 ½ English standard" and that this was a large shoe for a woman of five feet. He also stated that he would expect a woman of that size to wear size 4 to 4 ½. We now know that Bella was actually shorter than five feet giving her an expected shoe size range between 3 ½ and 4.

There is no reference to the shoe being 'packed out' to help with fitting. Other than DI WILLIAMS' report, I have not uncovered any formal documentation reflecting the observation that the shoes were too big for Bella.

Mr BARNES was asked to comment on the possible length of time the shoes had been exposed to the weather. Unable to offer an opinion, he directed DI WILLIAMS to the British Boot, Shoe and Allied Trades Research Association in Kettering.[2] I was unable to find any official documentation referencing this line of inquiry, and the Association does not hold any archive material.

Finally, on 1st May, DI WILLIAMS attended Clarence Bray Limited in Sileby, near Loughborough, Leicestershire[3]. The shoe was recognised, the company's record book identifying it as D.956—"a blue semi-chrome side Gibson Shoe, with three rows of pin punching on quarter and vamp. It was made on a 97 last with leather through crepe sole and fair stitched fore part, and crepe heel". They confirmed that this type of shoe was manufactured between April and June 1940. Also identified were the companies which the size 5 ½s were supplied to; C.A. ALLEN Ltd. of Bilston, Staffordshire received six pairs; 72 pairs were supplied to a mail order firm called Mr Ambrose WILSON Ltd. of London; and 54 pairs went to Mr DARNELL & Son in Shoreditch, London, who were suppliers themselves.[4]

It was indicated that the retail price in 1940 for these shoes would have been 13s 11d—worth around £48.70[5] today.

Armed with this information, the investigators concentrated their inquiry on the local area. On 4th May,[6] DI WILLIAMS visited

---

[2] Then at 30-36 Thorngate Street, Kettering. Now known as SATRA Technology.
[3] DI WILLIAMS, report dated 2nd May, inquiry regarding ladies shoes found in wood.
[4] BRAY Ltd. supplied four dealers; only three ordered size 5 ½.
[5] The National Archives Currency Converter 2005.
[6] DI WILLIAMS report dated 5th May, 1943, inquiry re ladies shoes.

shops owned by Mr C.A. ALLEN Ltd. in Bilston, Wednesbury and West Bromwich. At the Wednesbury shop, he met with the owner, Mr ALLEN, who indicated that the blue coloured shoe was known in the trade as 'ice'. He explained it was a popular type which retailed quickly, meaning that it would have been sold around June 1940.

Significantly, reference is yet again made to the fact that the shoes "were rather large for a woman of five feet". Therefore, if the shoes had been sold in June and endured six months' wear (as previously indicated), the earliest 'age in the tree' for the shoes would be December 1940—two years and three months before the discovery.

Professor WEBSTER and the police were immediately of the opinion that the shoes belonged to the victim. This is despite the fact that, within the shoes, there was no recovery or reporting of bones, flesh, leaf debris, material from socks, stockings, or padding to help with fitting. This opens the possibility that the shoes are not directly related to Bella at all; instead, they might be in fact replacements (along with other items), designed to confuse the investigators, or rubbish, or not related to Bella at all.

The laboratory clearly had an indication about the possible age of the shoes when they started to piece together what Bella was wearing. Did that knowledge bias the investigators towards a specific style and period of clothing when they were determining what the recovered scraps of her clothing came from?

Furthermore, on 26th April, the inquiry was to get its first lead, and a possible victim, a gypsy named Mary LEE. Did this information also influence the laboratory findings? Did they ignore the obvious and justify their observations by making Bella out to be "neglectful as to her appearance and habits", her social status and the 'make do and mend' culture because her shoes and clothing did not fit?

The next time the shoes would become the focus of the investigation would be in 1978, when a man named Leonard

COGZELL contacted the Black Country Bugle newspaper to tell his story about the shoes[7].

He recalled how he had watched a television programme sometime around 1970 that hosted Professor WEBSTER and discussed the Hagley Wood murder. During the programme, the Professor displayed the shoes recovered from the crime scene and COGZELL recognised them...

---

[7] Chapter 19

CHAPTER 2
ROMANY GYPSY STORIES

Introduction

First, I must explain why I will be using the colloquialism 'Gypsy' rather than the full title of Romani Gypsy, Traveller, or other.

Throughout the 1940s and '50s, the official documentation uses the term 'Gypsy', not just to describe a specific ethnic group, but to anyone who was a 'Caravan Dweller' or 'Hawker'. This even included people who were displaced during wartime and who ended up living in tents because no accommodation was available, or they had hit upon hard times.

In the 2005 Police Closure Report, the word 'Gypsy' had been replaced with 'Traveller', which had by then become the prescribed term. Subsequently, the Council of Europe has stated that the word 'Gypsy' is sometimes considered derogatory because of its negative and stereotypical associations, and that the word 'Romani' is more appropriate.

Just to confuse things further, the UK Equality Act 2010 recognises Gypsies as a specific ethnic group amongst other members of the travelling community with a nomadic lifestyle, and includes Romany Gypsies, Irish Travellers, Scottish Gypsies and Travellers, Welsh Gypsies and Travellers, New Travellers or New Age Travellers, Bargees and other people living in boats, and fairground and circus families, known as travelling showmen.

I am a non Gypsy, or 'Gorgio', but I did become a member of the Gypsy Lore Society in order to try and learn as much as I could about the people, their customs, culture and lifestyle. This certainly does not make me an authority on the subject, and I make no claim to be. Although the halo of false romance disappeared quickly, I have a profound respect, not just for those listed under the Equality Act, but for other Gypsy and traveller cultures, who refer to themselves as Rom, Romanichals, Cale, Sinti, Ludar and Romungre.

I feel comfortable and respectful enough to use the word 'Gypsy', not just within a historical context, but because the individuals themselves I believe were proud of who they were.

The following sections of this book look at all the different stories that have a 'Gypsy' theme, and I have hopefully presented them in such a way as to keep the official facts separate from the gossip, folk lore and different theories that have homogenised over the years into the modern narrative, so that the reader can see the origins of the different versions.

I provide commentary on the six Gypsy inquiries carried out by the police: one in 1942, 13 months before the discovery of the skeleton in the tree; three in 1943 immediately following the discovery; one in 1944; and another in 1949.

These six complicated and complex stories offer little insight when considered individually. It is not until you consider them in their entirety that you start to see a bigger picture of what could have happened and, who knows, the truth of what happened may lie within.

Everything is drawn from the original police files, supported by official documentation such as the census and 1939 Register. I have unpicked the facts from fiction, highlighted where the stories converge, and have provided new revelations along the way.

I also discuss a group of 'missing' Gypsies referenced within some police reports as camping on Hagley Wood Lane, but who do not appear to have been the subject of a dedicated police inquiry, unlike the others, as well as the relevance of the hop-picking workers' encampments, the communities and family groups that stayed there in the summer of 1939, and the Hagley Wood murder, is a significant element to this story. So much so that there is a dedicated chapter to this very topic, which will highlight the connections between the different, previously unconnected, inquiries.

The Mary LEE inquiry

Additionally considerable effort was expended attempting to identify the whereabouts of a Mary WENMAN@ LEE@ BEAVER, a traveller who at one time resided close to the location where the cadaver was recovered. A soldier HEYWOOD, who formerly was having a relationship with the woman and sought to re-establish the relationship, initiated this. By a number of guises he used the Police to initiate an investigation to ascertain her whereabouts. The reality of the situation came to light and HEYWOOD subsequently admitted the details.

The statement made in the 2005 Police Closure Report about the search for a missing girl called Mary LEE, is a single paragraph and would benefit from some correction.

HEYWOOD is spelt wrong; it should read HAYWOOD. The protagonist was a man called Bill FLETCHER and not HAYWOOD, who in fact never met Mary LEE. Also, there are people and places within this inquiry that link to other inquiries, which are not even referenced in the closure report.

The police search for Mary LEE was not as brief as indicated. Rather, it was a complicated and complex affair that lasted for seven months. The 'guise' mentioned was discovered within weeks, yet the search resumed.

This story had its origins in 1942, 13 months before the discovery of the skeleton. Two soldiers and an Army chaplain contacted the police, inquiring about a missing Gypsy girl called Mary LEE or LEA. The police investigated at the time, but being unable to trace her, filed the letters. When the skeleton was discovered, the significance of this potential line of inquiry was quickly identified and was highlighted to the murder inquiry[8] on 26th April 1943.

---

[8] Report: 26th April 1943. Skeleton found at Hagley, DC 215 John W LEE, Halesowen.

At the outset on 1st January 1942, a letter sent on 29th December 1941 was received by Halesowen Police. It was signed as being from a serving soldier named Private 4915824 H. HAYWOOD. He asked about a traveller known as Mary LEE who had been staying on Mr JAMES's Farm, at Illey, Halesowen, and stated that he was worried about her. The police inquired and responded in a letter on 12th January, indicating that, although it was confirmed a family named LEE had stayed at the farm, a Mary LEE was not known amongst them.

Six months later, on 20th July 1942, another letter was received, but this time sent to the police at Oldbury and from a different soldier, a Private 4920132 W. FLETCHER. He also asked about the wellbeing of Mary LEE.

A response was sent on 22nd July – no trace found.

The following month, a third (typed) letter was received, this time from an Army Chaplain, A.G.

Superintendent.

For information of
Insp. Bache.
Jes
20.7.42

I have been
informed that a certain person
bearing the name of Mary Lee
as been seen on several occasions
around your district and am
led to believe that she maybe
residing there so will you please
do me the favour of locating
her for me because I lost
touch with her when I went
abroad and I am going
frantic to find so will you
please for my sake as well
or for her do the best you can

Descriptions. Height 5ft 2ins. Black
curly hair, full set of pure
white teeth, and complexion
very dark. You will very
likely find her on a farm

2

because she is a traveller
and she maybe going round
with a basket hawking stuff.
Sir if you can't find anything
of her please write and let me
know

Your Most Humble
Servant.

Pte. W. FLETCHER
4920132. 2 No. BATT. S.S.R.
(A. COY) C/o. A. P. O.
NOTTINGHAM.

Subject: Missing People.

To:- The Chief Constable,
    The County Constabulary,
    WORCESTER.   AGH/G1/13.

A soldier in a Unit which is under my pastoral care is anxious
to trace a woman who is a labourere on farms etc., where she
helps in the gathering of fruit and hop crops. She has no
permanent address whatsoever. The last letter she sent him
was very despondent and in which she threatened to take her
life. I have told him that all I can do is to write to you
and see if it is possible for you to make enquiries as to her
present location, ~~if possible~~.

    I rather think that this woman may be of the 'gypsy' class.
She has usually worked in the county of Worcester, and she was
at ILLEY FARM, ILLEY, Worcs. on 13 June 42. Her description is as
follows:
    Age: 23 but looks about 18.
    Height: about 5'2.
    Blue eyes, very long and very black hair, very white pearly
    teeth, none missing.
    NAME: MARY LEA.

I should be glad if you will communicate with me if and when
you are able to trace this person.

                        A.T. Harper. C.F.
                    Chaplain.

3 August 42.   **THE REVD. A. G. HARPER C.F.**
2nd. Bn. Oxf. & Bucks. Lt. Infty.,
c/o Army Post Office,
    NOTTINGHAM.

Insp. Backe for attention.

*You have had a previous
enquiry respecting Oldbury Div.
this woman.*

        JS 1.8.42

HARPER, and was sent on 3rd August 1942 to the Chief Constable of Worcester[9].

The letter referred to an unnamed soldier in a unit under his pastoral care, who had told him he was anxious to trace a woman. The soldier had told him that the last letter she had sent him had been very despondent and that she had threatened to take her life. She was named as Mary LEA and was described as being a Gypsy, aged 23 but looking about 18, 5' 2", with blue eyes, very long and very black hair, very white and pearly teeth; none missing. Her last known whereabouts had been at Illey Farm, Illey, Worcester on 13th June 1942.

On 8th August 1942, PC 94 Edgar REYNOLDS responded[10] to the letter. He stated that Illey House Farm had changed hands twice during the last 18 months, and that on 13th June 1942, there were no travellers on the site. Furthermore, all the fields had been 'under the plough' for over 12 months.

These letters were then placed on file; that is, until eight months later when the skeleton was discovered.

Within days of the discovery of the skeleton, Mary LEE or LEA was named as a possible victim, and the police allocated a considerable amount of resources to tracing her.

The police contacted Mr Alfred JAMES, who was, by 1943, living at 29 Queen Street, Halesowen. He had been the owner of Illey House Farm on whose premises up to and around December 1939 there had been a permanent Gypsy encampment known as 'Alf JAMES's Ground' and 'Alfie JAMES's Farm'.

Alf was helpful and confirmed that, during the latter end of 1939 and the beginning of 1940, several families of travellers, including the LEE family, moved from the farm at Illey and went to live on land off Newbury Lane in Oldbury. He believed that the LEEs

---

[9] Letter: A.G. HARPER, 2nd Batt. Oxf. & Bucks. Lt. Infantry, Subject: Missing People. Ref: AGH/G1/13.
[10] Report: 8th August 1942: Frankley Station.

travelled with a family called WENMAN and collectively they were known as 'The Londoners'; the head of the family being a man called 'Bug' WENMAN[11].

He added that some families had stayed in Oldbury for about six months, until Oldbury Council had acted, and the camp was cleared. He did not know where they went after that but heard that some had moved to land in the Rowley Regis area.

Detectives also felt that both handwritten letters had been written by the same person, so they sent them to the forensic laboratory[12] for the handwriting to be examined. The laboratory soon responded, stating: *It was the opinion of the scientist that they were written by the same hand.*

It became the task of DC GAMBLE of Evesham Station to investigate and report the circumstances surrounding the letters. He interviewed both soldiers who were serving together in the 11th Battalion, South Staffordshire Regiment, which was billeted at Seaton Barracks in Plymouth. He also interviewed three other witnesses who knew the missing girl called Mary LEE: a Gypsy and serving soldier, 'Titch' SMITH, a Civil Defence Foreman called James HANDLEY, and a labourer called Norman TAYLOR.

On 9th May 1943, DC GAMBLE went to Seaton Barracks where he interviewed 'Bill' FLETCHER. Bill confirmed that he had written both letters; the first he said had been with HAYWOOD's permission. He told how he had lied to the chaplain about Mary LEE's threat to commit suicide, in order to convince him to write on his behalf. He told the investigators about how he had met

---

[11] 1939 Register shows John WENMAN OGJC1/1, his wife Patience as WENMAN OGJC1/2 and Mary WENMAN (BEAVER) OGJC/3 in LEDBURY at the Bosbury Hop Pickers Camp.
[12] Refs: CID.J/.135/43. & WRH/JD/C.1735. dated 10th May 1943; W.R. HARRISON.

Mary LEE at The Star Inn[13] in Halesowen and they started 'walking out' during 1939[14]. The last time he saw Mary was about three months before he 'joined up' on 2nd February 1940. He believed that when they parted company she was pregnant with his child.

Bill was asked why he had waited two years from the last time he saw her to when he sent the first letter. He said "that he was fed up and just thought he would like to get in touch with her".

He also indicated that Mary had been spotted shortly after the last letter was sent. A man he knew, called James HANDLEY, had told him that he had seen Mary in Bromyard carrying a baby around September 1942[15].

The following day, DC GAMBLE went to Dudley and interviewed Pte HAYWOOD, the supposed sender of the first letter, who was home on leave. HAYWOOD first met Bill FLETCHER whilst training in Newcastle, County Down, Ireland. They were together for about six months in 1940, and he had occupied the bed next to Bill, but since then he had had little to do with him. He recalled that he knew of correspondence between Bill and a Halesowen female called Kitty who worked at a gown factory, and that she was a married woman. He had never heard of him being worried about a person called Mary LEE, nor had he given permission to use his name to inquire.

When Bill was interviewed again on 12th May, whilst at home on leave, he continued to state that HAYWOOD had given permission.

---

[13] Also known as the 'Star' and 'Star Hotel'. The area has been developed and is now a Medical Centre – across the road from the Olde Queens Head.

[14] At the time, Bill was living at 6 Birmingham Road, Halesowen. 1939 Register QJFY 215/4.

[15] HANDLEY confirmed the possible sighting, but said it was around May 1942.

On 14th May, a 24-year-old soldier[16] and Gypsy named Nalie 'Titch' SMITH was interviewed. 'Titch' told how, for the past ten years, he had been living in the Illey district of Halesowen[17], and in the latter part of 1939 had become friends with Bill FLETCHER. He confirmed that Bill had been 'walking out' with a girl called Mary LEE. However, unknown to Bill, the woman in question was known within the Gypsy community as Mary WENMAN. He also confirmed that he believed Bill was the father of her first child.

He indicated that he had last seen Mary in September 1942 in Bosbury[18], Bishop's Frome, where she had asked after Bill – she also asked after his address, but he did not have it at the time. He confirmed that she was staying with other travellers from London and that she had been at Alf JAMES's Ground. He also said that she could be found in the Evesham District during pea-picking season and Bishops Frome during the hop-picking season.

James Merriman HANDLEY, of 53 Church Street, Cakemore, was interviewed. He told how Bill had been a member of his Civil Defence Section[19] before he joined the army. Their headquarters was next to the 'Star' and they drank together, along with a Gypsy called 'Titch' SMITH. He confirmed that Mary had been 'walking out' with Bill and said that "she took to FLETCHER because he is of gipsy breed"[20].

He stated that he had seen Mary carrying a baby whilst he was on a bus passing through Worcester about 12 months previously. He also told how he remembered seeing Bill in the 'Star' around May 1941 and that he had asked him, and a few Gypsy lads who were in at the time, about Mary, but no one had seen her. However, he

---

[16] Private 14505511 Nalie SMITH, 356 Company of Pioneers – stationed at Appleby, Westmorland.
[17] 1939 Register QKPD 156/4 at the Upton on Severn, Hop Pickers Camp with his family.
[18] Note: The HANDLEY sighting was in Bosbury four months earlier.
[19] No.9 Regional Column Rescue Service.
[20] On his mother Amy's side, née LOVERIDGE.

saw Bill again in September or October 1941, when on leave, but he had not asked about her then.

The last to be interviewed was Norman Walter TAYLOR of 22 Richmond Street, Halesowen; 35 years old, and a general labourer. Norman confirmed the relationship between Bill and Mary but added that James HANDLEY was, at the time, with another, much younger Gypsy, with light hair, and that all four were frequently together.

On 21st May, PC 7 Charles ELSTON[21] interviewed several Gypsy groups passing through his beat. A Mrs Henry SMITH and Sarah BAKER both said that they had seen Mary WENMAN in Evesham during the summer of 1942, when she was pea-picking at Byrd's. Of note is that they described her as being 20-25 years old, 5' 6", blonde, rather attractive, and with a child of about 18 months – contradicting other descriptions that specifically mention Mary having black hair.

By mid-June the police had still not traced Mary LEE/WENMAN.

One line of inquiry involved reviewing all the Pedlars' Certificates (also known as 'Hawkers Licences') that had been issued since 1937. They were checked in the hope of identifying Mary. None were issued to a Mary LEE, but there were several issued to women named LEE. Officers were sent to trace each one; although none fitted the description of the missing women, one inquiry provided a possible lead.

On 19th June, one of the LEEs who had been issued a certificate, was located travelling as Frances DICKSON (OGIV.534/26). She was living with, but not married to, a Mark DICKSON (OGIV.534/25). She was mother to four children; three with a Joseph ELMES, and a third, Michael (19 years), with James LEE.

---

[21] Report: CID Worcester, Sedgeberrow Station.

TWO A.R.P. workers created a scene in Dudley market place on Saturday night, causing a crowd to collect and eventually found themselves arrested by the police.

The sequel was heard at Dudley Court to-day, when James Merriman Handley, aged 32, of 63, Church-street, Blackheath, was fined 10s. for being drunk and disorderly, and William H. Fletcher, aged 23, of 6, Birmingham-road Halesowen, was fined 10s., with 5s. costs, for obstructing a police-officer.

A STRUGGLE

P.C. Lane said both men were arguing and pulling each other about. Several times he asked them to go home, but they would not do so, and caused a crowd to collect.

Fletcher called across the road to him " I wish you were in civvies," and Handley, who could hardly stand, brandished his steel helmet and shouted " This is what I do."

When he arrested Handley Fletcher tried to pull him away, and the three of them were struggling in the street for some time. Eventually another officer and a special constable went to his assistance.

At the station Handley expressed regret and Fletcher said: " I was only taking my friend's part."

Evening Despatch 27/11/39

Frances recalled seeing a Frank GURNEY in the company of a 15-year-old Gypsy girl called Mary LEE, the daughter of a Charles Henry LEE – known as 'Charlie Boy' – about ten years earlier. Frances's daughter, Ellen DRUMMOND (née ELMES) (WSJG.215/2), recalled that around August 1941 she had seen the LEE family and had asked Mrs LEE about her daughter, and was told she was married. In 1942, she saw 'Hughie' LEE, a son of 'Charlie Boy' and asked again, and was told "I don't know, we do not know where she is, we have not seen her for a long time".

Further information that supported this statement came from PC 115 BENBOW of the Malvern Station. He recalled that in 1936, 'Charlie Boy' had been in his district with his daughter Mary or Lilly, aged about 17 years. She was going about with a man age 20 called GURNEY. He remembers also seeing the couple again some time in 1937, but not since.

The group referenced by Frances was identified[22] as being Charles Henry LEE (OGAD.61/1), known as 'Charlie Boy', his wife Lilian LEE (OGAD 61/2), and son Charles Henry LEE (OGAD.61/3), known as 'Hughie'.

Frank GURNEY (aged 36 – much older than had been thought) was identified as the man mentioned by Frances DICKSON and PC BENBOW. He had stopped travelling and was now living at 7 Nailors Row, Evesham. GURNEY was known to the police because of a complaint alleging that he had unlawful carnal knowledge of a girl named Lillian LEE in July 1936. He told the police that he had not married the girl, had not seen her since 1936, and that he had heard she had married a gipsy named SHERRIFF.

Around the same time, information was received that Mary LEE/WENMAN may now be married and known as Mary BEAVER[23].

The SHERRIFF connection was ruled out and the inquiry concentrated on looking for a Mary (not Lilly or Lillian) LEE/WENMAN/BEAVER.

In July 1943, PC 7 Frank REDWARD of Stourbridge Station reported that he had seen a newspaper article about a Gypsy named Ethyl LEE, and thought she may be related and could help in finding Mary.

---

[22] Report: May 1942 PC 71 Charles ELSTON of Sedgeberrow Station. Reported moving Gypsies from the roadside in Aston Somerville.
[23] Report: Hampshire, 4th June 1943, DI BRIGHT: If Mary (Lillian/Lilly) LEE/WENMAN/BEAVER [OGJC1/3] is the same person (and the Register is correct) she was ~12 years old in 1936. GURNEY was ~29 years old.

Ethyl Lee, a gipsy, who milked
a neighbour's cow was fined 25s.
at Mansfield for stealing milk.

Sunday Express 25th July 1943

By November 1943, there had been reports that Mary had been
sighted at Mr TROTT's Farm in Bridgwater, Somerset, on the
Gypsy site behind the 'Dog' in Gloucester[24], and at Stow-on-the-
Wold. However, all these locations related to the fruit and pea-
picking seasons, which had finished by the time the information
was received and the Gypsies had left the district[25].

Therefore, formal identification by the police never occurred –
Mary was never traced.

The only other Mary LEE reference I found is in a 1949 report,
made during the SHERWOOD inquiry, written by DI
WILLIAMS[26]. He wrote ...*although Mary LEE was never interviewed
there was good evidence that she was seen alive and well at Pudge's Farm
at Bishop's Frome some twelve months after the discovery of the skeleton
and in any case her description as far as could be obtained did not tally
with that of the skeleton...* The only reference for a sighting at
Bishop's Frome is in the statement made by Nalie 'Titch' SMITH.

The description of the victim, provided by Professor WEBSTER,
was of a woman with brown mousy-coloured hair, aged between
25 and 40, but probably 35 years, plus or minus a few years, so
aged 31-35 in 1939. The witnesses all described Mary with black
hair, and she would have been ~18 years old, much too young.

I was unable to find a report or statement from Mary LEE's alleged
family group, Charles Henry 'Charlie Boy' LEE et al.

---

[24] Report: Birmingham CID 8th June 1943.
[25] 1st November 1943 Evesham Station Ref: CID.J.135/43(1a).

[26] Report: DI WILLIAMS, 5th October 1949.

The 1939 Register identifies Mary WENMAN/BEAVER as being with the WENMAN group at a Hop Pickers camp in Bosbury near Ledbury.

The LEEs were at a camp ten miles away in Bromyard, and are listed as being four members. Charlie and his wife Lillian are named but the remaining two entries are closed records. The police report would indicate that one is possibly the son 'Hughie', the other a daughter. It is possible that the fourth closed entry is 'the real' Mary or Lilly LEE, and that Mary WENMAN/BEAVER, being of a similar age, stole her identity. We will know in a few years once the records are opened up. It does pose the continuing question, however, of the whereabouts of that fourth member of their family.

The locations and connections between all the different people discussed in this inquiry, and all the others, are presented at the end of the section and this would also not be the last time Bill FLETCHER would appear in one of the police Gypsy inquiries...

Mrs LEE And Her Daughters

Another point of reference occurred during the early stages of the Mary LEE inquiry. DC 215 LEE reported[27] that a Mrs LEE, who had five daughters aged between 18 and 35, had stayed at 'Alf JAMES's Farm' in 1939, and that they were employed by a farmer named PALMER[28] somewhere near the Lyttleton Arms, Hagley.

The group was located on 11th May 1943 at Hinton Green by PC 258 LANGLEY. He reported that Mrs LEE was travelling with her son, Joe 'One Eye' LEE, and his (unnamed) wife, along with a Jonathan John SMITH[29], who was married to one of Mrs LEE's

---

[27] Report: Halesowen CID 5th May 1943.
[28] Possibly Spring Farm.
[29] Also known to travel as WEBB.

daughters called Richenda[30]. Also in the group was John's brother, Henry SMITH.

He describes Mrs LEE as being about 84 years of age and having four daughters (although DC LEE indicated five), named Lavina[31], Data, Bertha and Richenda. All the daughters except Bertha were married, and the report does not indicate (except for Richenda) that they are travelling together.

They said that they did not know a Mary LEE, although we now know that they were camped with Mary at 'Alf JAMES's Farm' in 1939.

I have been unable to locate this group within the 1939 Register.

At the same time as the police started to investigate the whereabouts of Mary LEE, another Gypsy inquiry was started following a discovery of clothing close to the tree and a group of Gypsies who had camped in the field adjacent to Hagley Wood.

The Nimmings Field Gypsies

In April 1943, during the search of the crime scene, a collection of old clothing and a 'root chopper' were found "thrown over the fence" inside Hagley Wood, approximately 150 yards from the tree. It was believed that they had been thrown away by a family of Gypsies who had had been living in the field several months earlier.

The root chopper appeared to have been made from the pointed end of a scythe and crafted to be used by Gypsies when peg making. All the clothing was described as filthy and in a ragged condition[32]:

• One piece of floral curtain material

---

[30] Also known as Hilda.
[31] Married John WEBB 26/01/1925.
[32] Report: 28th April 1943 PC POUND.

- One small boy's woollen jumper
- One boy's waistcoat
- Two gents' shirts; one red check, the other striped
- Four ladies' shoes; two are a pair, the others odd ones
- One gent's brown jacket
- One pair of boy's cloth trousers
- One brown blazer with school shield on pocket
- One pair of grey flannel utility trousers
- One pair of Jensen navy blue twill overalls
- One lady's artificial silk stocking
- Miscellaneous rags

The head of the family group was named as Arkie SMITH, but the police were unable to locate the group in the local area. On 30th April, an official request was made to the Worcester and Malvern districts, to locate Arkie and his family.

The first response came on 6th May from PC BENBOW of Malvern. He reported that, about a week earlier, he had seen Arkie accompanied by his son who was known as 'Baker'. They passed through his area travelling in the direction of Tewkesbury. He also reported that Arkie's wife Ellen was the sister of a Gypsy called Jim SMITH, also known as 'One Thumb Jim'. Arkie's family name was apparently BUTLER, but he used his wife's maiden name when travelling.

Another report at around the same time mentions that a Gypsy[33] in the Ombersley district had also recently seen Archie. However, he said that his name was Arkus BUTLER, but confirmed that he was going under the name SMITH. It took PC BENBOW two weeks to locate Arkie in Severn Stoke, Malvern where he interviewed[34] him and his family. The group consisted of:

---

[33] William James SMITH, National Registration Number OGIB.108/1.
[34] 26th May, 1943, PC 115 BENBOW of Malvern Station.

Arkus SMITH (OGIB[35].8/1) and his wife Ellen SMITH (OGIB.8/2), with their two sons and their wives.

Daniel BUTLER (OGIB.7/1) and his wife Ivy BUTLER (OGIB.7/A1).

Wisdom SMITH (YQKQ[36].231779) and a young woman named as DAVIS (YQKQ.I091205) who was travelling with Wisdom as his wife.

They confirmed that they had camped from a few days before Christmas 1942, for about a month, in a field off Hagley Wood Lane. They also confirmed that they had put the quantity of old clothing over the hedge into Hagley Wood. They recalled several articles, including one pair of lady's shoes overpainted red, and some odd shoes. They also left behind a knife made from the blade of a billhook. They also indicated that, if shown them again, they could identify the articles that they had left behind. They all assured PC BENBOW that this was the only occasion they camped anywhere near Hagley Wood Lane.

Felix TATE, aged 46 years of Holliers Farm, Hagley, added more background. He confirmed that the group had staying on his farm doing casual labour and lifting carrots prior to moving to the field[37], but he could not recall the reason why he had asked them to leave his farm. He had approached Charles Harry WILLETT, aged 70, the occupier of Hagley Hill Farm,[38] .to see if he could accommodate them, which he agreed to for ten shillings per week. Harry remembered that when the group moved on, they left a lot of rubbish behind: wood shavings, old clothing, and bits of tents and cloth that he burnt with the aid of paraffin. He noted that

---

[35] OGIB is Ledbury, 1939 registration district.

[36] YQKQ is replacement 'Y' in Upton-upon-Severn.

[37] 1949 SHERWOOD inquiry.

[38] His birth name and 1939 Register names him as WILLETTS. Father was also on the farm. No obvious connection found between him and the WILLETTS Timber Merchants. He retired shortly afterwards and went to live at the 'Old Castle' Hagley Park, Hagley.

some rubbish had been thrown into Hagley Wood but he had not interfered with it.

The interview also provided some additional information. 'One Thumb Jim' SMITH had seven brothers. Two of them, Ike and Harry, had been working for a person named HUPPER in the Hagley District.

Mrs Lennie SMITH

On 17th May 1943, another missing person inquiry was launched. Mr GABB, a farmer of Callow End, near Worcester, reported that a Gypsy called Daniel 'Danny' SMITH, who had been coming to his farm to work as a hop-picker for several years, had arrived a few years earlier without his wife. Although Danny had told Mr GABB she had died of pneumonia, he knew they had come from the Halesowen area and thought she could have been the murder victim.

It was quickly discovered that Danny's wife, Lennie SMITH, aged 55, had died of a cerebral haemorrhage at Alf JAMES's Farm, Illey, Halesowen on 16th February 1939, and was interred in Halesowen Church Yard. At the same time, Danny indicated that he had a daughter called Lallie who had just had a baby and was still living in Hagley.

The FORREST Inquiry

A popular story that is referenced in books[39] is about an arguing Gypsy couple, and a woman seen running away bleeding

Although the story has been elaborated upon over the years, it is based on an actual event in 1944 which was subject to a police inquiry.

---

[39] McCormick: Murder by Witchcraft p. 67.

At about 8pm on 10th April 1944, a Mrs Hannah BOLTON[40] overheard a conversation in her local pub, the Cross Keys Inn[41], in West Hagley. The storyteller was a Mrs Dorothy LEWIS of 'Glendale', Hayley Green, Halesowen. Dorothy had been heard telling others that two years earlier, a Gypsy couple had been living for some considerable time in a caravan on a piece of waste ground opposite the end of Newfield Road and behind Spout Farm[42] in West Hagley.

As Dorothy recalled they were an unhappy couple and often argued. The man had attempted to strangle the woman on several occasions and she was seen to run away from the caravan screaming with her neck bleeding – an incident that happened several times. At some stage, the couple left the farm and went to live beside Hagley Wood, but they soon disappeared and had not been seen since. Dorothy believed that the frequent quarrelling and violence meant that the woman in the tree could be her.

Hannah did not go to the police; rather she told what she had heard to an unnamed public official, who worked as a Civilian Clerk in Stourbridge, who, in turn, informed the police. The following-up was tasked to Sgt SKERRATT[43]. He first interviewed the land owner, Mr CUTLER of Spout Farm, and then the storyteller, Mrs LEWIS, to unravel fact from fiction.

It transpired that Mr Percy CUTLER of Spout Farm, West Hagley, owned a piece of land at the rear of Worcester Road, West Hagley, close to Vaughan's Nurseries (not on waste ground behind the farm as indicated), which he allowed tents and caravans to camp on. He said that during the summer of 1941, the storyteller, Mrs Dorothy LEWIS, was herself living in a caravan on the site.

---

[40] 36 years old, working as a 'servant' and living at 'Applegarth' on Newfield Road, West Hagley.

[41] Now a residential property.

[42] Also known as Sprout Farm.

[43] Sgt SKERRATT CID report 13th April 1944.

Percy recalled that, in July 1941, he was approached by a lady who asked to pitch her caravan on the site, which he agreed to. However, when she arrived, instead of a caravan, she pitched a blue square canvas tent, measuring twelve feet square. The lady also indicated that her husband was in hospital and that he would be joining her and her children later. Two weeks after they arrived, her husband joined them.

Percy confirmed that the couple had quarrelled. He remembered one incident that occurred around midnight, when the lady was seen running from the tent in her nightdress. Mrs LEWIS had complained about their behaviour; Percy confronted them, and they left a few days later.

When Mrs LEWIS was interviewed, she added some further detail, and indicated that after they left, she believed she saw the tent pitched in the field opposite the Gipsies Tent Inn, close to Hagley Wood. However, Charles HARRIS of Hagley Hill Farm, who farmed that area of land, was adamant that at no time had he given permission for anyone to camp in that field, although two fields above the one mentioned had been occupied by the Home Guard who had exercised, mainly at weekends, over the previous two years. PC POUND, whose beat covered that area, confirmed that he had never seen tents on that field.

Sgt SKERRATT soon identified the couple as the FORREST family, and located them living in a caravan on land at the rear of the Brickmakers Arms, Ladymoor, Oxford Street, in Bilston. He interviewed[44] Ann FORREST aged 42 years, who was, by then, estranged from her husband. Her son Hamilton had joined the army and she was living in the caravan with her two daughters, Margaret aged 20 and Mary Ann aged 14.

Ann confirmed that she had been the lady in question, and that she and her husband James and their children had stayed on the land in a tent for about a month in July 1941. She also recalled that

---

[44] Report: 17th April 1944, Ref: No.881/44.

she had had cause to flee the tent partly clothed on one occasion whilst her husband was in a temper.

On 16th April, having traced the woman, D/Supt INSIGHT closed the inquiry[45].

Eddie SHERWOOD Inquiry

Six years after the discovery of the body in the Wych hazel tree in Hagley Wood, on 23rd September 1949, 35-year-old George Frederick KING, of 30 Old Hawne Lane, Halesowen, contacted the police. The previous evening, he had been drinking in the Old Lyttleton Arms, Halesowen[46], with some friends. Amongst them was Bill FLETCHER (the Mary LEE inquiry) and his brother-in-law, a 33-year-old hairdresser called Eddie SHERWOOD[47]. At some stage during the evening the conversation had turned to the unsolved Hagley Wood murder.

Eddie told a story about an incident that had happened prior to him being called up to the army in 1940[48] (later clarified as happening in December 1942). At the time, he had been employed by Spaldings Ltd., Horse Slaughterers. He recalled that he was sent to collect a dead horse from a field near the wood. He told how he had seen some Gypsies fighting and that a woman was

---

[45]Bella in the Wych Elm Case Files\Original Documents\Folder 7 – Information 1943-49 Bunch2 1a.

[46] Note: In the town of Halesowen and not a pub of the same name in Hagley. The 1939 Register shows the Lyttleton Arms, 91 High Street Halesowen, with the residents the Pick family. It was also known as the 'Old Lyttleton Arms' and 'Billy Pick's. In 2007 it was renamed Picks.

[47]The 1939 Register shows spelling as SHEARWOOD and living at No. 27 Hancox Street with mother and father; the 1949 Electoral Register, living at No.25 with Alice née FLETCHER. He died in May 1987.

[48] Driver 2352818 SHERWOOD, Batman to the Lt/Col A.K. METCALF, Commanding Officer, of the 1st Command Signals, Royal Corps of Signals, Western Command. Joined 1940, wounded and discharged on 21st September 1943.

knocked down with a bar and didn't get up again. He suggested this might have been the murdered woman.

Eddie remarked that he would be able to identify the woman who was knocked down in the fight. He also said that he had been 'taken short' and went into the wood where he found a woman's black shoe. He had searched around for the other one but didn't find it.

George KING said Eddie was the type of person who liked to be the centre of attention and told tall stories but after thinking about it, he decided he ought to tell the police about what was said.

That evening, Eddie went to Oldbury police station, and the following morning gave a statement. A few days later he went with police[49] to the field next to Hagley Wood, and identified where he had seen several Gypsies encamped near a gate in a field adjacent to the wood about 120 yards from the tree in which the remains were found.

Eddie told how he had joined the army in 1940, but after being injured he was allowed to work periodically for Spaldings for a month at a time. On one occasion, sometime in December 1942, he had to go to a farm near Hagley Wood to slaughter a horse and collect it. The farm was situated over the brow of a hill, and to get to it he had to turn up a lane opposite the Old Tollhouse alongside Hagley Wood. It was getting dark and there was snow on the ground. Just inside a field about halfway up the lane and to the right-hand side was a single Gypsy caravan, which was standing about 15 yards from the entrance into the field. Slightly to the left when entering the field from the lane gate, about 10 yards from the caravan and higher up the field, were two canvas homes.

After he slaughtered the horse, he went to the Gypsies to ask them to help move the horse onto the road. There were three men and two women in the group. The old man and old woman were

---

[49] 2nd Oct, D/Supt INSIGHT, DI MOBBS, DI WILLIAMS, Sgt SKERRATT and PC POUND.

making clothes pegs and the young men assisted him in moving the horse down to his lorry, then left and went back to their caravan. Whilst securing the horse on the lorry, an argument broke out amongst the Gypsies. On the ground, he saw what he thought was an old cart wheel. All the men were fighting amongst themselves and they were armed with weapons, which he thought at the time were spokes from the wheel, but one of the men had what he thought was a crowbar. He recollected that the old woman was shouting and was trying to stop the fight, and remembered seeing the young woman amongst the men when she fell to the ground. He didn't see her get up again but got into his lorry and drove away. He described the young woman who was knocked down as being between 27 and 30 years of age, with black hair and of average height.

He added that they had a wood fire on the ground close to a 'four-wheeler' horse-drawn caravan. He described the young men as being about 25 years old, with black wavy hair and about 5'6" in height. The old man was about 60 years of age and was distinctively taller than the young men. The old lady was about the same age as the old man, short and stocky.

PC 187 JAYNES of Oldbury Station was sent to examine the log books at Spaldings Ltd., from 1939 onwards. He recorded entries relating to each visit, including the type of animal collected and which employee/driver had been assigned the job.

The log showed that on 23rd December 1942, it was a driver named BIRCH who had attended Mr. REECE's Penn Orchard Farm and collected a brown mare, and not Eddie. The log confirmed that Eddie had been working that day but elsewhere. The log also indicated that he had never collected from Penn Orchard Farm. Eddie suggested that the log was not always a true reflection as drivers often changed at short notice. Spaldings disagreed, indicating that their records were always accurate.

The Gypsy group in question had previously been identified in April 1943 (Nimmings Field Gypsy inquiry) when, during the search of the crime scene, a collection of old clothing and a 'root chopper' were found thrown over the fence inside Hagley Wood.

Another witness came forward who also challenged Eddie's version of events. John 'Jack' PALMER, aged 53, licensee of The George in Halesowen,[50] recalled that in December 1942 he was living on Spring Farm when he assisted a Spaldings lorry driver with the removal of Fred REECE's old mare called 'Jinnie'.

He remembered that the Spalding lorry was parked in Hagley Wood Lane at the top corner of the wood and within a few yards of the gate to the Nimmings field where some Gypsies were camping. The Spaldings man said he could not get his vehicle up to the horse, so he fetched his tractor and dragged the mare into the lane right behind the lorry. The mare was then chained, and the carcass dragged into the lorry. The chain broke when the carcass was part way on the lorry, but the second attempt was successful. They were very busy, and he remained with the driver and vehicle until he drove away. He did not see the driver go anywhere near the Gypsy camp and they had no help from the Gypsies.

He remembered that the driver was worried about getting back because it was getting dark, and that it was about 20 minutes from the time he dragged the mare into the lane. He remembered seeing the lorry drive off and down the lane before leaving.

He could not remember if the Gypsies had a fire at the time. He thought the caravan was possibly green in colour. He heard no noise of any description from the camp and was close enough to have seen and heard anything unusual. His description of the group was an old man and an old woman, two or three young men, and, he thought, three women. The men were on the small side, aged between 25 and 35. The women were smallish, of medium build, aged between 25 and 40. He did think that one of the women had fair hair and the others' hair was 'gypsy black'.

---

[50] Report: follow-up notes, 30th September 1949, DI WILLIAMS.

W.J.

RECORD OF EXTRACTS TAKEN FROM THE LOG BOOKS OF MESSRS. SPALDINGS, HORSE

SLAUGHTERERS, BIRCHFIELD LANE, OLDBURY, RELATING TO COLLECTION OF ANIMAL

CARCASES.

DATE	PLACE	ANIMAL	KILLED OR DEAD	VEHICLE DRIVER
6th March, 1939	REECE, PENN OR-CHARD FARM, CLENT	BROWN MARE 15.2 HNDS	DEAD	AMOS
18th April, 1939	DITTO	BLACK COB 13.2 hnds	DEAD	AMOS
22nd March, 1940	DITTO	RED ROAN HEIF-ER,	DEAD	
		RED ROAN HEIF-ER,	DEAD	
		4 SHEEP	DEAD	MORTON
Ditto	1. Brown, Forge Farm, West Bromwich.	Bay mare		
	2. Tedd, Stanton Farm, West Bromwich.	Chestnut mare	Killed	
	3. Wilkinson, Whitehall Farm, Romsley.	Brown Geld-ing. 16 hnds	Dead	SHEARWOOD
19th April, 1941	REECE, PENN OR-CHARD FARM, CLENT.	RED & WHITE HEIFER	DEAD	BIRCH
	(SHEARWOOD did not collect any animals about this time - in Army)			
15th Sep. 1942	REECE, PENN OR-CHARD FARM, CLENT.	RED & WHITE COW	DEAD	MORTON
23rd Dec. 1942	DITTO	BROWN MARE 16 HANDS	KILLED	BIRCH
23rd Dec. 1942	1. FLETCHER, DODFORD.	RED & white cow	Killed)	
		Red & White Sturk(Calf)	Killed)	
		Blue Roan Cow	Dead)	All in one journey
		Red & White Sturk	Killed)	
	2. MEACHAM, WOOD-ROW LANE, LYDIATE ASH.	Red & White Cow	Killed)	
		Red & White Sturk.	Dead)	SHEARWOOD
23rd Dec. 1942	1. TAYLOR, GROV-ELLY FARM, HOPWOOD.	White Bullock	Dead	
	2. ROUND, PRIORY ESTATE, DUDLEY	Bay mare 12.2hands	Killed	SHEARWOOD.
23rd Dec. 1942	WEBB, CARAVAN, PITT LANE, NETHEREND.	Bay Gelding 14 hands	Dead	BIRCH

DI WILLIAMS interviewed others who confirmed Jack's version. His brother, Charles PALMER[51], recalled that Jack had helped drag a mare named 'Jinnie' from a field off Hagley Wood Lane. His sister, Mrs Prudence May TATE (48 years) née PALMER, wife of Felix TATE of Holliers Farm, Hagley, told how she would walk up the lane to get to Spring Farm and remembered seeing Gypsies only a short distance up the lane, about three months before the skeleton was found. She also recalled a "very nasty smell" in the area where the skeleton was discovered, but never put any importance to it, thinking it was just a dead animal, but could not remember when that was.

The story also sparked interest with the media, highlighting the Gypsy theory.

1943 MURDER HUNT BEGINS AGAIN

C.I.D. meet round wych elm

WORCESTERSHIRE C.I.D. yesterday held a conference round a hollow wych elm in Hagley Woods in which a murdered woman was found six years ago.

Detectives have reopened inquiries into the murder because a man, who has been in the Army since 1940, has come forward with fresh clues.

Supt. T. N. Williams, of Stourbridge, who took part in the original inquiries, explained that this man said he had seen a party of gipsies in Hagley Wood-lane very near where the body was found.

Identity secret

Supt. Williams said: "We cannot afford to ignore any information, and this man's account of what he saw is being thoroughly inquired into. Police have visited the spot with him and are satisfied that some of the facts he has revealed are accurate."

The man's identity was not being revealed as it might hamper inquiries.

Det.-Supt. Inight told the Birmingham Gazette: "We hope the new line of inquiry may help to solve the crime, although the fresh information is somewhat vague and slender."

The body was discovered in April, 1943, by two boys who

Birmingham Gazette 04/10/1949

[51] Son of farmer PALMER of Spring Farm and in 1949 the licensee of the 'Hill Tavern', Adams Hill, Clent.

The Missing Gypsy Group

Within the archive material there are several references to a group of Gypsies who were camped at the bottom end of Hagley Wood Lane, near to the Birmingham Road. The only area that could be occupied without causing an 'obstruction to the highway', resulting in being moved on by the police, was approximately 100 yards up the lane. There are several references over a protracted period and within different police inquires. The reason for gathering them together is because it would seem to have been an obvious line of inquiry for the police to investigate; however, no documents exist.

In the SHERWOOD inquiry, Mrs REECE recalled that she had never seen any Gypsies, either before or since in Nimmings field, although she had seen them lower down. She recalled seeing two women in the lane, within a few yards of the camp in the field, and assumed they were with that party. One was about 40 years of age, 5' 7"-8", thin, dark, 'proper Gypsy type' with a black apron. The other woman was about 20 years of age, 5 foot tall, with fair hair, neither brown nor ginger, probably blonde, and with a fresh complexion. Mrs REECE was of the impression that she was the daughter of the older woman but had remembered her as *it wasn't often you saw a fair-haired Gypsy*.

In the same inquiry, Mrs TATE remembered seeing Gypsies only a short distance up the lane an, Mr and Mrs REECE said that the gossip at the time when the skeleton was discovered, was that 'one of those' Gypsies was missing when they went away, although they said they could not remember who said it.

A more detailed description was given by Mrs Sarah Annie LORRIE-PORTER, aged 60, of the Toll House store, which is approximately 1,000 feet from Hagley Wood Lane on Birmingham Road. She remembered that, before the skeleton was found, some Gypsies shopped at her store. They bought bread, sometimes groceries, and occasionally they begged a bucket of water.

This group stayed much longer than other Gypsies had in the past. She recalled that there were at least three women and two or three little children[52], one of whom was a young boy. One of the women was quite old and seemed to be the mother of them all. She was between 50 and 60 years of age, of slim build and medium height. The next oldest was a woman, about 22 or 23 years old. She was slightly taller, at about 5' 2 1/2", of slim build, and with dark hair plastered down with grease. The next was a young woman between 17 and 20 years of age, about 5' 2", of medium build, and good looking, with greased brown hair. She could not remember what they wore, except that they seemed to wear shawls crossed over one shoulder and passed round the waist. They used to make artificial flowers made of wood or paper, which they coloured.

There were two men, one being very old, who appeared to be the husband of the older woman. He was about 50 to 60 but shortish in height and of medium build. The other was about 20 to 22 years of age, 5' 4"-5", medium build to slim, and untidy, and he seemed 'dopey', as though he wasn't quite all there.

She thought that a name in one of the ration books was DAVIS[53]. They were described as a very quiet, inoffensive lot, and she had no idea where they came from or where they went, and had never seen them since.

During the 1943 Nimmings Field inquiry, reference was also made to a Richard SMITH (OGAD. 56/1), who was in Hartlebury and who had camped in the past in the Romsley area.

---

[52] The Nimmings Field inquiry established that there were no children in that group.
[53] Nimmings Field inquiry: A young woman named as DAVIS (YQKQ.I091205) was travelling with the Wisdom SMITH as his wife.

The 1939 Register

Whilst Gypsies are often described as being 'nomadic' or 'of no fixed abode', the evidence is that those who feature in the previous stories followed a more structured travelling lifestyle than is often imagined. They were known to see out the winter in the same place, return to a favourite church for baptisms, marriages and burials, and for those who were farm labourers, they moved in family groups from farm to farm, following annual crop harvests, often 'picking' for the same farmers.

Although the outbreak of World War II in 1939 did disrupt their annual routine, with enlistment into the armed services and war effort working opportunities, I felt I ought to try and identify the missing Gypsy group. Also, I should be able to map other family groups to see if that would provide any additional information.

It was not easy. Gypsy genealogy is full of traps for the unwary, and even when you know them and try to avoid them, you still fall into them. It is easy to misidentify someone, or their parents, spouse, or children. Therefore, I have tried to keep the information as simple as possible. I have done the best I can to eliminate mistakes, to avoid misleading the reader, and to reference the basis for my research. I have consulted original records whenever possible to test the accuracy and the relevance where links have been found in combination with other inquiries, before I have made any observations.

I was restricted by the availability of official documents whilst undertaking this phase of my people research. Although the census logs for 1921 and 1951 were helpful, because the 1931 census was destroyed by fire during WWII, I was greatly dependent on the 1939 Register to identify people during the period of the mystery.

The Register was completed during September 1939. At the beginning of the month, households, or in the case of this section of the book, caravans and tents, also known as 'Yardos', were given a blank Registration form to complete. On 29th September, officials checked, and amended if necessary, the forms before they were collected to be processed. The information was then used to produce identity[54] and ration cards, as well as monitor the movement of people.

Although it is only a snapshot in time, I found the Register helpful in identifying family groups and their locations. Also, neighbouring family groups were often close relatives or, at least, regular travelling companions. This then provided me with some help in mapping groups and the different stories. I was mindful that there is no guarantee that any of the information given by individuals was accurate; therefore, names, ages, marital status and occupations were taken at face value.

The 1939 records are also incomplete; Data Protection legislation prevents records of those born less than 100 years ago from being made available to the public. This means that the details of anyone indicated as being born after 1918, unless known to be dead, remains in a closed file. Therefore, although an annual review of the records may uncover additional details, we will have to wait until 2039 to see the full records revealed.

When viewing the individual stories in isolation, people and locations mean little. However, when I mapped the stories and people, I made some interesting discoveries. I identified that, in September 1939, many of the Gypsy family groups who feature in the Mary LEE inquiry were to be found at hop-picking camps in three locations in the Malvern area. Nalie SMITH (QKPD 156/4) was at the Upton-upon-Severn, Beauchamp Lane site, with his family. The LEE family, 'Charlie Boy' et al., were at the Bishop's Frome 'Broomtree' site in Bromyard (OGAD), along with Richard SMITH (OGAD56/1). The WENMANS were at (OGJC) Bosbury, near Ledbury. With nearly all the Gypsies away hop-picking, the Register indicates very few Gypsies in the local area at all. There

---

[54] National Registration Identity Cards, included Enumeration District 'ED' letter code.

were no Gypsies on Alf JAMES's Illy House Farm[55], and none on Spring Farm or camped on Hagley Wood or Uffmoor Lane. The records only show Emma LAMBERT aged ~51, Nora SMITH, age ~28, and the subjects of two closed records, camped on Illey Hall Farm. Arthur EVANS, aged 76, was camped on Dark Lane, Romsley, and Albert H HULL (or HILL), aged 71, was at Chapman's Hill, also in Romsley.

We know from the FORREST inquiry that farmer Percy CUTLER of Spout Farm[56] allowed people in July 1941 to camp on his land at Worcester Road, West Hagley but we don't really know what motivated Bill FLETCHER over Christmas 1941 to try and locate the girl he knew as Mary LEE. One obvious consideration is that he had heard that someone from within the LEE family groups/community had been killed, and he had been concerned it was Mary.

This time period is significant because it coincides with the time of death indicated for Bella (Oct-Nov 1941) by Professor WEBSTER. I therefore decided to have a closer look at the Bromyard location[57], specifically the LEE family and their neighbours. Mindful that Professor WEBSTER indicated that the victim was aged between 25 and 40, but was probably 35, plus or minus a few years, when looking at the 1939 Register, the victim would have had to be aged between 23 and 37, but probably between 31 and 35.

In the census the Mary LEE family are all OGAD61. I discovered that there are nine women who fall into the outer age range within their 'travelling community'. There are three who fall within WEBSTER's probable range, but there is only one who would have been 35 years old in Oct-Nov 1941.

---

[55] Just Alf (QFR72/2), his wife Mary (/1), Walter (/3) and one closed record.
[56] Worcester CID, Clent Division report 14th April 1944, Supt JJ HOLYHEAD.
[57] 1939 Register OGAD Bromyard, pages 82 and 83.

OGAD	Name	~age	M/S	Occupation
	Page 82 Bromyard R.D.			
50/1	John **WATTON**	53	M	Farm Work
/2	Zillah	50	M	Pedlar
/3	Joseph	29	S	Farm Work
/4	Kiah	24	S	Farm Work
/5	Harry	21	S	Farm Work
/7	William	14	S	Farm Work
	x3 closed.			
51/1	John Alfred **LANE**	38	M	Farm Labourer
/2	Amy	27	M	Farm Labourer
	x3 closed.			
52/1	Frank **SMITH**	56		Farm Labourer
/2	Amy	53		Farm Labourer
/3	Lily	21		Farm Labourer
/4	Rose (**REDMAN**)	19		Farm Labourer
/5	Alfred	17		Farm Labourer
/6	Amy (**LUTHER**)	15		[B/218/DWP]
/7	Joseph	12		School
	x1 closed.			
53/1	Thomas **SMITH**	24	M	Farm Labourer
/2	Mary	23	M	Farm Labourer
	x1 closed.			
54/1	Alfred **EVANS**	35	S	Pedlar
/2	Bella [Isabella] **EVANS**	33	S	Pedlar
55/1	Robert **WATTON**	46	M	Farm Labourer
/2	Rose	34	M	Farm Labourer
	x5 closed.			
56/1	Richard **SMITH**	53		Farm Labourer [YQKH/1789]
	x2 closed.			
/4	Janet (**BOSWELL**)	22		Farm Labourer
/5	Richard **SMITH**	17		Farm Labourer
	x2 closed.			
57/1	Robert **SNOW**	64	S	Scrap Dealer
/2	Margaret **SHORWELL**	60	M	Scrap Dealer
/3	Alfred **SHORWELL**	25	S	Scrap Dealer
	PAGE 83 Bromyard R.D			
58/1	John **WHALEY**	54	M	Farm Labourer
/2	Mary	49	M	Home Duties
/3	John Robert	24	S	Farm Labourer
/4	X1 closed.			
/5	George	66	S	Farm Labourer

/6	Anne (**COULSON**)	11	S	At School
/7	X1 Closed			
59/1	Andrew **WINTER**	52	M	Farm Labourer
/2	Mary	43	M	Home Duties
	X2 closed /3 half visible	21	S	Farm Labourer
/5	Celia (**DUNN**)	12	S	Farm Labourer
/6	William		S	Farm Labourer
/7	Closed			
60/1	Donald **LOCKE**	19	S	Farm Labourer
/2	Frances (**SYMANDS/LOCKE/JOHNSON**)	23	S	Domestic Work
Caravan Upper House Field				
61/1	Charles **LEE** (Charlie Boy)	59	M	Hawker
/2	Lillian	50	M	Hawker
	X2 Closed [/3 Charles Henry 'Hughie']			
62/1	Richard **EVANS**	36	M	Hawker
/2	May **ERNE**	44	M	Hawker
/3	Sarah **EVANS**	31	S	House Maid
/4	Robert **EVANS**	27	S	Unfit For Work
/5	Closed			
/6	Caroline **ERNE**	27	S	Household Duties
63/1	Fredrick **BOSWELL**	42	M	Marine Labourer
/2	Annie	37	M	Domestic Duties
/3	Louise (**EDWARDS**)	19	S	House Work
64/1	Pricilla **HUGHES**	44	M	Farm Labourer
/2	Albert		M	
	X2 Closed			
/5	? (**DOE**)		S	
65/1	X2 Illegible and x2 closed		M	Pedlar Hawker
66/1	? **HUGHES**	56	M	Farm Worker
/2	Edna	60	M	Farm Worker
	X2 Closed x1 partial - female	23	S	Farm Worker
67/1	Bertie **WATTON**	52	M	Scrap Iron Hawker

In Summary the nine within the outer age range are:

Amy LANE (OGAD51/2), age 27

Mary SMITH (OGAD53/2), age 23

Bella [Isabella] EVANS (OGAD54/2), age 33

Rose WATTON (OGAD55/2), age 34

Frances SYMANDS/LOCKE/JOHNSON (OGAD60/2), age 23

Sarah EVANS (OGAD 62/3), age 31

Caroline ERNE (OGAD 62/6), age 27
Annie BOSWELL (OGAD 63/2), age 37
Closed record (OGAD 66/3-4), age 23

The three within WEBSTER's probable range are:
Bella [Isabella] EVANS (OGAD54/2), age 33
Rose WATTON (OGAD55/2), age 34
Sarah EVANS (OGAD 62/1), age 31

Only one gypsy would have been 35 years old, as indicated as the probable age by Professor WEBSTER – a Pedlar (Hawker) named Isabella 'Bella' EVANS.

CHAPTER 3
MISSING PERSON INQUIRIES 1943

When I started to write this chapter, I had expected it to be a lengthy task because I have seen references[58] to as many as 3,000 missing women being checked against 'missing persons files' nationally as part of the murder investigation. Accordingly it surprised me to find that the 2005 Closure Report refers only briefly to the search for missing persons, and it acknowledges that there is no retained record[59] of any inquiries other than that for a woman named Dinah CURLEY/O'GRADY in 1943.

Document 112 outlines page two of details of a number of person reported missing for the time appropriate to the believed death, provides a number of persons albeit there is no reference to investigation into the circumstances of their disappearance.

The document, No. 112, relates to a report dated 27th June 1943, from Worcester CID[60], listing the names of 21 women who were reported as missing in the Birmingham district between May and December 1941[61]. Halesowen and Hagley are not within the Birmingham catchment area and I found no documentation listing any other missing women.

The reason for only investigating women missing outside the location of the murder, or, why only Dinah CURLEY/O'GRADY and not the other missing women, were investigated, is not stated.

I was unable to find any proactive missing person inquiries in 1943 other than those made for Mary LEE and Dinah. Furthermore, all the later inquiries, including those in 1944, which followed the appearance of the chalk markings and the search for

---

[58] J.M. COLEY p. 7, Murder Casebook No.71, p. 2538; D. MCCORMICK, pp. 64 & 107, Express and Star Newspaper; A. SPARKE 2016, p. 8.
[59] Mary LEE is not on this list.
[60] Ref: C.I.D./J.135/43(108a).
[61] MCCORMICK p. 107 indicates about 200.

a woman named 'Bella', all appear to have been instigated by reports from the public, rather than arising from missing persons reports.

The story of the only missing persons search has its origins in May 1941, when Mrs M LAVIN of 56 Stanley Street, Cheetham, Manchester reported to the Birmingham Citizens' Society[62] that a woman named Dinah CURLEY/O'GRADY had gone missing, apparently following a heavy air raid on the city. There is no explanation as to the significance of the two surnames, but the

---

[62] Birmingham Citizens' Society (No.161 Corporation Street) promoted and coordinated charitable and social work in the City and assisted in the distribution of special relief funds.

documentation shows that the police were concentrating on a woman named Dinah CURLEY.

First, the police went to interview Mrs LAVIN at 56 Stanley Street. When they attended the address, they discovered that the previous occupant (thought to be Mrs LAVIN) had left two years earlier, and there was some doubt as to whether her name was actually LAVIN. They did discover that she had lived for a while with a family named LYNCH (NKEK282) at 32 Robert Street, but they had also left in May 1942 and moved to Haverfordwest in Pembrokeshire.

On 13th July 1943, Pembrokeshire police were requested to help in the search for Mrs LAVIN and the LYNCH family. They reported that a Mrs Mary LAVIN had been living at 73 Belle Vue Terrace, but she had moved four months earlier, first to Dumfries and was now believed to be in Ripon[63].

Unfortunately, the LYNCH family had also moved again, this time to Kettering in October 1942. However, the police believed that a Mary LAVIN was friendly with, or possibly even related to, Mrs Annie LYNCH.

On 20th July, Harrogate police were requested to assist with locating Mary LAVIN and to obtain a description of Dinah CURLEY. However, when they went to the home address in Ripon, they discovered that it was a boarding house for men, and no one named Mary LAVIN had ever resided there. The house register did list a man named John Edward LAVIN (CJAH77/11) who had stayed there from 9th March for about six weeks. As the name and occupation times coincided, it was assumed he was the husband of Mary LAVIN. They were unable to locate Mary, and John had moved to Lincoln. Also, his previous address was given as Stockport and not Pembrokeshire.

---

[63] The police used the National Registration Office and Food Office to help with locations.

At the same time, the police were still looking for Annie LYNCH in the hope she could assist in locating Mary, so Kettering police were asked to assist. They were successful and, on 27th July, Sergeant H.E. WILFORD of the Kettering station interviewed Annie. She stated that she had "left South Wales about ten months earlier and that Mary had left a month previously". She also had no knowledge of Mary's whereabouts or of Dinah CURLEY[64].

The search now focused on finding John Edward LAVIN in the hope he was the husband of Mary and that he could assist with locating his wife. This became a complicated task because it appeared that John had exchanged ID cards with his father. John was also known as Jack, and this was the name he was known as. James, the father, had reported his ID card missing and had been given a replacement. Since, his son had been using the 'lost' ID card, it had been reported for unauthorised use.

Then Northampton police contacted the inquiry to report that John 'Jack' LAVIN was wanted for non-payment of a £15 fine and was 'on the run'[65]. Furthermore, he had lived at four different addresses over the previous two years.[66] The last recorded location showed him working as a lorry driver for Sir Lindsay PARKINSON, Public Works Contractor, in Leeds. However, when contacted they said they had no record of him ever being employed by them.

On 2nd September, Worcester CID reported that John/Jack had stayed in Ripon and previously Dumfries, providing another link with Mary.

There was a breakthrough on 10th September, when Haverfordwest police reported that they believed Mary's

---

[64] Ref: CID/J.135/108a 27/07/1943: Kettering.

[65] Absentee from (Ministry of Labour) work, Northampton Landing Grounds Corporation.

[66] White Hart Hotel, Penkridge; Ellerdine Hotel, Wellington; Claremont, Ripon; Queen Street, Dumfries.

National ID number was LCIL9/1. With this information, on 27th September, PC 71 Thomas KELLY finally traced Mary Ann 'Annie' LAVIN (LCIL9/1), as staying at 40 Lawrence Street, Stockport. Mary indicated that she knew no one called CURLEY, had never made inquiries, nor lived in Manchester, and did not know why or how her ID card was registered in Pembrokeshire. She also indicated that in May 1941 she was living at the same address, was not married, and her maiden name was DOWLING.

PC KELLY also interviewed Mary's sister, Mrs SOROHAN, and her husband, who corroborated Annie's account. He then interviewed the only other Mrs LAVIN in Stockport borough, who lived at 12 Bird Hall Lane. She also stated that she had been living at the same address for many years and had not heard of Dinah CURLEY.

Nothing further happened for six months until the 25 year old John/Jack LAVIN was arrested on 25th March 1944, in Crowborough, Sussex, a year after the search for him began. He had been living with his father at 28 Redesdale Street, Chelsea, London.

During interview, he explained that, although he was born John Edward, he was known as Jack LAVIN (which is what he was registered as in 1939), had been born in Balla, Castlebar, Co. Mayo, Eire on 7th June 1919, and worked as an excavator driver and mechanic. He also confirmed that he had accidently taken his father's[67] ID card when he moved to Leicester in 1940. He had married Mary Ann DOWLING on 21st December 1941 at St Joseph's Church, Stockport, and after they married they lived at 40 Lawrence Street. He confirmed that his wife had joined him in Haverfordwest, Pembrokeshire for a few months, which she had previously denied. He said that his wife was the only Mary LAVIN he knew, and that they have never lived in Stanley Street, Manchester. He confirmed that his wife was born and brought up

---

[67] Michael James LAVIN, born Bella, 02/05/1889, Labourer.

in Ireland, had moved to England six years earlier and had always lived in Stockport. He had never worked on the Birmingham/Worcester road, did not know Halesowen, did not know a Dinah CURLEY or O'GRADY, and his wife had only ever visited him while he was working one contract in Haverfordwest.

This is the only reference that I have found for the use of the name O'GRADY. The statement offers no explanation to the importance or background to that name. However, it is referenced in the Closure Report where, in summary, it indicates that the information supplied is insufficient in identifying whether CURLEY, aka O'GRADY, ever existed. It also states; there is nothing on the file to indicate that Mary LAVIN was interviewed and challenged about these issues but this is incorrect; she was interviewed by PC Thomas KELLY on 27th September 1943.

All the coincidences make it probable that the reporter for the missing person was Mrs Mary LAVIN, the wife of Jack (John Edward) LAVIN, despite denials by them both of any knowledge or links to the 56 Stanley Street address. The reasons for the denial and the report being made remain unclear but it is probable that it was for personal gain, and that the alleged missing person, CURLEY, aka O'GRADY, was fictitious. The Closure Report references several communications, which, it says, *would seem prudent not to follow as the basis for the content is at best questionable* but I am unable to identify to which documents this refers.

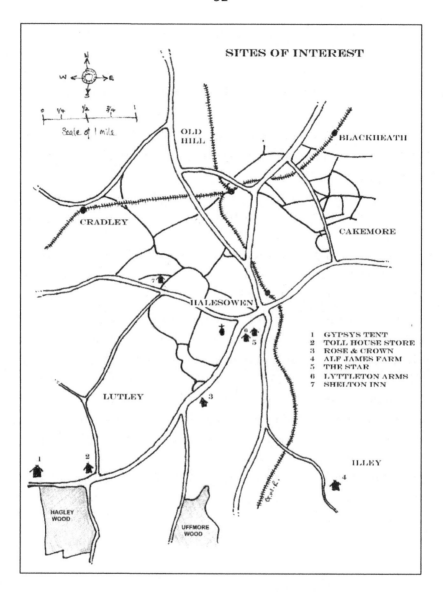

SITES OF INTEREST

1 GYPSYS TENT
2 TOLL HOUSE STORE
3 ROSE & CROWN
4 ALF JAMES FARM
5 THE STAR
6 LYTTLETON ARMS
7 SHELTON INN

CHAPTER 4
CHALK MESSAGES

The 2005 Police Closure Report indicates that the 'first issue' that took up considerable effort was the chalked messages. This statement would benefit from being amended, as messages did not start to appear until March 1944, 11 months after the discovery of the skeleton in the tree and the previously discussed gypsy, and missing persons inquiries.

The first issue, which took up considerable effort, was the series of chalked messages upon walls throughout the West Midlands conurbation from Wolverhampton, into the 'Black Country' and also into the city centre of Birmingham. The chalkings were undertaken over a protracted period of time. The reason for and also the author/s of the chalkings were not established despite considerable investment.

The first two messages appeared in Birmingham on 28th March 1944, when Mr Wilfred Lawson WHITE, a Stourbridge fruiterer who was visiting Smithfield fruit market, reported seeing underlined chalk writing on the wall adjoining WHITE's on Pershore Street: **'HAGLEY WOOD BELLA'**, and on the wall of WILLIAMSON's on Upper Dean Street: **'WHO PUT BELLA DOWN THE WYCH ELM HAGLEY WOOD'**.

The police conducted inquiries[68] at WILLIAMSON's and obtained a list of 14 names and addresses of people who had visited the premises early on the 28th. There was one visitor from Halesowen, Mr H. EDMONDS, of Halesowen Road, Old Hill. He was interviewed and said that he was not aware of the writing until it was pointed out to him. DI WILLIAMS apparently knew Mr EDMONDS and was satisfied that he knew nothing.

Whilst inquiring at WILLIAMSON's, they spoke with the son of a warehouseman called Raymond Thomas BOFFEY, aged 16 years. He named a boy – George BOND, the son of a Selly Oak greengrocer who had brought the writing to his attention.

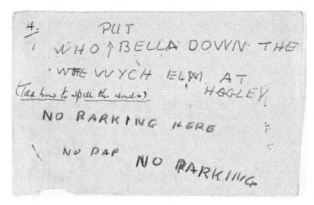

It was also noted that the words 'NO PARKING' and 'NO PARKING HERE' had been written on either side of the entrance to the premises. This writing was described as having 'some similarity' to the Bella message. Raymond first admitted that he knew about the Hagley Wood murder and that he had written the Bella message, but after being questioned further, he then strongly denied he had. DI WILLIAMS made him write in his pocket book and then indicated that he felt the boy was illiterate and, to his mind, did not write the message on the wall.

---

[68] List referenced in Closure Report bundle p. 48.

A few days later, on 30th March, Mr James William ROWLEY reported[69] seeing a message on a cottage wall along, Haden Hill, at the Barrs Road end in Old Hill, Halesowen, with the caption, **'WHO PUT LUEBELLER IN THE WYCH ELM'**. All three writings appeared similar in style, and the Old Hill message also had the words LUEBELLER and WYCH ELM underlined[70].

Mr ROWLEY stated that the message had *"...been there for some time"*. This was confirmed by the Head Master of Old Hill School, Mr John COX[71], who told Officers *"that to his personal knowledge it had been on the wall since before Christmas 1943"*.

On 5th April, all three messages were photographed, and samples of the chalk recovered then submitted for analysis at the Forensic Science Laboratory (South Wales and Monmouthshire area). Shortly afterwards, the laboratory reported that *...the inscriptions were by the same person and that the chalk was more or less similar*[72].

The Birmingham Gazette ran an article on the messages, which raised interest in the murder. It also encouraged what was believed to be a 'copycat' message on 12th April 1944. This message appeared on a wall that adjoined the premises of Messrs Walter SEAMERS and was opposite the Laminated Springs works on Mucklow Hill, Halesowen. DC LEE investigated and produced a hand-written note: of the messages which read:

WHO PUT BELLA IN THE WITCH ELM HAGLEY WOOD
JACK THE RIPPER?
JACK THE RIPPER
ANA BELLA DIED IN HAGLEY WOOD

---

[69] Insp HUGHES, Old Hill, report dated 4th April 1944.
[70] Referenced by Victor CROMPTON Chapter 15, previously called Barge Road
[71] 31st, John COX, 'Sunset' Haden Hill.
[72] R. HARRISON, Director, Forensic Science Laboratory (South Wales and Monmouthshire area) report dated 12th April 1944, Hagley Wood Murder. Ref: WRH/ML/C.2082.

On 12th April 1944, an anonymous letter was received by the City Police in Birmingham[73]. It was postmarked Kidderminster and dated 7.15 p.m. 11 APR 1944. This is the same day the chalk markings appeared on Mucklow Hill, which were believed to have been produced by a 'copycat' or 'practical joker'.

Sgt SKERRATT, who viewed the chalk markings, investigated the letter and reported[74] that the man referenced was Arthur W EDGINTON, a 58-year-old signalman employed by the Great Western Railway at Churchill & Blakedown Station. He was living at the Blakedown Station House, Kidderminster, having been separated from his wife, Ada May EDGINTON,[75] since May 1942.

He says that, '…*From information received she appears to be a woman of peculiar mentality for she has frequently written to her husband and the people with whom he has been lodging, accusing him of all kinds of silly things'*.

Two anonymous letters posted in April and July 1943 to Arthur, and believed to have been written by Ada, were recovered by Sgt SKERRATT and are contained in the archive. Of note is that the text is all in capital letters and the word DIRTY is underlined in a similar way to other chalk marking words.

---

[73] D.E.H Copy J 135/43(75).
[74] Report, Clent, Stourbridge Division 20th April 1944.
[75] Living at 2 Little Park Street, Worcester.

Hagley Murder
What woman was 030930
signalman EDGINTON
with up the Hagley
road. One Sunday night
near midnight.
Came through
Blakedown. 5 oclock
next morning. Going
up the Birmingham
road Kidderminster.
Where he then lived
Very fishy.

Postcard dated 1st July 1943

On 15th April, Sgt SKERRATT and DI WILLIAMS viewed the writing for themselves and reported that they believed it was not the same as they had seen before at Old Hill and Birmingham but was the work of a 'practical joker'. DI Williams also noted that the spelling *[Wych]* is WYTCH not WITCH, as did DC LEE in his formal report on 12th April.

Nothing further happened for nearly four months, until on 1st August, another three messages were reported.

The first was by a Mr RAY,[76] who was walking from Heath Town towards the railway station along Sun Passage (now Sun Street) in Wolverhampton, when he saw on his right, underneath an archway, the caption, **'HAGLEY WOOD LUBELLA ADDRESS OPPOSITE THE ROSE AND CROWN HASBURY'.**

The next two messages were discovered on the same day in Halesowen by DC LEE who was serving a summons, and were investigated by PC PITCHER on 2nd August. One was written on a fence (or part of a gate) at Shelton Lane, opposite the Shelton Inn[77]. The caption was similar in style to the Wolverhampton message and read, **'ADDRESS WAS OPPOSITE ROSE AND CROWN HASBURY HAGLEY WOOD LUBELLA'.** The other was nearby, on a wall underneath the railway arch[78], and read, **'I USE TO HAGLEY WOOD LUBELLA WAS NO PROSS'.**

---

[76] Stanley Arthur RAY, aged 24, Chemist, 133 Shenley Fields Road, Selly Oak.

[77] Chapter 14.17 discusses an anonymous letter from Canada, which references Bath Meadow which is nearby.

[78] PC 231 Albert PITCHER's report: Hasbury Station, dated 2nd August 1944, & DI WILLIAMS' report: Chalked writing on wall and fence at Belle Vale Halesowen, dated 4th August 1944.

Although the Halesowen sightings were officially reported at 9.40 a.m. on 2nd August, on investigating, it became apparent that both had been seen there at least a fortnight earlier.

PC PITCHER made inquiries at the ten houses and Timber Yard[79] on Hagley Road, which were opposite the Rose and Crown. He inquired about the movement of all persons visiting or staying at the addresses during the previous six years. The occupancy was as follows:

No. 390 Ernest WILLETTS (Jnr), wife and child.

---

[79]Which in 1943, had the forestry rights ...to cut the trees and purchase the timber—in Hagley Wood...

No. 392[80] Walter WILLETTS (Snr)[81] and wife.

Timber Yard J.T WILLETTS & Son.

No. 394 Harry MOORE, wife and three daughters.

No. 396 Colin Edward WITHERS[82], wife and child.

No. 398 Francis Hilda ARGENT[83] and child.

No. 400 Alfred Thomas HARDWICK, wife and three children.

No. 402 Albert ALLSOPP and wife.

No. 404 Samuel ALLSOPP and wife Emma (née BASTERFIELD[84]).

No. 406 Arthur JAMES, wife, daughter Janet, and son-in-law Howard HEART.

No. 408 Mabel BASTERFIELD (widow) and son.

No. 410 John LAIGHT, wife and three children.

During his inquiry, the occupants of No. 404, Mr and Mrs ALLSOPP, told how a woman, who was a distant relative named Bella JAMES, aged 60-70 years, used to visit them, but they had not seen or heard from her for the past four years. They thought that she lived at No. 39 or No. 49 Hurcott Road, in Kidderminster[85]. Because Bella's age fell outside the parameter of the investigation, no follow-up inquiries were made.

---

[80] Sometimes listed as a single (No. 390) house.

[81] Kelly's Trade Directory 1940 names Walter as Director of Timber Yard. Birmingham Daily Post 4/12/61 Walter's death announced. London Gazette 18/08/70 p. 9232, Liquidation of Timber Yard. Also, his father had once been the Publican at the Rose and Crown.

[82] Serving soldier.

[83] Aircraftman 1st Class 1177764 Trevor John ARGENT, aged 38, 993rd Balloon Squadron, RAFVR. Died 29/06/1942.

[84] A Mr BASTERIELD is named as the source of the Home Guard stories in chapter 22.

[85] 1939 Register indicates that Isabella JAMES (b. 15/03/1876 d. Mar 60) was living with her husband Albert (b. 23/6/1865) at No. 37 Hurcott Road. Isabella was 67 years old in 1943.

Three months later, on 2nd November, PC LAYCOCK reported two more messages, this time specifically referencing No. 404. The first read, **'HAGLEY WOOD LUBELLA ADDRESS WAS 404 LOWER HASBURY HALESOWEN'**. This was chalked on a wall that extended from the railway bridge on Station Road, Old Hill to the entrance of William Henry PALMER & Co. Timber Merchants. On inquiring he was told that the message had appeared between Sunday evening 29th October and the following morning.

PC LAYCOCK then made his way up Station Road towards Gorsty Hill, where he discovered another similar chalked message on a wall opposite the mouth of Coombe Hill: **'404 LOWER HASBURY HAGLEY WOOD LUBELLA ADDRESS WAS'**.

This time DC LEE conducted an inquiry, reporting that the ALLSOPPs had lived there for the last 56 years. He also noted that they had one daughter who had died aged 18 months, and one son, Samuel Charles Geoffrey ALLSOPP, aged 23 years, who was serving in the RAF[86] having been 'called-up' in 1940.

DC LEE closes the report by stating … *I have been unable to ascertain nothing of a doubtful character in the history of either of this young man's parents or in the history of the young man himself* – meaning this inquiry again led nowhere[87].

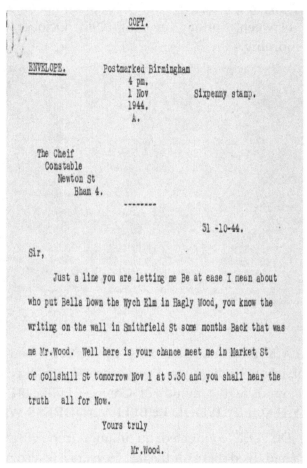

COPY.

ENVELOPE.   Postmarked Birmingham
4 pm,
1 Nov   Sixpenny stamp.
1944,
A.

The Cheif
Constable
Newton St
Bham 4,

----

31 -10-44.

Sir,

Just a line you are letting me Be at ease I mean about who put Bella Down the Wych Elm in Hagly Wood, you know the writing on the wall in Smithfield St some months Back that was me Mr.Wood. Well here is your chance meet me in Market St of Collshill St tomorrow Nov 1 at 5.30 and you shall hear the truth   all for Now.

Yours truly

Mr.Wood.

Police transcript of the letter and envelope

---

86 1534798 LAC ALLSOPP, S.C.G. RAF, Section 19G, Rowley Mile, Newmarket, Suffolk. Married Lillian Mavis née JONES 1914, died 14/11/1983.
[87] DC 215 LEE, Halesowen Section report dated 31st October 1944.

The following month, on 16th November, D/Sgt RICHARDSON of Birmingham City Police CID reported that a letter had been received, offering advice about one of the chalked messages. The author, a 'Mr WOOD', asked that someone meet him at 5.30 p.m. on 1st November. However, the letter was only received at the postal sorting office at 4 p.m. on the 1st and did not reach the police until the next day – too late for the police to make the appointment. The postmark indicated that the letter had been posted within the Birmingham Head Post Office district, which extended over an approximate eight-mile area. Identifying where it had been posted was an impossible task.

Mr WOOD specifically mentions the writing on the wall in Smithfield Street. Although there is no reference to this street in any reports, in 1944 it was an adjoining street between the two named locations – Upper Dean Street (27th March) and Pershore Street (30th March).

The next reference I discovered was in the Birmingham Gazette on 28th November 1953.

The article reports a quote from DI WILLIAMS who says, "It was the work of a crank who we are satisfied knew nothing and had nothing to do with the case. So, it seems that 'Bella' wasn't Bella after all".

This article was published during a phase of increased interest in the mystery following the revelation that Bella could have been a spy.

There is no supporting police documentation in the archive to support this statement.

Scrawl clue to 'Bella' is false

ONE of the few clues in the 10-year-old unsolved mystery of "Bella"—the skeleton of a murdered woman found in a wych elm in Hagley Wood—has proved to be false.

Worcestershire police have traced the man, who a year after the skeleton was found, scrawled on walls in Birmingham and Old Hill the words which gave her her nickname: "Who put Bella down the wych elm, Hagley Wood?"

Det. Supt. Tom Williams, head of the County C.I.D., said yesterday: "It was the work of a

crank who we are satisfied knew nothing and had nothing to do with the case. So it seems that 'Bella' wasn't even Bella after all."

Of note is that another newspaper article[88] published around the same time discusses the possibility that the chalk markings were not a hoax; that they were made by a member of a witchcraft circle who was trying to point the police in the direction of the murder(s).

There is also reference in a 1973 Black Country Bugle article[89] that chalk messages were also 'scrawled on pavements', but I found no supporting confirmation in the police files.

Nothing more happened for 40 years, when on 27th August 1984, the words, **'WHO PUT BELLA IN THE WYCH ELM'** appeared on the car park wall at the rear of Hagley village library.

It would not be until 1993 that similar graffiti was daubed on the Wychbury Obelisk. It appeared after the Express and Star newspaper ran an article[90] titled, Fifty Years On: The Riddle Of The Mysterious Body, Munitions And MI5... Day death went down to the woods.

---

[88] Wolverhampton Express and Star 20th November 1953.
[89] Black country Bugle 18th September 1973 p16.
[90] Express & Star, 11th November 1993, p. 6.

Date	Location	Message
28/03/44	Pershore Street, Birmingham	HAGLEY WOOD BELLA
28/03/44	No.19 Upper Dean Street, Birmingham	WHO PUT BELLA DOWN THE WYCH ELM – HAGLEY WOOD
30/03/44	Haden Hill, Old Hill, Halesowen	WHO PUT LUEBELLER IN THE WYCH ELM
12/04/44	Mucklow Hill, Halesowen	WHO PUT BELLA IN THE WYTCH ELM HAGLEY WOOD JACK THE RIPPER? JACK THE RIPPER ANA BELLA DIED IN HAGLEY WOOD
01/08/44	Sun Passage, Wolverhampton	HAGLEY WOOD LUBELLA ADDRESS OPPOSITE THE ROSE AND CROWN HASBURY
01/08/44	Shelton Lane, Halesowen	I USE TO HAGLEY WOOD LUBELLA WAS NO PROSS
01/08/44	Shelton Lane, Halesowen	ADDRESS WAS OPPOSITE ROSE AND CROWN HASBURY HAGLEY WOOD LUBELLA
31/10/44	Station Road, Old Hill, Halesowen	HAGLEY WOOD LUBELLA ADDRESS WAS 404 LOWER HASBURY HALES-OWEN
31/10/44	Coombe Hill, Halesowen	404 LOWER HASBURY HAGLEY WOOD LUBELLA ADDRESS WAS
16/11/44	MR WOOD LETTER	
28/11/53	SCRAWL CLUE TO 'BELLA' IS FALSE	
27/08/84	Hagley village library	WHO PUT BELLA IN THE WYCH ELM
1993	Wychbury Obelisk	WHO PUT BELLA IN THE WITCH ELM

Chart showing the messages in chronological order and highlighting the two linked clusters.

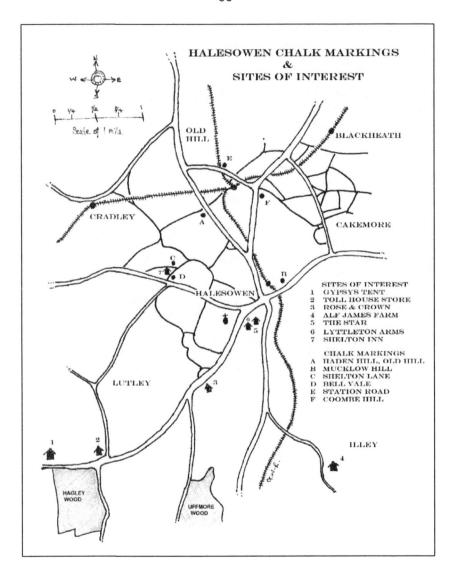

HALESOWEN CHALK MARKINGS
&
SITES OF INTEREST

OLD HILL

BLACKHEATH

CRADLEY

CAKEMORE

HALESOWEN

SITES OF INTEREST
1 GYPSYS TENT
2 TOLL HOUSE STORE
3 ROSE & CROWN
4 ALF JAMES FARM
5 THE STAR
6 LYTTLETON ARMS
7 SHELTON INN

CHALK MARKINGS
A HADEN HILL, OLD HILL
B MUCKLOW HILL
C SHELTON LANE
D BELL VALE
E STATION ROAD
F COOMBE HILL

LUTLEY

ILLEY

HAGLEY WOOD

UFFMORE WOOD

Wychbury Obelisk 2018

CHAPTER 5
JOHN JONES – ARMCHAIR SCIENCE

Three days before the first chalk marks appeared in Birmingham, a 20-year-old man named John JONES called into the Birmingham police office.

He said that, in August 1942, he had stayed with his sister Helen (aged 33) at the Clent Youth Hostel. Whilst returning home the following day, they passed Hagley Wood, and he had the feeling that something terrible was going to happen.

After reading a five-page article in a booklet called 'Armchair Science', he believed that the article related to him, and he fancied his chances at solving the crime. He had visited the Birmingham office in order to refresh his memory in respect of certain details and to see whether the police had overlooked anything in their investigation.

DOCTOR
DETECTIVES

By A. M. Barbour

After the first two messages were discovered, John was interviewed on 5th April. He was described as a 'peculiar youth', over 6 feet in height, with protruding ears and teeth. He lived at 106 Reservoir Road, Erdington, Birmingham, and worked as an electrician at the BSA factory in Small Heath. He was also a member of the Birmingham Home Guard, attached to the Intelligence Section of 26th Battalion, C Company. His role was map reading and the identification of uniforms.

On 17th April 1944, DI WILLIAMS reported that he was quite satisfied that John knew nothing about the case and that he was possibly mentally unbalanced.

After the interview, John called Digbeth police station no fewer than 20 times, each time with some new ideas, either about the writing on the wall or the type of man who, in his opinion, had committed the murder.

He was also questioned about being the author of the writings on the wall but was ruled out because he had difficulty in spelling some of the words. Handwriting samples were also sent to Professor WEBSTER for analysis; he presumably concurred.

CHAPTER 6
MISSING WOMEN 1944

The police checked their local Burgess Lists[91], and local Food and Registration Offices for the names Bella, Luebeller, Christabella and other similar names, and were unable to glean any information that would assist the investigation.

After the first two messages appeared in March 1944 referencing the name 'Bella' and newspaper articles were published, the inquiry started to receive missing persons reports from the public of women named Bella. This resulted in five inquiries:

April
Violet GOODE
Bella TONKS
Bella SHEWELL
Bella LUER
May
Isabel Helena BEECH

Violet GOODE

On 3rd April, PC VENABLES was conducting inquiries relating to the chalk marks discovered on 30th March, when he was told of a conversation in which it was alleged that a man openly said that he knew who had committed the Hagley Wood murder[92]. The potential victim was called Violet GOODE[93], and a man called Thomas Henry 'Harry' TRUMAN[94] was the murderer.

---

[91] Electoral Roll.
[92] Information passed to Inspector F.R. BACHE of Halesowen.
[93] Report CID030930, dated 4th May 1944.
[94] Age 49 QBVZ167/1.

> Violet GOODE was a female who had been involved in a relationship with Thomas Henry TRUMAN resulting in his relationship with his wife Gladys TRUMAN failing. Subsequently TRUMAN returned to his wife and a spurious assertion was made that GOODE had been killed to make way for this return. GOODE was identified as being alive and well, working and living in Stourbridge.

The informant had overheard a conversation in the Star Inn, Halesowen[95] to the effect that the Hagley Wood murder was probably carried out by a local man who had left his wife for another woman. He had returned to his wife after several years and his girlfriend then went missing. It was believed that the man was living next to Dean Street, a few yards from one of the Bella chalk markings.

The story goes that Harry TRUMAN was married to Gladys TRUMAN[96] (née TAYLOR) and it was said that "he gave his wife little money, spent freely himself, and was fond of the company of women". Gladys suspected that he was intimately associating with a woman from Birmingham and that he was the father of her son. It was said that they were seen together in Halesowen by one of Harry's daughters. Gladys is said to have traced this woman to her home in Birmingham and to have appealed to her to give up her husband, but the appeal proved unavailing and Gladys left her husband and obtained a separation order in 1935. After living in Halesowen for a short time, Gladys and her two daughters went to live in Birmingham. She later opened a shop that was very successful, and she made a lot of money.

After Gladys and Harry separated in early 1935, Harry lived with Violet[97] for about two years, first living in lodgings in Bearwood and for short periods with his mother on Friday Road, Hasbury.

---

[95] Report dated 5th April 1944, also the same public house that featured in the Mary LEE inquiry.

[96] May Gladys: married March 1918, Stourbridge.

[97] Aged 32 years, no fixed address, one child aged 8 years.

However, on hearing of Gladys's good fortune in opening a shop, Harry persuaded her to let him return[98]. He eventually moved back in with his wife in Birmingham

The police quickly located Harry and Gladys living together as the caretakers for Dr WISEMAN at his surgery at 142 Bromsgrove Street, Birmingham. Gladys was also the owner of a fish and chip shop at 156 Bromsgrove Street.

Harry stated that he had not seen Violet since going back to his wife. He said Violet was employed as a polisher by J. H. STRONGER Ltd., in Stourbridge. The police contacted the firm and spoke with the manager, Mr WEST, who confirmed that Violet had worked for them for nine years and was still working for them, and now lived at 56 Green Street, Stourbridge. It was agreed that she would not be made aware that the police were inquiring about her welfare.

Of note is that Harry's mother Emma is referenced in the report as living at Friday Road, Hasbury in 1935. In the 1939 Register, she is living with her husband Thomas and daughter Maisie BROWN (née TRUMAN) at 328 Hagley Road, which is on the same road and a short distance from the Rose & Crown, which is the location referenced in the August 1944 Shelton Lane chalk markings and those at Station Road, Old Hill in November. Harry is also listed in a police report[99] as living at No. 324 Hagley Road at some time.

Bella TONKS

Within the 2005 Closure Report under the heading 'Investigation', DCI NICHOLLS briefly references Bella TONKS and indicates

---

[98] 1939 Register: Harry, Gladys and daughter Kitty (GRAZIER) living at 156 Edward Street, Birmingham. Harry is a Capstan Lathe Hand and Gladys performs domestic duties.
[99] Birmingham City Police CID. Ref: 030930, dated 4th May 1944.

that she was identified as living under her maiden name in Heath Hays[100].

Bella TONKS was raised as a possibility following a media circulation. The name 'Bella' was seemingly derived from the chalk writings on the walls throughout the West Midlands conurbation, and as such the link to the enquiry was questionable. That said, the individual Bella TONKS was identified as living under her maiden name in Heath Hays.

This is incorrect and is a reference to a completely different inquiry (Bella SHEWELL). Furthermore, unlike the other inquiries in this chapter, which report the outcome of the inquiry, there is no reference of Bella TONKS ever being identified.

The background to this story is that an 'informant' contacted the police on 4th April, indicating that a woman named Bella TONKS had gone missing around the time of the First World War. Bella had lived with her brother Wilfred in a detached cottage, next to the grocer's shop opposite Clent Church. Both parents were dead, Wilfred had been killed in WWI[101], and Bella's younger sister Beatrice, also known as 'Trix', had been brought up in a Wolverhampton orphanage.

In 1908, Bella had been a school teacher at Clent School, and was described as around 20 to 22 years old, attractive, plump, with golden-brown hair and between 5' 3" and 5' 5" tall.

That is all that the archived material and the Closure Report tells us about this inquiry. There is nothing to support the Heath Hays statement. It feels as though some of the paperwork has gone missing, although there are similarities with the lack of detail and content in an archive bundle labelled 'miscellaneous', which contains missing women reports (not referenced in the closure

---

[100] Correct spelling is Heath Hayes.
[101] Sergeant 998 Harold Wilfred TONKS, Machine Gun Corps (Motors), died 21/05/1917, aged 24, son of the late John and Lucy TONKS, of Clent.

report), where women were 'ruled-out' of the investigation because their profile fell outside the investigation parameters.

Bella was born on 24th May 1887, which would have made her ~57 years old at the time proposed by Professor WEBSTER, too old to be the victim.

I investigated further, and the public records confirm that Lucy TONKS (née BRADLEY) gave birth to three children: Lucy Isabel 'Bella', Beatrice Annie 'Trix', and Harold Wilfred. Bella TONKS married Arthur KIBBLE[102] in December 1919, and when 'Trix' died in 1962 (spinster), Lucy Isabel KIBBLE was granted Letters of Administration. Bella KIBBLE née TONKS died aged 103 on 21st September 1990 at Lillington Nursing Home, Leamington Spa.

Bella SHEWELL

At the same time as John JONES (Armchair Science) went to the police, a Birmingham prostitute (from Halesowen) contacted them, wanting to discover the whereabouts of a woman she knew as Bella. The informant had good knowledge of the circumstances surrounding the murder and indicated that Bella had been missing for about three years.

The inquiry was led by Sergeant RENSHAW and was concentrated at various houses and licensed premises at Ladywood, Moseley, and the Bristol Road districts of Birmingham. They eventually traced Bella to her last known address of 34 Trafalgar Road, Moseley. The landlady remembered having had a Christmas card from Bella in 1942 but had heard nothing since. They also discovered that she was known by two other names: KENDRICK and LAWLEY.

The landlady was also able to supply the address of Bella's mother who lived in Hednesford, Staffordshire. It was from here that this

---

[102] b. Aug 1894 d. Dec 1983.

missing Bella was identified, under her maiden name of Bella SHEWELL, alive and living at 93 Gorsemoor Road, Heath Hayes.

On 17th April 1944, DI WILLIAMS[103] closed the inquiry.

It seems the Heath Hayes location referenced in the Bella TONKS story has been drawn from this inquiry although the name is not referenced in the Closure Report.

Bella LUER

This inquiry was instigated in April 1944 by a Mr Alfred RICHARDSON, a 52-year-old factory hand from Darenth Road, Stamford Hill, London. He had read an article in the Sunday newspaper headed, Do You Know Bella? He went to Tottenham police station to report that a woman named Bella LUER had gone missing about two years earlier. She had lived in lodgings next door to him, before she went to work in a factory in the Midlands. He believed it was possibly a powder factory about 12 miles outside Reading.

Do You Know Bella?

POLICE in the Midlands are chasing a murder clue which is proving as fantastic as any in a crime "thriller."

The story began last year when four boys bird-nesting in Hagley Wood, near Stourbridge, found inside a hollow wych elm the skeleton of a woman.

At the inquest last April a verdict of murder was returned.

A pathologist gave the police a rough description of the woman after an examination of the bones which he said must have been pushed into the trunk at least eighteen months before.

Then just before Christmas these words were found written in chalk on a house in Hayden Hill-road, Old Hill: "Who put Luebella down the wych elm?"

That message was not brought to the notice of the police till the Friday after they had found a similar message on the wall of empty premises in Upper Dean-street, Birmingham.

Sunday Pictorial, 02/04/1944, p. 3

Soon after she left, he had received a letter from her saying that she was going to marry a soldier and that they would be coming to London and would visit him, but he had not heard from or seen her since. He also recalled that, after receiving the letter, he had read in the newspaper that a Bella LUER had been prosecuted for absenteeism from the factory, but he was unable to recall when he saw the article. He described her as being about 24 years old, 5 feet tall, with mid-brown hair, and a good set of her own teeth, not false.

Coincidentally, the following month, a Mr I J LEVAINE, who was working at the Ordnance Parachute Factory, Sialkot, Punjab, India, also reported to Tottenham police a missing woman named Bella LUER[104]. He described her as being 'identical' to the description of the Hagley Wood murder victim and gave her last known address as Railway Cottages, Goring-on-Thames, Oxon, which is approximately 12 miles outside Reading.

Despite this, the closure report indicates that there was no definitive link with the Bella from Stamford Hill and the Bella in Goring.

Bella LUER was a woman who moved from London to undertake factory work. The contact chain with persons in London was broken and thus she was raised as a possibility as being the deceased. Again the major factor was the term 'Bella'. Enquiries traced a Bella LUER as being resident at Goring on Thames however this individual was not definitively linked to the Bella LUER who was formerly resident in the Stamford Hill area of London.

It has been difficult to add any detail to this story as I was unable to find Bella, Alfred or Mr LEVAINE in the 1939 Register. The only birth for a Bella LUER I found was in 1922, mother's maiden name of BRADSHAW, and I was unable to find a marriage for her parents, or indeed either of them on the 1939 Register – this could be because they were dead.

---

[104] Metropolitan Police, Tottenham: 201/43/63, dated 5th May 1944.

I did, however, find a Bella LEUR living at 49 Pentonville Road, Islington on the 1945 Electoral Register, but have no proof that this is the same person. However, if it was, then she was still in London in 1965, married Fred E. CRANE in September 1961, emigrated to America, and died in December 2004

Isabel Helena BEECH

Bella BEECH was drawn to the enquiry's attention following her disappearance from bombed premises in West Ealing, London. She had left the bombed premises to live in the Birmingham area, and contact had ceased. Enquiries traced this woman to a hospital in the London area where she was working as a nurse.

Bella BEECH[105], a dental nurse, was reported missing by her twin brother, George Alexander BEECH, in May 1944. George had been serving in the army when their mother Emily[106] was killed on 19th April 1941, aged 52, during an air raid at the family home of 46 Talbot Road, West Ealing. George had lost contact with his sister and was concerned for her welfare.

BEECH Emily of 46 Talbot-road West Ealing **Middlesex** widow died 19 April 1941 Administration **Llandudno** 17 July to James Charles Beech railway guard. Effects £1927 7s. 2d.

Following her mother's death, Bella moved to Birmingham to be with her other brother, James Charles 'Jim' BEECH (QJBL.385-1.83/1), who lived with his family at Rose Cottage, South Road, Bromsgrove[107]. Initially, they believed that she had gone to live at

---

[105] Middle name Helena, although sometimes referenced as Eleanor. Born 30/08/1915, died March 1984.
[106]Widower, Donald BEECH.
[107] Spent about ten years as a Porter at Kingsbury L.M.&S Railway Station before moving in 1934 when he married.

Upper Dean Street[108] (chalk message location), but inquiries found no one of her name living in the area.

The police quickly traced her, living and working at Woodside Hospital, Muswell Hill, London[109][110]. She would go on to enrol as an assistant nurse[111] on 21st December 1945, and died in March 1984.

---

[108] Ipswich Police Report Ref: D)*/H.22(1)/44 dated 3rd May and Birmingham CID J.135/43(74) 17th April.
[109] Sunday Pictorial, 02/04/1944, p. 3, Do You Know Bella?
[110] Memo Ref: CIDJ135/43(74) dated 17th May 1944.
[111] Roll of assistant nurses 1947-8, p. 54.

CHAPTER 7
THE HANDBAG

The only other inquiry that took place in 1944 followed the recovery of a handbag discovered by Special Constable R SHEPPARD from Hagley Section[112] in Hagley Wood at 10.15 a.m. on Friday 17th November 1944. He was working on an issue over the shooting rights within the wood when the discovery was made.

The handbag was brown leather, 9 ½" by 6 ½", with nickel-plated corners and a snap fastener. It was described as 'falling to pieces and the upper side was covered in moss', having been exposed to the elements for some considerable time.

Being covered in moss is an important observation. Dr LUND recorded the lack of any moss or growth on the bones that were recovered outside the tree, which provided him with a timeline for the murder.

The following day, PC POUND recovered the handbag and recalled that "the handbag was at the base of a Birch tree, which was located in relation to the Wych Elm tree approximately 170 yards to the north side, and was about 20 yards to the north of the Birmingham Water Works 'Ride' (Elan aqueduct) and 25 to 30 yards west of Hagley Wood Lane".

PC POUND noted that on the Birch tree, about three feet from the ground cut into the bark, was the letter 'T', which appeared to have been cut at least three to four years previously.

The records at Clent Police Station showed that a Dr Dorothy MARKHAM[113], had her handbag stolen from her car on 16th December 1939 when it was parked on Hagley Wood Lane. Inside

---

[112] PC 302 POUND memorandums 20/11 & 23/11/1944; Lady's handbag in wood.
[113] 1939 - 25 Elgin Road, Alexandra Park, London, N22.
1944 - No.1 Compton Court, Compton Road, Wolverhampton.

the bag was 15 shillings in cash, her driving licence, and a fountain pen.

If I had expected to find considerable police activity following the discovery of the skeleton I was wrong. What I discovered was that 1943 was dominated by the Mary LEE inquiry, with a few weeks spent on the search for the Nimmings Field Gypsies and the search for the owner of the shoes recovered from the crime scene. Nothing happened at all in 1944, until the chalk messages appeared, resulting in four brief inquiries in April: the gypsy FORREST, Bella TONKS, Bella SHEWELL and Bella LUER. This was followed in May with two cursory inquiries for Isabel Eleanor BEECH and Violet GOODE. In November came the search for the owner of the handbag. Then nothing happened for nearly five years until 1949.

CHAPTER 8
THE CHARLES WALTON MURDER

I must raise the unsolved murder of Charles WALTON in 1945, because it is the principal source behind the witchcraft theories, although the association did not really feature until 2nd August 1950, with an article in the Birmingham Gazette titled, Midlands 'Black Magic' Murders...Witchcraft Lives On –Scientist. It was published following an interview with Dr Margaret MURRAY, who believed WALTON had been sacrificed and that the Hagley Wood victim was also a victim of devil-worshippers.

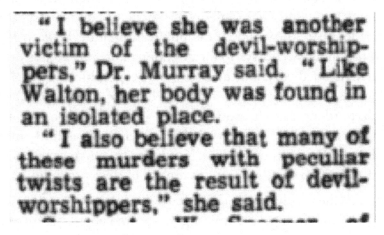

"I believe she was another victim of the devil-worshippers," Dr. Murray said. "Like Walton, her body was found in an isolated place.
"I also believe that many of these murders with peculiar twists are the result of devil-worshippers," she said.

Extract from the Birmingham Gazette article

Furthermore, both murders would later be linked by author Donald McCORMICK in his 1969 book, Murder By Witchcraft. Both McCORMICK and Dr MURRAY are discussed in detail later but the facts which lead to the linkage of the cases are set out briefly here.

On 14th February 1945, Charles WALTON, a 74-year-old agricultural worker, was murdered[114]. The autopsy showed that he had been beaten over the head with his walking stick and his arms were cut where he had tried to defend himself. His throat

---

[114] FABIAN of the Yard, p. 105-111.

had been ripped away with a sickle blade of a trouncing hook, which was then buried in his neck. The prongs of the pitchfork were embedded into either side of his neck, pinning him to the ground. The handle of the pitchfork had then been wedged under what was described as *'a cross member of the hedge'*.

His body was discovered at around 6 p.m. The first policeman on the scene was PC Michael James LOMANSNEY, who arrived at 7.05 p.m., followed by members of Stratford-upon-Avon CID later in the evening. Professor WEBSTER arrived at around 11.30 p.m. and the body was recovered for post-mortem at 1.30 a.m.

The Chief Constable of Warwickshire had sought the aid of Scotland Yard, and help came in the shape of famous inspector, Robert FABIAN. It would be the publication of his book in 1950 that brought Dr MURRAY to the attention of the press and started the witchcraft theory and an assumed geographical connection was made between the two murders because there is a suburb which borders the Halesowen ward called Quinton. Charles WALTON was killed in a place called Lower Quinton, thirty miles south in Stratford-upon-Avon. The similarity in names belies the fact that the two murder locations are not in close proximity at all.

Although the involvement of Dr MURRAY was not revealed until 1950, her part in the 1945 investigation came about because the police were aware of another similar murder and its links with witchcraft at Long Compton in 1875. Ann TENNANT[115] (née SMITH), aged 79, was murdered by James HAYWARD with a hay fork because he believed she had bewitched him. He also said he would kill all 16 witches in Long Compton.

It was thought that the mode of killing was a survivor of the ancient Anglo-Saxon custom of dealing with witches by means of 'stacung', or sticking spikes into them.

---

[115] Folk Lore, Old Customs and Superstitions in Shakespeare-land. J. Harvey BLOOM, 1930; NOTE: Sometimes referenced as Ann TURNER.

CHAPTER 9
JOHN THOMAS SWINDON

The last police inquiry had been the search for Violet GOODE in May 1944. Five years and five months later, the investigation would once again become headline news.

On 4th October, the Birmingham Gazette and the Courier and Advertiser became aware of the EDDIE SHERWOOD inquiry and published articles indicating that Gypsies were to blame.

Courier and Advertiser 04/10/1949

The following day, John Thomas SWINDON[116], a library caretaker, aged 58, of 71 Church Street, Smethwick, Birmingham, telephoned Birmingham CID to tell them he had information that could help the murder inquiry. John related that on reading the story in the paper about a soldier giving information concerning Gypsies, he thought he had better tell about a couple who had been in the back of his mind for some time. The following day he was interviewed by D/Sgt JONES of the Oldbury office.

John told how, on 16th June 1942[117] (he remembered the date because it was the start of the fishing season and he went fishing at Bewdley), he had caught a bus from the King's Head in Bearwood sometime before 9.00 a.m. and sat on the bottom deck of the bus about halfway back. He recalled that the bus halted at a bus stop by Hagley Wood, near a gate leading into a coppice on the left-hand side of the road before reaching The Gypsy's Tent public house.

He noticed two people got off at the bus stop; one a soldier and the other a woman. They came down from the upper deck and he presumed that they were on the bus prior to him getting on. The soldier was of medium height, dressed in khaki without a jacket. He was wearing a cap but John couldn't remember what sort, and was aged between 34 and 38. The woman was very plain and looked as if she had just left the 'washing tub'. She was wearing a coat and hat, and appeared to be wearing an apron. She was a bit shorter than the soldier, but probably about the same age. They did not speak to each other and when they got off the bus they went through the gate and straight into the coppice.

There are no more reports about this incident. However, of note is that at this time, the papers were reporting that an arrest had been made, which was quickly denied by the police.

---

[116] 1939, living at 71 Church Street with wife Lilian May and two sons, Henry and George, working as a Millwright at Smethwick Gas Works. He was also an ARP.
[117] He stated 1943 in his initial call.

Tree murder: arrest denied

POLICE SUPT. T. N. WILLIAMS, of Stourbridge, last night denied rumours that an arrest had been made in the Hagley Wood murder, reopened after six and a half years.

In 1943 the skeleton of a woman with a rag stuffed in her mouth was found by boys inside a hollow wych-elm tree.

New information by an ex-soldier has now started extensive police inquiries about a band of gipsies heard quarrelling near the scene of the crime in 1942.

Birmingham Gazette 05/10/1949

CHAPTER 10
SHEILA

A few weeks after John Thomas SWINDON made his approach to the police, a woman named Vivian Mary 'Biddy' CROSS (née WILLIAMS), aged 28, of 'Hoarstons', No. 27 Sweetpool Lane, West Hagley, also contacted the police to make them aware of an incident that had occurred during the autumn of 1942[118].

Biddy said that in mid-October 1942, she was employed delivering milk in the West Hagley area for PARSON's dairy. One morning, whilst in Hagley, a man stopped her and made a comment about one of the front wheels on her vehicle wobbling. She said that she was aware of this fact, but Mr PARSON was unable to get a replacement. The man called himself Pat GRAHAM, but Biddy now knew that was not his real name.

After that meeting, Pat went to see Mr PARSON, which resulted in him being offered some mechanical work. He subsequently became friends with Mr PARSON, and was often seen around the dairy. Sometimes, when there was nothing to do, he would accompany Biddy on journeys in her van.

Pat told her that he was on a month's leave from the Rolls Royce factory where he worked, but he had taken a firm van without permission that he had hidden in Hagley Wood. He said he was staying with friends in Hagley and Biddy recalled that he was often seen in the company of a Land Army girl by the name of Sheila. Pat also told Biddy that his fiancée, a former 'racing motorist', had been killed in a crash, and that he was getting over her death, but he would never forget her screams as she died because he was present in the pits at the time.

---

[118] HQ CID Report: 25th October 1949.

Biddy also recalled Pat was always singing an RAF ditty[119] with the words, "...my wife she died, I laughed, and I cried, to think I was single again...".

At first Biddy found him to be 'very plausible', but she became somewhat suspicious of him and it came as no surprise when she heard that the police wanted to see him. One day towards the end of October or the beginning of November 1942, Biddy told how she was at the dairy when Lord COBHAM arrived in his car accompanied by a police officer wanting to speak to Pat GRAHAM.

He was not around, and Biddy left to do her milk round, stopping off at home on route for lunch. At some point she saw a van from Hagley driven by Sheila stop outside the house then drive off. A few seconds later, there was a knock on the door, and it was Pat.

He was aware that the police were looking for him, explaining it was because he had obtained some tyres without a permit and that he needed somewhere to stop whilst he thought things over.

Biddy let him into the house and agreed to help him. He asked that she drive him somewhere later and lend him her Red Setter dog – he refused to give her any more details until they were on the road.

He stayed at the house until dusk and at about 6 p.m. they left. Biddy recalled that Pat gave her directions, but during the journey he was singing hysterically and had a very queer look about him, and she became very nervous and upset by his behaviour. Eventually, Pat asked her to pull over at the entrance to Hagley Wood Lane.

She recalled asking what he was going to do, and he replied, "I can't possibly tell you, but one day you might know".

After he made her promise not to say anything, Pat got out of the car. She remembered he hid his face when a bus passed by before

---

[119]A folk song: I Wish I Was Single Again, made famous by Wilf CARTER.

he walked up the lane with her dog. She watched them disappear into darkness before driving straight back to the dairy. At the dairy she saw Mr. PARSONS who was concerned about the length of time she had had the van and that she was not looking too well. She did not tell him anything about where she had been or about Pat GRAHAM, and then went home.

The next morning, when she went to collect her van, she met Mr PARSONS who had her dog. He explained that Pat had brought the dog back at about 10.30 p.m. the previous night.

The next time she saw Pat was possibly a few weeks later when he turned up at the dairy. She remembered that his dress and appearance were much smarter and that he explained that he had been in Manchester driving taxis. He was told that the police were still looking for him and he went away, not to be seen again until sometime later when he was in Stourbridge Court, charged with stealing a Mackintosh coat. Biddy remembered that Pat was often seen wearing a coat that was later found to have been stolen from a stable at Hagley Hall.

After being in court, Pat came to the dairy and that was the last time she saw him, talking with Mr PARSONS.

Biddy explained that when in April 1943, the skeleton of a woman was found, she did not connect the incident, especially because the body was stated to have been in the tree for at least 18 months and Pat was around only about six months prior to that. However, it had always been in the back of her mind, and she became aware that the case had been reopened so decided to inform the police.

The police identified Pat GRAHAM as Kenneth Francis 'Pat' PATTEN[120] who, in October 1949, was in Wandsworth Prison, halfway through an 18-month prison sentence.

---

[120] 1939 Register (RMAN130/2) living with father at 127 Valley Road, Nottingham.

He was interviewed and he stated he had been discharged from the RAF on 1st February 1942 and was living in Cheltenham. When he left the district, he travelled the country, hitchhiking from place to place. By October he had reached Stourbridge, where he met a Land Army girl called Sheila who worked on the Hagley estate. He told the Police how she had invited him to live with her in a cottage that she occupied, situated off the lane leading to Hagley Hall main gates, but he could not recall Sheila's surname.

He said that he spent about three weeks in the district and during that time met 'Biddy' WILLIAMS who was employed by Mr T.F. PARSONS. He also remembered a friend of Sheila's called Peggy BOTTOMLEY who was from Manchester. They were visiting Peggy when he was arrested by the Manchester police for the theft of a raincoat in Hagley for which on 18th December 1942, Pat was *bound over to keep the peace.*

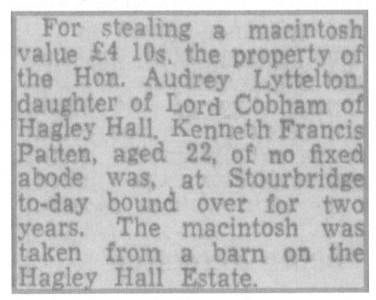

For stealing a macintosh value £4 10s. the property of the Hon. Audrey Lyttelton, daughter of Lord Cobham of Hagley Hall, Kenneth Francis Patten, aged 22, of no fixed abode was, at Stourbridge to-day bound over for two years. The macintosh was taken from a barn on the Hagley Hall Estate.

Evening Despatch 18/12/42

He said that he knew nothing of the Hagley district and spend most of his time between the cottage, Biddy WILIAMS's home, and the dairy, where he worked on some motor vans. The last he had seen of Sheila was when he was arrested in Manchester in 1942.

The premise of this inquiry appears to be about the suspicious activity of Pat PATTEN, rather than identifying the victim. Once he was interviewed, there was no more information held in the archive.

I was unable to find Biddy on the 1939 Register. This could be because she is still alive (aged ~98) or simply because she would have been about 18 years old in 1939, so her record remains closed.

The same goes for Sheila if she were of similar age. However, I did find three women named Sheila whose 1939 entry states their occupation as Land Army, but none in the Hagley area. One was in Newcastle-under-Lyme, Staffordshire, born 1912, died 2003; one in Suffolk, born 1903, died 1992; and one in Leicestershire, born 1924, died 2002. It is of course possible that as at 1939 Sheila may not have been recorded as being in the Land Army.

I was unable to find a Peggy BOTTOMLEY in Manchester, although her real name could have been Margaret and there are quite a few of those. I was unable to find Mr PARSON either.

CHAPTER 11
DR MARGARET ALICE MURRAY (1863-1963)

Dr Murray c. 1933

Dr Margaret MURRAY was a suffragette, archaeologist (specialising in Egyptology) and scholar, who led excavations in Malta, Menorca and Palestine[121]. Margaret also wrote extensively on folklore and witches.

Margaret was 82 years old when she was asked to assist with the murder inquiry of Charles WALTON in 1945, but she would not be linked to the Hagley Wood murder until September 1950, when she was interviewed by the Birmingham Gazette.

---

[121] William KIMBER (1963) Autobiography: My First One Hundred Years.

Witchcraft lives on—scientist

MIDLAND 'BLACK MAGIC' MURDERS?

by A. E. H. TAYLOR

A FRAIL, grey-haired woman scientist of over 80 sat in the lounge of Birmingham's Queens Hotel last night and told me that she thought the victims of two Midland murders had been human sacrifices.

DR. MURRAY

She was Dr. Margaret Murray, eminent Egyptologist and writer on folk-lore and witches, visiting the city for the British Association.

"I think there are still remnants of witchcraft in isolated parts of Great Britain," she said.

"I believe that Charles Walton, a 74-year-old hedger found murdered on St. Valentine's Day, 1945, in a field at Lower Quinton (Warwickshire), was one of the people sacrificed.

"I think this because of the peculiar way in which he had been killed. His throat had been cut and a pitchfork had been used after he was dead to prevent him from being moved.

"The sacrifices are carried out by people who still believe in a religion practised in Britain before Christianity whom we call devil-worshippers. They still practise black magic.

"The belief is that if life is taken out of the ground through farming it must be replaced by a blood sacrifice.

"I am not interested in the murder, only in the witches.

"I think it was a murder without normal motive — no money was missing and there was no other reason why the old man should have been killed.

"He died in February—one of the four months in the year when sacrifices are carried out."

Hagley Wood case

Then Dr. Murray, who is a Fellow of London University and a former professor, turned to the Hagley Wood murder, where a woman's body was found in a tree trunk in April, 1943. Her identity has never been established and her murderer never found.

"I believe she was another victim of the devil-worshippers," Dr. Murray said. "Like Walton, her body was found in an isolated place.

"I also believe that many of these murders with peculiar twists are the result of devil-worshippers," she said.

Supt. A. W. Spooner, of Warwick C.I.D., said yesterday that the professor was helping him with the five-year-old investigation.

"I am confident I shall clear up this case one day," he said.

Ex-Supt. Robert Fabian, in a newly-published book, devotes a chapter to the Walton murder, and in it he says that at the time it was believed to be the work of witches.

Birmingham Gazette 02/09/1950

The interview with the Birmingham Gazette coincided with the release of a book[122] by a famous police investigator of the time, Chief Inspector Robert FABIAN of New Scotland Yard. He had assisted with the WALTON investigation, and the case was discussed in his book along with 'slight' references to the witchcraft theory, although he does not reference the involvement of Margaret in the inquiry.

In the Birmingham Gazette article, Superintendent SPOONER of Warwick CID confirmed that Margaret was helping him with the WALTON investigation, but despite the fact that she commented on Bella's murder there is no confirmation that she was ever consulted in the Hagley Wood inquiry.

---

[122] Robert FABIAN (1950) FABIAN of the Yard: p. 105-p111.

CHAPTER 12
Billy GIBSON

In February 1951, Leonard 'Len' HUGHES of 15 Albert Road, Halesowen, contacted the police. He was concerned about an acquaintance called 'Billy' GIBSON whom he had not seen since September 1938, when her husband had gone to work in India. It was believed that he returned home after the war married to another woman. The police note in the archive[123] provides details of the initial contact:

Len was employed at STEWARTS & LLOYDS (S&L), Coombs Wood Tube Works, Halesowen, Birmingham.

He told of a 6′ 2″ man named Oswald GIBSON who came to work at S&L as the Department Manager in 1936. It was said that Oswald had travelled widely before joining the company; he was well educated, and his father was a Professor of Hydraulics at Manchester University. He left S&L in August/September 1938 and went to India to take charge of an ordinance factory.

At the time, it was believed he was married, or possibly living (as husband and wife) with, a woman called 'Billy', in the Manor House at Hagley. Billy was thought to have been born between around 1912 and 1916, and was described as attractive with fair hair, highly strung, fond of the company of men, and a bad drinker with a bad temper. She also had an upper gold tooth. He did not know if Billy had gone to India with Oswald, but he had received letters from Oswald during the war and had been surprised that no mention was ever made of Billy despite asking many times for information.

Len provided a photograph of the three of them and a letter from Oswald.

---

[123] Stamped Hindlip Hall, 5th February 1951.

The significance of the reference to the upper gold tooth is that Professor WEBSTER indicated in his post-mortem report on Bella that the left lateral incisor and the second right molar were missing. He noted that they had dropped out post-mortem having been present in the head at the time of death. These missing teeth were never recovered.

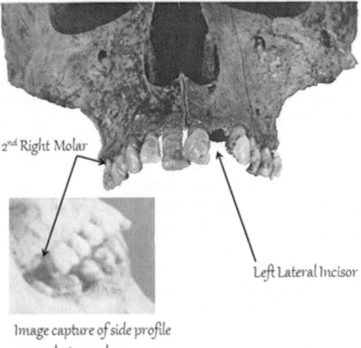

2nd Right Molar

Left Lateral Incisor

Image capture of side profile
scene photograph

A copy of the letter provided by Len from Oswald is on the file, dated 24/01/1943 from Lieutenant Colonel O. GIBSON C/O M.G.O. Branch, G.H.Q.(I)., New Delhi.

Dear Leonard, how goes things in Coombs Wood? It seems ages since I heard from any of the old crowd. Please remember me to them all and particularly to Mrs HUGHES. I hope she is fit. I often think of the days when we used to shoot rabbits – do you remember? I have just been posted back to GHQ after some active service on the Burma border. We were in a district which was stuffed with wild elephant, tiger, leopard, buffalo and that very rare animal the Indian Rhinoceros. Not to mention snakes, mosquitoes and millions of other pests. I should very much have liked to have a go at them, but we were kept too busy with more important matters to have time to think of big game shooting. Of course, if you walked into anything big and your tommy gun is handy – well, it's a matter of self defence then!!!

Well, all the best Leonard.

Yours bye, Osborne Gibson.

On 5th February,[124] a response was sent to Len from an unknown officer. He thanked Len for his interest and for the documents he had loaned, which were returned with the response. The officer made some observations:

About her height; the officer estimates Billy to be 5' 4 1/2" and notes that Prof WEBSTER has the victim as 5'. Although references that another expert who reconstructed the skirt indicated that [the skirt] would be on the ankles of a 5' woman. From the height he thought it could be Billy.

He then discussed the mouth, noting that, in the picture, Billy had her mouth closed, which was not helpful, referencing that Len indicated that Billy had a gold tooth. He enclosed an image of the upper jaw showing where the tooth had been extracted, noting that was about where Len mentioned. He also inquired about irregular teeth, noting that 'if she had been a clever girl, she would close her mouth when having her photograph taken'.

The officer also sent a photograph of the shoes, clothes worn by the victim, and the ring – inquiring if she dressed like this. He also asked if she might have fallen on 'evil days' since he last saw her, noting that the victim's hair was mousy in colour and inquiring if Billy dyed or bleached hers.

He finished by saying that they would be glad of any further observations.

On 9th February 1951, Len responded with a letter:

With reference to the attached correspondence re 'Billy'. Would it be possible for some old acquaintance to get in touch with GIBSON whose whereabouts are presumably ascertainable and attempt to obtain the last

---

[124] Typed letter REF: SWI/J dated 5th February 1951.

known location of Billy probably on the pretence of returning to her some artefact of value which belonged to her, or some other excuse.

It would be obviously best to start from the beginning i.e. by trying to trace Billy rather than to presume that the dead woman was Billy and trying to contact them.

It might even be worth the direct approach i.e. through official channels, to GIBSON to ascertain his last knowledge of Billy and if my first suggestion is not possible for some reason, I respectfully suggest the later course before any further enquiry is made re the teeth etc.

Len wrote again on 21st February[125], hoping to get some information as to when the couple had divorced, as he had tried himself without success.

He also told how he had asked the opinion of a colleague, L. WHYLEY, 'who knew the lady well', and they had both concluded that the possibility of 'Billy' being the female concealed in the tree was very remote. Whilst they were of that opinion, they pointed out that they were not competent to inquire on the question. Therefore, if they secured any further data, they would advise the police.

That is all the information contained within the archive bundle marked 'Miscellaneous' on the Billy GIBSON inquiry. It is also not mentioned in the Closure Report along with other reports that appear to fall outside the time parameters and description of the victim set for the scope of the investigation. In this case, Billy went missing in 1938, not 1941. She was between 29 and 33, not 35, and her estimated height was 5' 4 1/2", not 5'.

Not having any more information about why Billy was not investigated further, despite the obvious similarities between Billy and the victim, intrigued me, so I have tried to progress the story beyond where the police apparently stopped.

---

[125] Received 23rd February, Hindlip Hall.

Being unable to find Billy, I concentrated on finding Oswald, who I discovered was born Osborne and not Oswald on 25th December 1906 and had died in 1972.

The only other information that I found that was helpful is that his army service record shows that he was divorced from Billy and remarried Hilda Louise (née PAYNTER), a nurse,[126] on 9th June 1945 in Calcutta. He had a distinguished military career, was awarded a mention in dispatches when serving in Burma, and received an OBE in February 1946.

From this information I was able to obtain a copy of Billy and Osborne's marriage certificate. They married on 8th June 1935, and Billy is named as Millicent Evelyn ORRELL, aged 25, a spinster, and her father's given profession as 'Gentleman'.

Armed with Billy's information, the next stage was to locate a death certificate and close the inquiry; however, I was unable to find one, or even a birth certificate, at first. What I discovered was that Billy was born illegitimately on 27th February 1907, and not in 1910 as indicated on her marriage certificate, or between 1912 and 1916 as noted in the police note. This meant Billy was the same age as her husband (28) when they married and would have been nearly 35 years old in 1941, the probable age of the victim we know as Bella according to Professor WEBSTER.

Her mother, Jessie Constance ROBERTS, married Edward ORRELL in 1913. It is possible that because Edward would have only been 15 years old when Billy was born, the different birthdate would have made her 'father' 18 years old when she was born. However, Edward was killed[127] during WWI at the Somme in 1917. Billy's mother died on 6th August 1945. Her will names all her children, including a Millicent Evelyn KING. From this, I

---

[126] Register of Nurses for 1946 – No.60014: From Clevedon, Somerset: Qualified Bristol 1925-1928. 1939 Register OAAP391.1.223/1, Richmond Grove, Bristol.
[127] Sergeant 72188 E. ORRELL, 144th Heavy Bty., RGA. Killed 29/04/1917 aged 25. Also served with 168th Heavy Battery.

discovered that Billy died on 10th August 1983, at 28a Park Road, West Kirby.

Her death certificate names her husband as David Halford KING[128]. The anomaly of her birthdate continues to the end, although it is consistent as her death certificate gives her birthdate as 27th February 1913 – the same date as her mother married Edward ORRELL.

---

[128] Died on the 10th July 1985.

CHAPTER 13
WILFRED 'BILL' BYFORD-JONES

Byford-Jones Berlin 1945

Introduction

Wilfred 'Bill' BYFORD-JONES was a journalist with Wolverhampton's Express & Star newspaper who wrote under the pennames 'Quaestor Seeker' and 'Quaestor'[129]. He was also a radio reporter, author, playwright[130] and soldier, with books published under the names Quaestor, W. BYFORD-JONES, and later as Lieutenant Colonel W. BYFORD-JONES. Bill is a

---

[129] Latin for 'investigator'.
[130] The Almighty Petticoat & Broken Nail.

significant character in the story as he wrote about the Hagley Wood murder. He is credited with introducing witchcraft to the mystery and for being the instigator of the many spy theories that are discussed in the next chapter.

Because of his close link with the story from a journalistic perspective, it is not surprising that his name is associated with the mystery. However, what does surprise is how much of a connection he has with so many different elements of the story. For that reason, within this chapter I will present Bill alongside different events and stories, and show the geographical links. First, I will discuss his personal life, his career including his military service, his whereabouts at the time of the discovery of the skeleton, and the subsequent police investigation until 1953. Then I will provide a more detailed sequence of events and actions relating to his articles in the Express & Star newspaper, which did so much to popularise the mystery.

Pre 1953

1905: Wilfred JONES was born[131] on 26th July 1905, in Dudley in the West Midlands; however, his birth was registered in Machynlleth, Wales. His birth name was JONES, his mother's maiden name was BYFORD, and as a child he lived with his family at 149 New John Street, Halesowen[132].

1923–29: Aged 18, Bill became a reporter and a black and white artist between 1923[133] and 1929, with the Midland Newspaper Association. He then joined the Express & Star newspaper in 1929, initially as Foreign Correspondent and then as Feature Editor. He remained with the Express & Star until his retirement, when he and his second wife, Cynthia, retired to Wales. He died on 16th May 1977 in Llandaff.

---

[131] Father Ehud, mother Mary Elizabeth.
[132] 1911 Census. His father was a fruit dealer.
[133] Express & Star 18th & 21st May 1977, military service record – qualifications.

1930–31: On 19th August 1930, he married his first wife, Swedish-born Winifred Louise née DAWSON[134], 22, and they lived briefly at 126 Lea Road, Wolverhampton. They had a child, Charles Miles, born in Bilston on 11th September 1931, and by then the family had moved and was living at 'Eversley', Mount Pleasant, Bilston, Wolverhampton.

1932–36: In June 1932 it is reported that he was the Best Man to Anne and Bernard[135] COOPER at their wedding, which took place at the British Embassy in Paris[136]. It was around then that he started to publish. Bill's writing career went through two specific phases. First, prior to WWII Bill wrote several books, which are described by the Express & Star's News Editor, B. D. WHITEAKER as a collection of 'features' or articles telling of life in the Midlands. Bill refers to them as collections of essays. By whatever name, these stories had previously been published within the newspaper but were reproduced in book format.

After the war, his books took on a more 'serious' social and historical theme. His first three books were: 'Both Sides of the Severn' (1932), 'Midlands Leaves' (1934), and 'Vagabonding Through the Midlands; (1935) followed by 'Death By Order', his first and only novel[137] featuring a heroine called Miss Isobel ARNOLD. He also used the artwork of an Express & Star[138] illustrator called Arthur ARROWSMITH in many of these and future books.

---

[134] Born 8th August 1908: In 1930 Winifred was living at 56 Inverness Terrace, Paddington, London. They married at the Swedish Protestant Church, Harcourt Street, Marylebone, London. Her father was a timber merchant. Died 1975 in South Africa.

[135] Lived at Gower house, Quinton.

[136] Birmingham Daily Gazette, 16th June 1932.

[137] A book titled Death By Order is referenced as being a novel he wrote but I have been unable to find a copy.

[138] Also, for Shropshire Star and Shropshire Journal.

Also in 1935, Bill took an interest in ghost hunting and the work of psychic investigators. He got into a dispute with the Wolverhampton Temple of Spiritual Progress after he openly expressed doubt about the ability of a Spiritualist and Materialising Medium from Leeds called John JONES after attending a 'challenge séance'. Later in 1937 he wrote[139] about this and other spiritual experiences saying that he had *'...slept in haunted houses and a monastery, visited scenes of current hauntings all over the Midlands without seeing anything...'*. He described himself as a confirmed sceptic. He was known to visit sites with Elliot O'DONNELL, who at the time was a well-known 'celebrity' ghost hunter.

I also found several references to Bill in 1936 becoming the Express & Star's War Correspondent[140], and that he was sent to Spain to report on the Civil War. However, I was unable to find any official cooperative sources.

1937: Despite being a sceptic on the issue, he wrote several books on the subject of ghosts: 'The Shropshire Haunts of Mary Webb' (1937), 'I Met Them in the Midlands' (1937), 'Midland Murders', 'Hauntings and Odd Characters' (1937), and 'Earl Baldwin's Country' (1939).

Of note within this collection of books are references to 'The charming Midland village of Claverley'. In the book Midland Leaves, a photograph of the village features as the frontispiece illustration, and is the topic of a chapter titled 'Back To The Good Old Days'[141]. In his book, 'Both Sides of the Severn'[142], Claverley is again the subject of a chapter called 'Procession Of Pain', again with a photographic illustration. This is relevant as the village of

---

[139] Midland Murders, Hauntings and Odd Characters p. 81-p99.
[140] Birmingham Daily Post 14/12/1967, Coventry Evening Telegraph 05/12/1957.
[141] Midland Leaves – A Travel Notebook, Quaestor 1934, p. 208.
[142] p. 70.

Claverley features within several future chapters, specifically with reference to spy theories[143].

It is also worth noting that in his 1937 book, Midland Murders, he writes about unsolved murder mysteries that baffled the police and references a £100 reward[144] to help solve a crime. Also, in October 1937 it was reported that he was one of the coffin bearers at the funeral of Mrs Frances Ellen PURCE at Bilston. Bill's wife Winifred was listed as attending a Royal Garden Party at the Palace of Holyrood House in Edinburgh in 1938[145]. The event was in honour of the Jubilee Council for International Woman.

1939: The 1939 Register indicates that Bill[146] and his family had moved again, this time to 18 Park Dale, Wolverhampton. The Register shows him living with his wife, Mavis Irene BICKFORD[147] (domestic servant) and one closed record; most likely their son, Charles Miles.

The Register also provides some additional information. Winifred would later remarry, to a Mr CALCRAFT. It also shows that Bill's father had by then retired, and he and his family (younger brother William, aged 19) had moved a short distance to 16 Narrow Lane, Halesowen[148].

There is also reference to Bill visiting Berlin twice in 1939[149], first in January for the opening of the Reich's Chancellery, and again in June. He would visit again six years later just after the end of the war.

---

[143] Chapter 13.3. Chapters 14.1, 14.2, 14.3, 14.5, 14.10 & 14.16. Chapters 16.1 & 16.2. Chapter 22.

[144] p. 37; also referenced later in Chapter 14.1.

[145] The Scotsman, 19th July 1938, p. 7.

[146] 1939 Register OQAU114/1, /2 Winifred, /3(closed) and /4 Mavis.

[147] b. 1918 d. 1975; married G.H. HARDY 1942.

[148] Also referenced as Fair View House.

[149] Berlin Twilight (1947) p. 19 & p. 87.

On 2nd August 1939, Bill was interviewed and considered suitable for a temporary commission on mobilisation[150] for the war. He was then affiliated to his local Territorial Army unit, the 5th Battalion, South Staffordshire Regiment. Whilst waiting for his mobilisation, which occurred in September 1940, Bill continued working as a journalist. He is credited with helping to raise £25,000 between September 1939 and September 1940, through the West Midlands and Express & Star Comforts Fund. Also, in June 1940, he helped raise £6,000 during the 'Gift a Spitfire Scheme'.

1939–45, The War Years: During this period, the most significant events in the Bella mystery were the discovery of the skeleton in 1943 and the appearance of the chalk messages in 1944. In Bill's life, he went to war and his marriage failed.

I found that, in different newspaper articles during the late 1950s and early 1960s when reporting on Bill's military service during this period, there were differing accounts of what he did, some even alluding to the fact that he had been a spy. For example, the February 1957 publication of the London Sphere newspaper, describes Bill as *'having the aura of a cloak-and-dagger man with just that touch of mystery necessary to sustain the role'*.

In others, his career variously includes being a correspondent or serving[151] in the Spanish Civil War 1936–39, as the Chief Liaison Officer in Field Marshal MONTGOMERY's staff during WWII; being in Greece during the revolution of 1944–45, and working as a senior member of the British legal team at the Nuremberg trials of 1945–1946.

Furthermore, in September 1959 he is quoted in the Western Mail[152] as saying that he had 20 years' active service in the regular army.

---

[150] Brig FJH PRING, Referees: Colonel Baldwin WEBB & Sir Robert Bird BART.
[151] The Sphere 14/04/1961 – Book review; Quest in The Holy Land.
[152] Western Mail 30th September 1959, p. 4.

What is certain is that in April 1940, Bill applied to join the Intelligence Corp. He was unsuccessful, and in the September[153] was mobilised for the war, appointed to the rank of Second Lieutenant, and received orders to report as a Press Conducting Officer to No.2 Section Public Relations Overseas Unit (Middle East) in Kenya.

Bill departed for the Middle East on 7th October 1940, but never got to Kenya. Instead, his orders were changed, and he was sent to GHQ in Alexandria. Here he was appointed as the Conducting Officer with the Press and Photography Service, splitting his time between Cyprus and Egypt until April 1944. I could not find any reference to his being any kind of Liaison Officer to General MONTGOMERY.

1944: Following the German withdrawal from Greece in October 1944, CHURCHILL arranged for a small British force to accompany the Greek government back home. On 7th September, Bill was assigned to this force, known as 'Force 140'. He left on 12th October, returning on 19th January 1945. It's during this time that Bill recounts[154] that he saved the life of 'General' Georgios GRIVAS[155] in Athens when he was threatened with execution by communists in December 1944.

A referenced association with Bill and the mystery is with the 1944 chalk markings because the family homes were situated close to all the Halesowen chalk markings. His father was a fruit dealer, which is significant because the location of the Birmingham chalk markings was next to Birmingham's Smithfield fruit market and Bill worked in Wolverhampton, as a journalist, near to that location. However, Bill was serving in North Africa at the time.

---

[153] London Gazette 18th Oct 1940 p. 6065.
[154] Western Mail 02/12/1959 p. 9.

[155] During WWII, GRIVAS led a resistance group against the Axis occupation of Greece. After the war he focused on ridding Cyprus of British colonial rule.

Bill wrote about his experience with Force 104 in his book 'The Greek Trilogy'. Also, in October 1949 he was awarded the Greek Medal of Military Merit, a decoration awarded for meritorious wartime service.

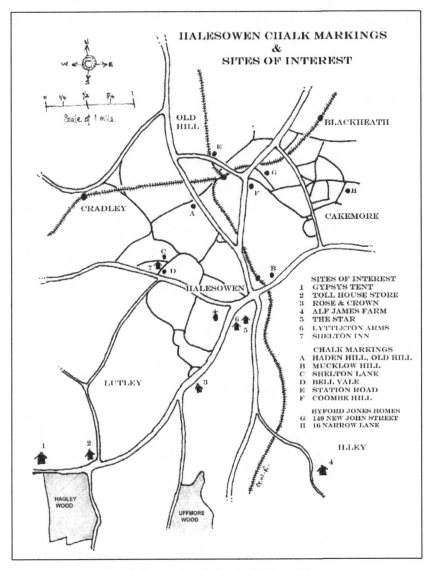

Family homes in relation to chalk markings

1945: On 15th June 1945, Bill was taken off the military strength of Mediterranean Expeditionary Force under 'Python'[156], returning to Britain on 12th July. Instead of demobilising, Bill applied to waive his rights under *Python* for continued service. He was then posted as SO2[157] to Berlin in the newly formed Information Services Control Branch. The full title of his unit was Control Branch for Germany and Public Relations Branch, Political Division, Control Commission for Germany.

In his book, 'Berlin Twilight', he tells how, two months after the fall of Berlin and the end of WWII, in July 1945, he flew from London to Bunde, then travelled by car to Berlin along with Vincent EVANS[158] and Lucia LAWSON[159].

Shortly after arriving in Berlin, Bill visited Adolf HITLER's bunker, the scene of his suicide, and the shallow trench where HITLER and Eva Braun were cremated. He says *"...I bent down, took up some of the ashes in my hand, and put them into an empty tobacco-pouch. They might have been the remains of burnt wood, or they might have been the remains of a cremated HITLER. I could not know..."*.

On 6th August 1945, Bill's appointment changes to SO2 Berlin Section, Information Services Control and Public Relations Branch. On 28th September, it is revised to SO2 Assistant Controller (Operations and Liaison) Public Relations Branch.

In July 1946, he tells how he interviewed prominent citizens about Adolf HITLER's death, with most of them believing that HITLER had escaped and not committed suicide on 30th April, and the cremated body that of HITLER's 'double'.

---

[156] Python was the codename given for the repatriation for long-serving personnel abroad.
[157] Staff Officer 2 (various locations).
[158] Daily Express's War correspondent and the first British journalist to visit Belsen.
[159] Control Commission.

On 29th September 1946, Bill became Deputy Controller SO1 and was promoted to Lieutenant Colonel. He returned to the UK on 1st October 1946, reporting to the Depot in Chelsea then proceeding home, which was named as being Fair View House, Narrow Lane, Blackheath.

There are newspaper accounts that reference that, in Berlin, he was the Chief Liaison Officer[160] and that he was a senior member of the British legal team at the Nuremburg trials. Bill made no such claim, only indicating that he went to the Nuremburg Major War Criminal Court at some time in 1946.

On 21st March 1947, Bill was released from military duty as a Major, but was granted the honorary rank of Lieutenant Colonel. However, this was not the end of his military career…

1947–1952: On 20th February 1947, Bill was now 41 years old and living at Birches Court, Codsall, Wolverhampton. He was remarried, to Cynthia Louise née JOHNSON, 22, who had been living at St Ermins, SW1[161]. Their wedding certificate indicates Bill was going by the name of JONES, was divorced, and was a Lieutenant Colonel in the army. The certificate has his age as 39. Once married, they lived at Lower Hall, Madeley Road, Beckbury[162], close to the village of Claverley.

There were two children from this marriage: Jeremy L BYFORD-JONES, born in 1947, died in 1948, and Jennifer, born in 1950, died in 1951. On 17th June 1963, the couple amended their wedding certificate to read BYFORD-JONES, and Bill changed his age from 39 to 41. He also published the book, Berlin Twilight, in 1947.

On 19th April 1949, Bill requested again to join the Intelligence Corp in the Army Reserves. This time he was successful, and on 29th November 1950, he became a Major (Honorary Lt Col) in the

---

[160] Liverpool Echo 09/05/1947 & The Scotsman 05/06/1947.
[161] Father Harry WILLIAMS former captain in the army, deceased.
[162] Express & Star Obituary, 16th Oct 2007.

Regular Army Reserves. He would relinquish his commission on reaching the maximum age limit on 26th July 1955.

Interestingly, Bill got a mention in two different papers on the same day in November 1951. First, he is listed as a guest at the inaugural ball to raise money for the county's welfare fund for pre-service units[163]. The other is because he made an offer during a village debate to introduce electric street lighting in the village of Beckbury. Bill offered to provide, for free, a 17th century stable-yard lantern, fitted to burn four candles. He said, *"This light would provide a pilot for the clients of inns who grope their way along the road. It would be easily erected on an electric-cable pole"*[164]. The article indicates that the introduction of street lighting was rejected.

In 1952, Bill was reported in the Birmingham Daily Gazette[165] as demanding action to stop radio comedians ridiculing the Home Guard. He did not like the suggestion that ...*the men are inefficient, drink, and use the Home Guard as an excuse to get out of washing-up at home...*

Also in 1952, Bill was the Deputy Editor of the Express & Star newspaper, but became involved with the (Midland Radio) BBC Home Service 'Sunday Out' television programme[166]. He was a member of the show's team of broadcasters and was principally involved in several of the programmes with reporting on people of interest. He was also solo presenter on 'A Holiday I Remember', where he recalls a holiday on the Albanian Frontier, which was broadcast on 3rd September 1952.

---

[163] Staffordshire Advertiser 23/11/1951 – Cross-service cadets.
[164] Birmingham Daily Gazette 23/11/1951.
[165] 2nd May 1952.
[166] Banbury Guardian 04/09/1952: Broadcast on 20/06, 18/07 & 12/09/1952.

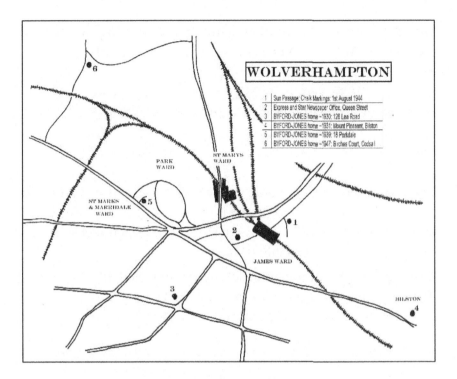

Map legend (Wolverhampton):

1	Sun Passage: Chalk Markings: 1st August 1944
2	Express and Star Newspaper Office, Queen Street
3	BYFORD-JONES home ~1930: 126 Lea Road
4	BYFORD-JONES home ~1931: Mount Pleasant, Bilston
5	BYFORD-JONES home ~1939: 18 Parkdale
6	BYFORD-JONES home ~1947: Birches Court, Codsall

The 1953 Bella Articles

In November 1953, Bill wrote two newspaper articles[167] that would result in the development of the spy theory although their purpose was an exploration of the witchcraft theory. The first article was published on 19th November, and provided the reader with a factual background of the circumstances surrounding the discovery of the skeleton, the chalk markings; it introduces Dr MURRAY, and discusses links with the WALTON murder.

He also discusses how some of the bones were 'discovered in a different part of the wood', and references an explanation favoured by those who believe that the woman was the victim of ritual murder by a strange circle of devil worshippers – that the hand was cut off and placed or lost in another part of the wood.

---

[167] No other articles found in the Express & Star between 1st and 18th Nov 1953.

This is the first quote I found regarding a hand being cut off, and contradicts Professor WEBSTER's post-mortem report.

WRITING ON WALL AT DEAD OF NIGHT BAFFLES MIDLAND MURDER HUNT TEAM
By QUAESTOR

The significance of the hand, known as 'the Hand of Glory', is explained as being a prized relic in witchcraft when cut from the arm of one who had been executed. It could open locks, reveal treasure or cast persons into deep sleep.

The second melodramatic article was published the following day, and tells how he took a walk in Hagley Wood on the anniversary month of the murder.

Night visit to Hagley Wood...

THE CONCLUSIONS I REACH ON THE FACTS
By QUAESTOR

...and the ghoulish tree coffin

Bill once again references Dr MURRAY and the WALTON murder, questioning whether the victim was sacrificed. He writes, *'I took a grip of myself, for those who argue that the girl had been the victim of devil worshippers nearly frightened me away. I am not ashamed of this and there must be few people who have not at some time been seized by a half-belief in the supernatural. It was easy to think of devils and witches here, of hellish brews and severed hands for spells. It was easy to fancy one heard the snap of a nutcracker jaws when it was only a twig beneath the foot or to hear the crackling laugh of witches when it was only an owl...'*

He also references a devil worship theory: *'Why were the bones of one hand found far from the body, suggesting that the hand had been removed after death in the manner of the old Hand of Glory rites of witchcraft?*

Whilst he discusses the possibility of witchcraft, he does say that he does not accept it and he also discusses a meeting with the vicar's warden, Mr A.H. HODGETTS, at St Kenelm's Church, who tells that he believes that the victim *'was a gypsy, that was tried and condemned by her tribe of Romanies, could be for the evil eye'.*

He challenges why the victim had so little clothing considering how cold it would have been; the absence of coat, hat and handbag. He also challenges the theory that she was asphyxiated, noting that the cloth could have got there via various means.

He says that he visited the tree, and the article includes a popular reproduced image of it. The source of this image is not known, and the Express & Star archives no longer have a copy in their files, nor any knowledge of its origin.

He explores the possibility that the chalk markings were not a hoax, indicating that this was a co-conspirator pointing the police towards the witchcraft circle or gang and finishes by appealing for whoever produced the chalk markings to contact him with the victim's family name and, if possible, her address before death.

He got a response, but it was not what he had expected and that is discussed in the next section.

Post 1953

When he wrote under the pseudonym 'Quaestor Seeker' for the Express & Star newspaper,[168] he was still a reserve officer in the army[169].

1955: In 1955, he was Vice Chairman of the Staffordshire Army Cadet League[170] and after resigning his commission in 1955[171], he wrote several more books: 'Adventures with Two Passports' (1956), 'Acceptable – Oil on Troubled Waters' (1957), 'Forbidden Frontiers' (1958)[172], 'Grivas and the Story of EOKA' (1959)[173],

---

[168] The Express & Star newspaper HQ was in Queen Street Wolverhampton.
[169] Regular Army Reserve of Officers General List. Major (Hon. Lt-Col) Army No. 150240.
[170] Birmingham Daily Post, 11th May 1955.
[171] London Gazette, 22/07/55.
[172] Coventry Evening Telegraph, 23/12/1958.
[173] National Archives CO926/1110.

'Quest in The Holy Land' (1961), 'Uncensored Eyewitnesses' (1961), 'Africa: Journey out of Darkness' (1962) 'Four Faces of Peru' (1967), 'The Lightning War' (1968), and 'Severn Valley Stories' (1968).

1956: In late April 1956, Bill reveals that he discovered the plot to oust Lieutenant General Sir John Bagot GLUBB[174], also known as 'Glubb Pasha of Jordan', even before the Foreign Office got word of it. Later the following month, on 21st March 1956, Bill was having lunch with Field Marshal Sir John HARDING, the Governor of Cyprus. Bill tells how he saved the Governor's life when a bomb was planted under his bed[175]. He also tells readers that he personally knew Colonel NASSER, King HUSSEIN and David BEN-GURION[176].=

1959: In 1959, Bill published his book Grivas and the Story of EOKA[177]. The Foreign and Commonwealth Office's Mediterranean Department undertook a review of the book as it was apparently critical of the government. Prior to its publication in April 1959, he wrote to the Governor of Cyprus frustrated that the authorities would not discuss intelligence matters with him. He then visited and met with the Governor in May. There are records of this event in the National Archive[178]. Of interest are briefing notes to the Governor about Bill. They say he *joined the Officers' Emergency Reserve before the war, having had no previous military experience. He spent the whole of the war upon public relations work in East Africa and the Middle East (spending two years in Cyprus). He was engaged on similar work in Greece during the troubled period immediately after the war, and after a time with the Control Commission in Germany and left the Army in 1947. He has since been associated with*

---

[174] Led Transjordan's Arab Legion 1939-56.
[175] Western Mail 30/09/1959 & Aberdeen Evening Express 14/10/1959.
[176] Kensington Post 12/01/1968.
[177] Original titled and sometimes referenced as Grivas Face to Face and the EOKA Story.
[178] CO926/1110.

a Midlands news agency, apparently as news editor for a daily newspaper. He is the author of a number of books. He has from time to time applied to the War Office for further military work and, on the strength of his wartime knowledge of the Middle East, has suggested that he might be employed in obtaining information, but there is no record that he has ever actively engaged in intelligence work. Although he has made himself a slight nuisance on occasions, there is nothing on record which is to his personal discredit.

At the end of September 1959, prior to its publication on 14th October, a copy of the book was made available to the Cyprus MOD's Mediterranean desk. A review of the book in the Illustrated London News was by E. D. O'BRIAN[179], who indicates he knew Bill when he was a Captain in Cyprus during the war. He describes Bill as having *a lively intelligence with a small "I" which is not necessarily always allied to the branch of the service he belonged!*

All in all, Bill presents as an enigma conundrum, a man with either a varied and fascinating history or one with fantasist tendencies. Where the truth lies remains to be discovered.

---

[179] 24th October 1959, p. 518.

CHAPTER 14
SPY STORIES

Introduction

The most popular theory for those who follow the mystery, is that Bella was a spy, or involved in espionage. What often surprises people is that the story they are familiar with is one of (or is created from) seven different spy stories, and that the seven versions offer completely different and often conflicting accounts around the circumstances, sequence of events, locations, and people involved. This chapter visits all the different versions, as well as the relevant police inquiries. Hopefully, seeing all the different elements will allow each reader to identify the sources of the version they are familiar with and to sort fact from fiction.

Anna of Claverley

The two articles written by Quaestor were published in the Express and Star on Thursday 19th and Friday 20th November. On the morning of Saturday 21st, the newspaper received a hand written two-page letter at its Wolverhampton office on Queen Street. It was dated 18th November (a day before the first article was published) and signed by a woman using the pseudonym *Anna from Claverley*, a village 13 miles north west of Hagley Wood, and the neighbouring village to where Quaestor lived.

Anna wrote that the person responsible for the crime had died insane in 1942, and that the victim, who was Dutch, had arrived illegally in England in about 1941. Of particular note is that there is no reference to espionage within Anna's letter. The newspaper informed the police, photographed the letter, and sent[180] copies to

---

[180] Newspaper letter and photographs, police stamp and Supt WILLIAMS, signed and dated 23rd November.

Assistant Chief Constable S. INIGHT, noting that pencil marks on the letter were made by a sub-editor..

Claverley Near Wolverhampton
18/11/53

My Dear Quaestor
Finish your articles re the Wych Elm crime by all means, they are interesting to your readers, but you will never solve the mystery
The one person who could give the answers is now beyond the jurisdiction of earthly courts the affair is closed and involves no witches, black magic or moonnight rites
Much as I hate having to use a nom-de plume I think you would appreciate it if you knew me.
The only clues I can give you are that the person responsible for the crime died insane in 1942, and the victim was Dutch and arrived illegally in England about 1941.
I have no wish to recall any more.
I am no 'hoaxer', what happened to our mutual friend ----- did he return to -----
Yours sincerely
Anna

The last paragraph of the letter has the sub-editor's pencil marks as indicated and the writing is also hard to decipher. The name of the mutual friend and where he returned to are unclear.

On Monday 23rd, the Express and Star published an article with their edited version of the letter, omitting the last paragraph and naming the writer as Anna of Claverley. They also note that the writer adds a personal post-script, which gives a clue to her identity and disposes of the suspicion that the letter is a hoax.

The article also quotes ACC INIGHT as saying, *"Until the letter had been studied it was impossible to say whether the case would be actively reopened"*. This is the only reference I found indicating that the case had been closed.

The article features several readers' letters, including one from Major R MONCKTON of Stretton Hall, Brewood, Stafford and former Master of the Albrighton Hunt. He makes several points: that the Albrighton Woodland Pack hunted and shot in Hagley Wood regularly at the time the body was said to have been hidden (from November 1941 to April 1943). He notes that the tree was within 40 yards of a public lane and the area frequented by trespassers. He felt that the body could not have been there during the period of decomposition or else hounds would have gone straight to it, or some person would have noticed the smell, 'which is so offensive to the nostrils.' He also suggested that a reward for information be offered.

National interest in the story can be seen from a handwritten note in the file. Mr ALMAN at the Express and Star made contact to let the police know that London papers were asking for permission to publish photographs of Anna's letter, indicating that 'they' would want the opportunity to publish first. The police indicated that they were aware and provided reassurance that nothing could be published without their permission.

Two days later, the Express and Star published[181] another article reporting that the police had enlisted Quaestor onto the investigation, and that experts had scrutinised the letter and noted that the letter 'F' was continental (I was unable to find any supporting evidence in the police file). Therefore, they concluded, Anna was herself a foreigner!

There is also a reference in the article that gives a possible clue to the meaning and missing details in the letter's last paragraph. It says, *...that the letter made mysterious allusions to a distinguished foreigner as 'our mutual friend' - of pre-war days...* then indicates that Quaestor has *...interesting information to pass on about this foreigner,* with an appeal that Anna makes contact again.

The article tells how Claverley had been visited by scores of newspaper reporters and the only Dutchman in Claverley, William VERMEULEN, is quoted as saying, *"We have no Annas around here",* but he did confirm that many Dutch girls came to Britain during the war. He also confirmed that, in 1941, Wolverhampton was the centre of the Dutch colony in England, and Wrottesley Park was the Headquarters of the Dutch Army.

Reference is made to private investigators anxious for information to help them solve the murder and claim the reward of £100 offered by the paper – this is the first reference I found of a reward being offered for information.

Several readers' letters were also published, including one containing the first mention of 'Foreign Agents'. It was made by Mr and Mrs C SILVERS of Shrewsbury, whose theory was that Bella was an agent being hotly pursued by British counter-espionage men. After that nothing happened for just over a week, until on 3rd December another hand delivered, handwritten letter arrived at the Express and Star in Wolverhampton, marked *Urgent.*

---

[181] Generic article also in the Birmingham Gazette, 25th November.

3-XII-53

Dear Quaestor,

Had so much publicity not been given to 'Anna' I would have contacted you before.

I will meet you and officers of the Worcestershire C.I.D. at the Dick Whittington (it is beyond The "Stewponey" from Wolverhampton) tomorrow night (Friday) at about 8.30 p.m. and maybe I can help them with their investigations if they are still interested subject to my conditions to which I think they will agree

you of course, will not advertise this meeting in your press. you have had many wild goose chases during the last few days maybe this will be the last or the beginning of many who knows?

At the Whittington they have a bar on theleft of the entrance called the "priest's hole"

Sincerely,

Anna

This meeting took place on 4th December but there are multiple possible versions of what happened and what was said. There is the journalist BYFORD-JONES's version written on 16th January 1958. Then, whilst there is no official police record of the meeting, there are some follow-up notes and reports that appear to be lines of inquiry generated from the meeting and there is also a formal statement taken several weeks after the meeting, on 30th December 1953.

The BYFORD-JONES version #1

Whilst there is no official record of the meeting, which happened on 4th December 1953 at the Dick Whittington pub, the first published account was made by BYFORD-JONES on 16th January 1958, in an article titled: *Kinver inn meeting sheds light on the mystery of Bella*. The reason he gives for not writing anything earlier was because he says he had been sworn to secrecy[182] by the police. However, he had been prompted to write following a TV interview reported to be with Professor WEBSTER, who is quoted as saying, *"After extensive inquiries by the Superintendent[183] he was able to identify her. It was a classic piece of detection"*. This revelation, he believed, freed him from his obligation.

---

[182] Nothing to support this statement in the police files.
[183] Detective Superintendent T WILLIAMS, of Worcestershire CID, is named in the article.

Kinver inn meeting sh on mystery of Bella

16-1-58

By QUAESTOR

who describes the part he played in enquiries made with the police into the Hagley Wood wych elm mystery.

IT was late in April, 1943, that the remains of Bella were found by three youths in a hollow tree in Hagley Wood. A picture of what the girl had been like was soon built up by a pathologist and the robot figure he created told the police much—but not her name and address and the secret of her death.

No indication that either of these mysteries had been solved was given until recently, when a pathologist said of Bella in an I.T.V. programme: "After extensive inquiries by the superintendent (Detective Superintendent T. Williams, of Worcestershire C.I.D.) he was able to identify her. It was a classic piece of detection."

So now a pledge I made to keep secret further facts of the death of Bella of the Wych Elm is purged, I can tell of my dramatic meeting with a woman who claimed to know how Bella died. It began with the receipt by me of a letter from a writer who signed herself Anna. It was marked urgent and gave what purported to be some of the facts of the murder. It is to these facts that the pathologist referred as the solution.

★

AFTER the first I appealed to her through the *Express and Star* to meet me to discuss the crime.

It was obvious that she was afraid to do this since the facts she had given involved a relative. She said he was present when Bella, or to give her her full name, Lubella, died in what the writer knew as a bluebell wood. It was not until ten days later that "Anna" wrote again. She fixed a rendezvous in a way that could not have been more melodramatic if it had been written in a Dorothy L. Sayers detective story.

The place of the meeting was arranged in the Monks' room at the Dick Whittington Inn, Kinver, at 8 o'clock one dark rainy night. No clue was given in the letter of how I should know "Anna." She did not describe herself. All she said was "You will know me when you see me," Outside the inn I met Detective

into the Monks' room, a quiet cell like place off the left of the corridor that led from the mitred back door.

Then a girl entered. She was tall and curvaceous and blonde. Her clothes were fashionable. She looked in astonishment when she saw three people sitting expectantly, and without a word between them, in a quiet corner of the otherwise empty chamber.

She mounted a staircase, still looking at us curiously, but without a word or sign.

★

IN ten minutes at least 20 girls entered, mounted the staircase, then descended it and left.

All of them looked at us, it seemed, with apprehension and bewilderment.

Then I set off to investigate and I found that the stairs led to the ladies' toilet.

The little earnest group of sleuths were too tense to see the humour of the situation.

All we knew was that none of the dozen girls had been Anna. The question was which ?

Taking separate routes, the chief, the girl detective and I converged on the long bar in a room reached by descending several steps at the end of the corridor outside.

Here we searched among the female faces for a guilty or a knowing look.

Chief Detective Williams, one of the smartest men in his line, found that he was converging on the same woman as I. She looked quickly first at me, then at him. Then she began to talk rapidly to

lieve?" She caught her breath, nodded to her companion. "I'll follow you back to the monk's room," she said. She and her companions joined us five minutes later.

★

THERE followed for me, and, I think, for the detectives, a fascinating half hour.

Anna gave us her name and address.

Speaking with great solemnity she told us that she had for ten years guarded her story with great secrecy. Only one person, her husband, who accompanied her, knew the story she was about to tell. No one else would ever have heard of it, but for the fact that I had reopened the case. The details given, the new revelations made, had deprived her of sleep.

Then she told us her dramatic story, answering satisfactorily questions asked her without warning to check her grip on the facts. She gave us the name and address of an officer. He had come to her one night in late April, 1943 — in fact, on a day which was consistent with the expert assessment of the day of Bella's death—and told her that something terrible had happened to him.

He confessed to her under secrecy that he had been with a friend, a male trapeze artist then appearing at 'xxxxx' Hippodrome, and a Dutchman, in a car. The officer was driving it. Between the other two men in the back was Bella. Suddenly, as the car was descending Mucklow-hill, Halesowen, something happened. The officer stopped the car. The two men then told him to drive on. "She's dead," they told him curtly. The order to drive on was repeated, far more peremptorily than before.

The car was driven through the blacked out town of Halesowen, then Hasbury. Finally, after several tentative halts, he was told to turn to the right off the main Bromsgrove road. He found himself in Hagley Wood.

Here the body of the girl known now as Bella, was carried out and the officer was called on to help

voice that the officer was terrified. Next night he went again to Hagley Wood to make sure he had not been suffering from hallucinations.

He came back late at night. "There's no mistake," he told Anna, "the body is there all right, just as we left it." She said he had given the details exactly as I had done. She told her husband long ago.

16 JAN 1958

ANNA then said that the officer told her that he did not trust his two male companions of that tragic night. He said that he believed that the Dutchman was actually a Germany spy and he could not understand why the police did not pick him up. He and the trapeze artist asked him if he could give them details of the location of certain munition factories. All these were concerned with the manufacture either of aircraft engines or aircraft accessories. Anna said the officer came home at times with large sums of money and he could not

the officer that he had had a nervous breakdown. He was taken to a mental home which she named, where he died.

Inquiries proved that such an officer had in fact died on the date and at the place stated.

Other facts were also verified, but the Dutchman could not be found although efforts to locate him were made in Holland.

It is impossible for me to say if the police ever discovered the whereabouts of the trapeze artist but M.I.5 was brought into the case.

Detective Superintendent T. Williams, when asked last year to comment on the case added to the air of prevailing mystery by saying: "I can't make any comment about it at the moment. The case is still not closed. I do not think it would be advisable to say anything at the present time."

But the pathologist who appeared on I.T.V. said about Bella: "But after extensive inquiries by the superintendent he was able to identify her. It was a classic piece of detection."

The article itself is full of inaccurate facts, people, places, and dates; some that he had even previously reported accurately himself. I will not go through the whole article, but rather tell his version whilst highlighting where there are areas of contention between varying versions using footnotes to references.

He says: *The meeting took place in the Monk's Room at the Dick Whittington Inn, Kinver, at 8 p.m.*[184]. The meeting took place with

---

[184] Second letter calls it the "Priests Hole" and requests an 8.30 p.m. meeting.

himself, DI WILLIAMS, a policewoman, and a male detective shorthand writer[185].

He tells how Anna did not make herself known and he, DI WILLIAMS, and the policewoman went looking for Anna within the pub. It tells, dramatically, how their search was successful when they approached a couple and he asked, *"Anna, I believe?" She caught her breath, nodded to her companion. "I'll follow you back to the monk's room."*[186] Anna confirmed her real name and address as Una Ella HAINSWORTH, Four Acres, Long Common, Claverley and told them her story:

Her former husband, Jack MOSSOP, came home one night in late April, 1943[187] . Jack confessed to Una that he had been out with two men,: a Dutchman and a trapeze artist friend who was appearing at the Coventry Hippodrome. They were travelling in a car that he was driving, and in the back was the trapeze artist and the Dutchman, with Bella between them. Whilst travelling down Mucklow Hill, Halesowen,[188] Bella collapsed. *"She's dead"* they told him, and ordered him to drive on. After driving through blacked-out Halesowen, then Hasbury, he was told to turn to the right off the main Bromsgrove Road into Hagley Wood[189] and he helped to stuff her into the hollow trunk of the Wych Elm.

"Anna" stated that the next night he went again to Hagley Wood to make sure he had not been suffering from hallucinations. He returned and told her "There's no mistake, the body is there all right, just as we left it."

---

[185] Possibly WPC 4 Florence HILL, but no indication anywhere else that there was another Officer.

[186] The companion was possibly her husband 'Jack' HAINSWORTH.

[187] The skeleton was discovered in April 1943, and this date is different in her statement.

[188] The location of chalk marking 12/04/44.

[189] Travelling from Halesowen/Hasbury, the turn is left not right. BJ is a local man and would have known this.

Jack told Una that he did not trust his two male companions and believed that the Dutchman was actually a [German] spy and he could not understand why the police did not pick him up.

The Dutchman and the trapeze artist asked him if he could give them details of the locations of factories involved with war manufacturing. Anna said that Jack came home at times with large sums of money and he could not explain where he got it. Jack had said that Bella had entered the country illegally in 1941 "after Dunkirk". He thought she worked for the spy as an emissary, and had fallen foul of them or become dangerous and had been murdered.

Anna then said that the incident had such an effect on Jack that he had had a nervous breakdown and was taken to a mental home where he died.

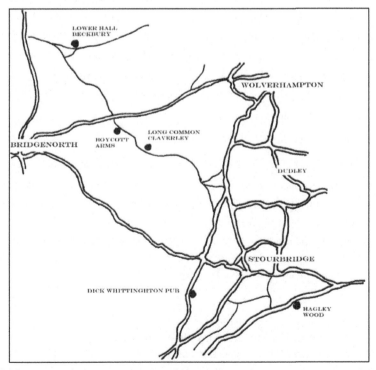

Orientation Map Of Principal Locations

Quaestor said that the Dutchman could not be found, though efforts to locate him were made in Holland, and that it was impossible for him to say if the police ever discovered the whereabouts of the trapeze artist but that MI5 were brought onto the case[190].

It may be significant that Wilfred BYFORD-JONES and family lived at Lower Hall, Madeley Road, Beckbury. While Una HAINSWORTH/MOSSOP and family lived at Four Acres, Long Common, Claverley. The Boycott Arms was the childhood home of Jack MOSSOP and the Dick Whittington Pub was Una's meeting location.

The Una HAINSWORTH version #2

On 30th December 1953, Una HAINSWORTH gave a formal statement at Kenilworth Police Station. Her statement totally contradicts the 'murder' account given by BYFORD-JONES; it does, however, provide some additional background information that, although not wholly accurate, introduces other people into the story. What follows is Una's unedited statement in italics with my added footnotes:

30th December, Kenilworth Police Station.

Una Ella HAINSWORTH, Four Acres, Long Common, Claverley.

I was married to Jack MOSSOP in 1932 and we went to live at the Bridge House, Wombourne. At that time he was studying to be a surveyor. The only child of our marriage was born in 1932[191] and he was christened Julian and at the present time, he is somewhere in America. My husband joined the A.S.T. in 1937 as a Pilot Officer and was stationed at Hamble near Southampton. In 1938 he commenced work for the Armstrong Siddeley Works Coventry and

---

[190] There is no record of MI5 being involved in the case.
[191] Not true; Jill Kyra MOSSOP was born on 19th November 1941 at 124 Warwick Road in Kenilworth. Jack MOSSOP is named as the father. However, Jill died in March 1942, her death certificate names her as Jill M HAINSWORTH.

subsequently he went to work at the Standard Aero Works at Coventry (Banner Lane).

It was in 1940 that a man named 'VAN RALT[192]' came to our house, No. 39 Barrow Road, Kenilworth. I believe this man was Dutch and as far as I know he had no particular job, and I have a suspicion that he was engaged on some work that he did not wish to talk about, but in my opinion it might have been that he was a spy for he had plenty of money and there were times that my husband appeared to have plenty of money after meeting him.

It was either in March or April, 1941[193] that my husband came home and was noticeably white and agitated. This was about 1 a.m. in the morning and he asked me for a drink. I made a comment that I thought he had had enough as he had been out all day but I gave him a drink. He then said that he had been to the Lyttleton Arms[194] with 'VAN RALT' and the 'Dutch Piece'[195] and that she got awkward[196]. My husband was driving the car, which belonged to 'VAN RALT' she got in beside him[197], 'VAN RALT' was in the back and then she fell over towards my husband, and he said to 'VAN RALT' that she had passed out[198]. 'VAN RALT' told him where to drive to and they went to a wood, stuck her in a hollow tree. 'VAN RALT' said she would come to her senses the following morning, and as far as I know, my husband came home. He came home in 'VAN RALT's' car which was a Rover[199].

I lived in Kenilworth until December 1941 and between April and December, my husband appeared very jumpy and it was noticeable that he had more drink than usual, and appeared to have more money to spend. He was nearly always away from work and this led to my suspicions that in some way, he was obtaining money and may have been meeting 'VAN RALT'. I should mention that my husband had an old Standard Car of his own and he used to go off for days on end and I did not know where he was.

---

[192] No reference to VAN RALT in the BJ article.

[193] BJ article states April 1943.

[194] Note: the town (Halesowen or Hagley) is not referenced.

[195] BJ article names her as 'Bella or to give her full name Lubella'.

[196] No reference to the trapeze artist, and the BJ article makes no reference to the Lyttleton Arms.

[197] Different location than BJ article, and he references two men and Bella in the back of the car.

[198] BJ article "she's dead".

[199] BJ article states that Jack returned to the scene the next day.

When I left my husband in December 1941 I went to Henley in Arden, and we lived there for ten years. We lived at Nuthurst House, Shrewley, near Henley in Arden, and we finally returned in 1951 to Kenilworth and came to our present address in August, 1953.

I saw my first husband Jack MOSSOP at Kenilworth on three occasions after I was forced to leave him in December, 1941 and tried to get my possessions including furniture from the house and on one of these occasions, it would be the last time I saw him, he told me what I thought at first, was a feature story to put me off and it was as follows:- That he thought he was losing his mind as he kept seeing the woman in the tree and she was leering at him. He held his head in his hands and said "it was getting on his nerves, I am going crazy". It was about June 1942 when I heard that he had taken to the Mental Hospital at Stafford where he died in August 1942. I was not informed of his death at the time and I did not attend the funeral because of this. The first I knew was when my present husband told me that an application had been made at the works claiming money that was due to him and sending a doctor's certificate.

I had no knowledge whatever of the Hagley murder until an article appeared in the Express and Star newspaper, neither had I read anything before which could in any way be connected with the incident, I have told you about. I have not discussed the matter with anyone and it was not until I was reading the details and bearing in mind the possible date when the woman met her death that I, in any way, connected this with my husband's statement to me in March or April 1941, and because of the articles referring to witchcraft etc., I decided in the first place to write a letter and signed it 'Anna'. I put sufficient clues in the letter which should have helped to have identified me and it was only because of a subsequent appeal in the newspaper and because I felt I ought to say what I know of this matter that I decided to arrange to meet you. I cannot add anything further and because I am now married again with three small children, I hope that what I have said to you will only be used to aid the course of justice and it is this which has prompted me to take the action I have. I was not treated too well by my husband and do not wish in any way to rake up the past but if what I have told you will help you in this matter, then the foregoing statement has been made by me voluntarily and with that end in view.

I, of course have no proof, that what I have told you now is the truth, but bearing in mind my husband's condition and what he said have to be at the time, I have done my best to recall it to help in the inquiry.

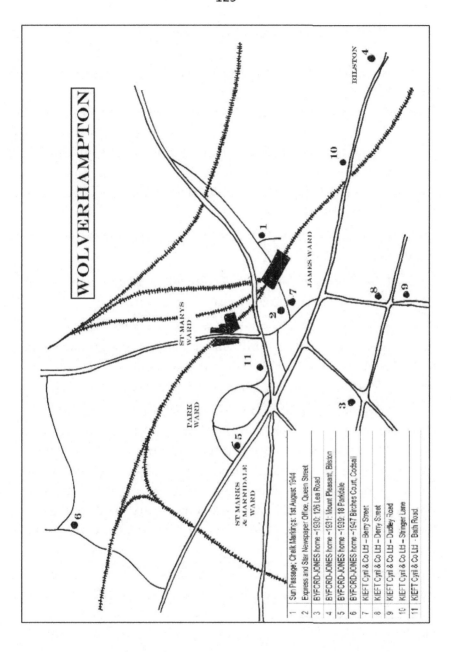

WOLVERHAMPTON

1	Sun Passage; Chalk Markings: 1st August 1944
2	Express and Star Newspaper Office, Queen Street
3	BYFORD-JONES home ~1930: 126 Lea Road
4	BYFORD-JONES home ~1931: Mount Pleasant, Bilston
5	BYFORD-JONES home ~1939: 18 Parkdale
6	BYFORD-JONES home ~1947 Birches Court, Codsall
7	KIEFT Cyril & Co Ltd – Berry Street
8	KIEFT Cyril & Co Ltd – Derry Street
9	KIEFT Cyril & Co Ltd – Dudley Road
10	KIEFT Cyril & Co Ltd – Stringer Lane
11	KIEFT Cyril & Co Ltd - Bath Road

The 1953 Police Inquiry

So far, we have the conflicting versions of what happened from Wilfred BYFORD-JONES and Una HAYWARD. To confuse the story even further, the police case file contains handwritten notes and reports that document their lines of inquiry prior to Una providing her formal statement. The notes are helpful because they add some missing elements, but also confuse, because they contradict elements of the two previous accounts. The notes are in italics and my observations follow:

She met Van RELT or RAALT twice in 1940 – In her statement this would become 'VAN RALT'.

Lived at Brick Bridge Cottage, adjoining Brick Bridge Inn[200] - Her statement names it as Bridge House, Wombourne.

She names one of Jack's friends as *Bill WILSON,* described as *probably being 50 years old* – Bill was more than just Jack's friend; he had known them both for several years and was one of their lodgers. His version of events is discussed in the next section.

There are references to the *Coventry Hippodrome and a man with the stage name FRUCK[201] who appeared there in 1938* – There is no context as to why he is of interest or that he was a trapeze artist. The BJ article indicates he was Jack's friend and the 'second' man in the back of the car. Una makes no reference in her statement; however, the police did carry out an inquiry. It is not clear, therefore, if VAN RALT and the trapeze artist are the same person.

Una *finally left her husband on 13th December 1941, and stayed at a house on Grosvenor Road, Coventry with a Mrs MURPHY* – Her statement only references Nuthurst House, Shrewley, near Henley in Arden. This address does however feature, but in 1937.

---

[200] Known locally as 'Brick Bridge' but officially the Waggon & Horse.
[201] An inquiry names Frick and Frack, discussed in chapter 14.6.

HAINSWORTH *works for Cecil KIEFT racing cars Bury*[202] – It is not clear if this is reference to Una or her husband. There was a Bury Street in Wolverhampton but it became part of Wheelers Fold around 1880. There is, however, a Berry Street adjacent to the Express and Star Offices in Queen Street.

One of the notes states; Typewriter taken, and photographs taken, but there is no further reference in the files.

There is another note regarding a telephone conversation between Inspector BUCHANEN, Warwick, and Inspector MORGAN, Kenilworth, dated 11.45 a.m. on 28th December 1953.

Inspector MORGAN reports that Una HAINSWORTH was well known. She had left 71 Randall Road, Kenilworth on 31st March 1953, and that 'she was in debt to all and sundry and they would like to get their hands on her'.

This chapter continues with additional and supplementary stories.

Bill WILSON

On the same day as Una gave her statement, so did William Phillip 'Bill' WILSON of 45 Birch Lane, Kenilworth. In his statement, he says he was very friendly with Jack MOSSOP, and that he had lived with the MOSSOPS at their three bedroom house, 39 Barrow Road, along with Jack HAINSWORTH. He left the house after Jack went to the asylum, and moved to 45 Birch Lane, Kenilworth. He never saw their son Julian, who apparently lived with his grandmother or sister.

He had known Jack before they started working together at the Banner Lane factory. They were together in rooms at 9 Grosvenor Road Coventry,[203] and Bill named Mrs GALBRAITH as

---

[202] Actually, KIEFT Cyril & Co Ltd. Edge Tools (racing cars). With several offices/works in Wolverhampton, Derry Street, Dudley Road, Stringers Lane and Bath Road.

[203] Destroyed during WW2, still undeveloped in 1954.

landlady[204]. He believed it was sometime between 1936 and 1938, after Jack had been discharged and was working at the Armstrong Siddeley factory, and Bill was working at the Baginton factory.

When Jack became ill, a man called Terry MITCHELL from his work took him to his family in Claverley, and from there he was admitted into hospital. Bill tried to visit Jack in Claverley but was told only relatives could see him, and he never saw him again.

Jack had told him he had been invalided out of the RAF after crash landing a plane and suffering head injuries. He was very moody and suffered from headaches and nightmares. Bill said that Jack *'was friendly with the opposite sex but wouldn't heart a fly – he did not have much backbone'*. He tells how Jack was having trouble with his wife and drank a considerable amount. He was a very heavy drinker and spent a significant amount of time away from work. He knew something was bothering Jack but put it down to the marriage. Finally, Jack had a car, a standard black saloon, four-door 1934 model.

On some specific points, Bill had no recollection of the Lyttleton Arms. He recalled that lots of people called at the house but none were foreigners or theatricals, and he knew nothing about a VAN RAALT or a Rover car. He did recall an Englishman with lots of pimples, aged about 20, called Vic, who also worked at the Banner Lane factory, and who, after the war, had started a car business.

Bill followed up his interview with a letter dated 3rd January 1954. He referenced the conversation at the police station the previous Wednesday. He said that the only tall, fair-haired man whose name he could not remember was Vic or Niv DRACO, pronounced 'DRARCS'. He had spoken with Ted PECK and Terry MITCHELL who knew Vic DRACO and the MOSSOPS quite well. The MOSSOPS knew him as Vic, so would not confuse the name with VAN, and they had no recollection of anyone called VAN or any connection with the Hippodrome.

---

[204] Police notes reference Grosvenor Road and Mrs MURPHY.

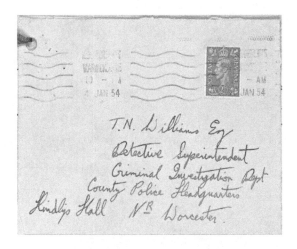

The police responded on 5th January, thanking him for the letter.

The Frick and Frack Inquiry

Within the file there are several reports compiled by Policewoman 4 Florence I HILL, dated 1st January 1954.

Florence had inquired at Tom Arnold Productions and spoke with a Mr LAKE about an act called 'Frik and Frack'. Although no records were kept after five years, he remembered that they were Swiss aliens and their correct 'stage' name was 'Frick and Frack', but he could not recall which agency they had come from. Further inquiries revealed that Frick and Frack were Swiss comedy ice skaters[205] who performed in an ice show. They were part of a touring London-based group and had performed two week-long shows in Coventry from 4th April and 12th September 1938.

"Frick" was Werner GROEBLI (b.21/4/1915 d.14/4/2008) and "Frack" was Hansruedi (Hans Rudolf) MAUCH (b.02/05/1919 d.04/06/1979).

---

[205] Coventry Herald 17th September 1938, The Stage; 22nd September 1938, 5th April 1956, The Whig 22nd August 1945, Lincolnshire Echo 20th February 1945.

Julian 'Jack' MOSSOP (Jnr)

Julian Michael 'Jack' MOSSOP was born on 3rd August 1932, in Wombourne, Wolverhampton. He was initially brought up by his grandmother and aunt at Gravel Hill, Wombourne until the age of 11. After his mother remarried in 1943, Jack went to live with them at Shrewley Common in Warwick. He went to Campion Street School, Leamington Spa, and left at the age of 14. He was then employed by his stepfather at a florist's shop and worked on a pig farm in Nuthurst before moving to London in 1949, aged 17.

There are then two different versions as to his employment once he arrived in London. His account[206] is that he had a brief job as a kitchen porter at J. Lyons and Company between 27th August and 8th September. He then says he worked for three months at the Grosvenor House Hotel, before returning to J. Lyons where he worked as a commis waiter until 20th April 1951. The police were only able to confirm the initial brief kitchen porter appointment. There is another (unreferenced) note in the bundle that says he moved to London in early 1949 and was employed as a porter at the American Embassy, whilst living at 77 Chippenham Road, London in 1951.

A Criminal Record Office[207] (CRO) report provides further details of his activities after he arrived in London, including the fact that he used the aliases 'Michael John KELLY' and 'Abel'. On 4th May 1950, he received probation for 12 months after being convicted of 'receiving' ladies clothing valued at £15. He broke his probation, resulting in being sent to Borstal on 7th June 1951, and being disqualified from driving for five years. He was convicted of entering a flat, where he had been previously residing, with a key and stealing an unattended motor car. He then escaped from Borstal on 25th September but was recaptured two days later.

He was conscripted for National Service into the Royal Artillery on 4th December 1952. Whilst undergoing basic training at No.66 Training Regt. RA Corps in Catterick[208] on 28th December 1952,[209] he deserted.

On 25th August 1953, now 21 years of age, Jack emigrated aboard the Anna Salen. The ship's manifest indicates he was a student

---

[206] Flying Squad Office, New Scotland Yard, dated 6th June 1951. DS FOSTER C.O. C.8.
[207] CRO Ref:19068/50.
[208] Army number 22749128.
[209] Police notes 11.45am 28/12/53.

destined for Canada. However, when the ship arrived in New York on 3rd September, Jack went no further.

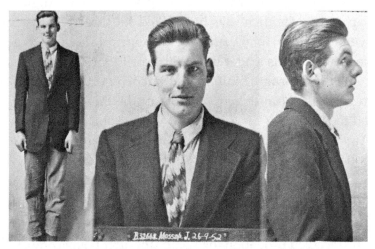

Prison photograph the day after he was captured

On 9th October 1954[210], Julian, now 22 years old, married Odette MONPLAISIR, aged 26[211].

However, public records show that in 1958, Jack applied for a marriage licence with Maria VICISOSO; there is no record showing that he married her.

Jack died in New York on 16th October 1998, aged 65[212].

The archive file shows that a copy of the custody photograph was sent to Empire News and Sunday Chronicle by DI WILLIAMS on 24th February 1960. It does not give a reason.

---

[210] Living at 6 East 94th Street, New York.
[211] Odette's Naturalisation Certificate (01/03/1954) indicates born 19/03/1918 in Kingston, Jamaica. Her death certificate (10/04/2008) states 18/03/1918, so she was 36 years old when they married.
[212] Hart Island, Potter's Field Plot 270: S1/G8.

Laura Frances Ryllis VAN-RAALTE

Laura was born in London[213] of German parents on 17th June 1899. In 1940 she was in lodgings at 2a All Saints Street, Nottingham. She was single and since September 1936 had been employed as a German teacher at Mundella Grammar School, Nottingham. Prior to this post she had taught in Chester, Bedford, Leytonstone, Brighton, York, Castleford and London.

On 30th May 1940, an anonymous letter was sent to the Chief Constable of Nottingham[214]. It complained that Laura was teaching her pupils the words and music of the German National Anthem, *'Deutschland über Alles[215]'*. It was considered a gross insult as the country was at war with Germany. The letter also noted that, in those days of fifth column treachery, a call for immediate and drastic action was needed.

The author left the matter with the police to resolve; however, if they didn't, the warning was that the Minister of Defence would be informed, and then a parents' meeting would be called to demand her internment.

Laura contacted Worcester police on 17th August 1940, requesting permission to purchase a guide book of the Malvern District whilst she stayed for a week in Malvern, in order to go walking and sightseeing whilst on holiday. They were aware of the complaint against her.

On 25th August, she stayed at the Beauchamp Hotel, Malvern with Miss M CHAPMAN[216] between 17th and 24th August. Nothing suspicious was observed.

Laura married Philip K HAYES in Nottingham in 1976. Philip died in 1980, aged 87, and Laura died in May 1995, age 95, in Basford.

---

[213] Living at 59 Ashburn Avenue, Golders Green, London.
[214] Letter dated 6th Jan 1954 CID Nottingham.
[215] Official title was: Das Lied der Deutschen
[216] 18 Elmcourt Road, London.

Martious Pieter VAN RAALT

The police file contains the briefest of notes on a man called Martious Pieter VAN RAALT. The note indicates that he was born on 16th March 1911, that his passport was issued in Leiden on 8th October 1948, and that he landed in England in the same year. His identification number was A225685, and he was living at 'The Grange', Grange Hill, London, SE25. There was no photograph nor any reference to his profession.

Jack and Una MOSSOP

I have presented the main (conflicting) versions of what was supposed to have happened to Bella from the different accounts; however, there are also numerous adapted published versions – too many to include in this book! What is fascinating were the inconsistent facts around Jack and Una MOSSOP's marriage and their 'family life'. In this section, I will tell my version of their story, by using official documentation and the accounts given by those interviewed by the police. Sadly, this is without contributions from Jack or his son Julian. I will follow Jack's story and introduce people and places along his lifeline.

Edward 'Percy' MOSSOP,[217] a steeplejack, married Charlotte 'Lolla' née CRUMP on 2nd December 1911[218]. They had two sons: Jack, born 29th August 1912, and Louis, born 31st October 1913.

Lolla died on 2nd November 1918, aged 27, during the Spanish Flu epidemic and her parents, George CRUMP[219] and Mary Anne née SMITH, raised Jack at their home, The Boycott Arms in Claverley. It is not known who raised Louis, but in later life he

---

[217] (b. 1881 d. March 1936) In April 1911 Percy was 28 years old and boarding at 211 High Street Smethwick (Harborne) Birmingham. In December he was living at the Boat Inn, Compton, Wolverhampton.

[218] In 1911 Lolla was 21 years old and living with parents at New Lanes, Claverley. They would later move to The Boycott Arms, Claverley.

[219] Died 14th January 1913 age 48, 3 Church Street, Claverley.

kept the Ivy House pub on Birmingham New Road[220] in Coseley, and passed away in 1982.

Jack's father, Percy MOSSOP, had another five children with Violet Catherine VANT, but they never married.

On 28th July 1932, Jack was a surveyor's assistant when he married Una Ella née ABEL[221] in Wolverhampton. On 14th November, their son Julian Michael MOSSOP was born. Julian was also known as 'Jack'. They first lived at Bridge House, Wombourne, Wolverhampton, whilst Jack was training as a surveyor. However, Julian did not live with his parents but was brought up by Una's parents, Frederick Rawlinson ABEL[222] and Rhoda Gertrude née SMITH, who lived a mile away at Gravel Hill, Wombourne[223].

In 1936, Jack was working for an automotive parts manufacturer called Lockheed, based in Leamington Spa. In 1937, he joined the A.S.T. as a Pilot Officer and was stationed at Hamble, near Southampton, but was discharged, possibly following an accident.

On 3rd November 1939, Jack got a job as a fitter at the Standard Aero[224] Works' No.1 Factory, at Fletchamstead, Coventry, and he and Una moved to lodgings at 9 Grosvenor Road,[225] Coventry. Another lodger at this property was a man called Bill WILSON.

In September 1939, work had started on the No.2 factory on Banner Lane in Kenilworth. It came into production in August/September 1940. On 27th November 1940, Jack transferred to the factory where he worked in the assembly shop manufacturing Bristol Hercules aero engines, and Jack and Una

---

[220] 1939 Register, living at Ivy House, 22 Birmingham New Road, Coseley.

[221] Born 14th November 1913, died June 1979 age 65.

[222] Died 7th January 1951.

[223] Some accounts indicate he was brought up by Mary CRUMP, like his father.

[224] Armstrong SIDDELEY.

[225] Mrs GALBRAITH, landlady, and about a mile from the Hippodrome Theatre.

moved to No. 39 Barrow Road. Here they took in two lodgers; first they were joined by Bill WILSON and a short while later by a man called Alfred HAINSWORTH.

Three months later, in February 1941, Una became pregnant, and Jill Kyra MOSSOP was born on 19th November 1941 at 124 Warwick Road in Kenilworth. The following month, on 13th December 1941, Una left Jack and moved to Nuthurst House, Shrewley, near Henley in Arden,[226] with Alfred HAINSWORTH. Sadly, baby Jill died in March 1942, but her death certificate names her as J.M. HAINSWORTH.

In June 1942, Jack's health started to deteriorate significantly, and he was taken by a work colleague named Terry MITCHELL to the 'family home' at The Boycott Arms, Claverley. He was then admitted to Stafford County Mental Hospital where he was declared insane. Jack died on 15th August 1942, in hospital, his cause of death being: (a) cerebral softening, (b) myocardial degeneration, (c) chronic nephritis, and (d) acute confusional insanity. Jack is buried in the churchyard cemetery in Claverley.

Una married Alfred J HAINSWORTH in 1943 and they went on to have four children: Andre, born in 1944; Eugene, born in 1945; Heather, born in 1946; and Terese, born in 1956. They were joined in 1943 by Julian, by now 11 years old, until he moved to London in 1949.

On 27th January 1944, Alfred was transferred to Aircraft Production at Ansty Aero, and he left there at the end of the war in 1945. We know from Julian's story that Alfred worked at a florist's shop. In 1951, they moved back to Kenilworth, and lived at 71 Randall Road until 31st March 1953, when they moved to Four Acres, Long Common, Claverley.

The two articles written by Quaestor were published in the Express and Star on Thursday 19th and Friday 20th November 1953.

---

[226]Also referenced as Knuthurst, Shrewley Common in Warwick.

The only other records that I could find are of the family travelling to Montreal and back again in 1957, with the ship's manifest showing their home address as Mill Cottage, Mathon, near Malvern, and of Alfred travelling to the USA in 1959, where he gave his address as Middletown, Studley, Warwick.

Alfred James 'Jack' HAINSWORTH

Not a lot is known about Jack HAINSWORTH[227], with the police reports making very little reference. He appears to have been discharged from the RAF on 30th August 1940, after serving for four months. Prior to that he had been working at Station Garage, Berkswell, as a fitter for three years.

He commenced work as a fitter in the assembly shop at the Banner Road factory on 3rd September 1940, along with Jack MOSSOP, and shortly afterwards he moved into 39 Barrow Road as a lodger. What happened next has been discussed in the previous section.

2005 Police Closure Report version #3

The Police Closure Report loosely follows the Una version, but makes several statements that I found confusing and was unable to corroborate.

In the first paragraph, it says that *'Julian remained with his mother until 1949'*, which is incorrect.

> In 1932 the relationship of MOSSOP and the now HAINSWORTH produced a son, Julian MOSSOP, who remained with his mother until 1949, when he went to London and there became involved in criminality.

---

[227] DOB 13/05/1917, also named as AINSWORTH in some reports.

Paragraph three says, ...*Following their divorce...* There is no record of Una and Jack MOSSOP ever getting divorced.

Paragraph four says, *At that stage some assertions with regard to witchcraft had been made and she wished not to be associated with it.* There is no account that Una wished this.

The report references a public house in Hagley called the Lyttleton Arms, despite Una's statement not indicating in which town it was in. This is even though the Lyttleton Arms in Halesowen is referenced in the Eddie SHERWOOD inquiry (Chapter 2) and was still known by that name until 2007.

The Donald McCORMICK version #4

In 1969, Donald McCORMICK published his book, Murder by Witchcraft. In chapter 17, I discuss why several academics and specialists of his writing career use terms such as 'fraudulent', 'hoaxer' and 'liar', and how this book and subsequent newspaper articles have, along with BYFORD-JONES's contributions, distorted the mystery.

In one section of his book,[228] Donald gives his account of the first meeting with Anna – an enhanced version of BYFORD-JONES's, and then writes about his own investigation in Paraguay and Holland, a possible Dutch woman, and a secret agent called Clara.

Donald quotes the source of his findings as the *'Abwehr Diaries[229]'* where he discovered that in March and April 1941, five agents were inserted into England from Holland. One was a woman whose codename was 'Clara' who was (possibly) parachuted into the Midlands area under cover of an air raid, somewhere between Kidderminster and Birmingham. He indicates that the Abwehr

---

[228] Chapter 7, p. 102–p120.
[229] The Abwehr was the German military intelligence service for the Reichswehr and Wehrmacht from 1920 to 1945.

records reveal that she failed to make contact and was presumed missing. Donald writes that he had no confirmation that Clara was dropped, or that the authorities in Britain had any knowledge of a Dutch agent in the country.

However, Donald's quest to identify 'Clara' resulted in him first tracking down a former Nazi living under an alias in Paraguay called Franz RATHGEB. Franz had been involved with the steel industries before the war, and had spent time in England, mostly in the Midlands and South Wales areas and he said he knew Stourbridge. Donald suggested that Franz and his colleagues had been actively recruiting Nazi sympathisers inside Britain and occupied territories.

Franz knew Clara, and told how she had been the 'Dutch Mistress' of an Agent whose codename was 'Lehrer'. He described her as being well educated, intelligent, attractive, and about thirty years of age. Clara apparently knew Britain well, having lived in Birmingham for five years before the war; she spoke fluent English and had had an unhappy love affair with a Stourbridge man. He recalled that she had irregular teeth and that, because she was attractive, this 'blemish' was noticeable. She wasn't tall, probably well below average height for a woman. He also indicated that he thought she was possibly from Utrecht; however, it was also possible that she was not Dutch at all, rather she just posed as Dutch for the purpose of espionage. He also said that Clara read horoscopes.

Franz provided Donald with another contact – a Frau CREMER who lived in Amsterdam. She told Donald that although she could not identify Clara, she felt sure that the woman in question was known as DRONKERS and was a relative of Johannes Marius DRONKERS,[230] a German secret agent, executed in Britain for spying. Also, she was friends with another German spy, Jan Willem Ter BRAAK, who was found dead on 1st April 1941 in a

---

[230] Hanged, Wandsworth prison, 31st December 1942.

deserted air raid shelter in Cambridge, where he had committed suicide.

Frau CREMER also told Donald that Clara acted as though she was a friend of the Dutch Resistance, but her frequent trips to Germany led many to believe she was a double agent. She also recalled that Clara was a student of astrology and once wore a garter of green snakeskin, which was apparently a witch's badge.

The John STALKER version #5

The former Deputy Chief Constable of Greater Manchester Police, John STALKER,[231] hosted a television show called Crimestalker Casebook and in 1994[232], the show featured the Bella In The Wych Elm case.

.

That said, the case was subject to a television program produced by John STALKER, broadcast nationally, which resulted in no additional material being forthcoming.

The reason for including this version is because both the programme and John STALKER are referenced in the 2005 Closure Report, and a section of the show is dedicated to the spy theory. A more in-depth review of this programme is discussed in chapter 20.

This version starts with John in the Express and Star's vaults discussing the first Anna letter, which is shown to camera. The letter presented is not the same as that in the police file.

---

[231] Died 15/02/2019.
[232] ITV's Central Broadcasting, Birmingham. Transmitted 14th September 1994.

There is then an interview with an Express and Star journalist, Jonathan LEAKE, who says, *"Anna wrote that the woman found in the tree was a Dutch woman who had been parachuted in by the Germans to spy on British munitions factories...and that the woman had subsequently been involved with some conflict with the spy ring she was meant to join and that they had then murdered her and placed her in the tree"*.

I was unable to find any other correspondence from Anna to support this statement.

Jonathan then goes on to say, *"Part of the story Anna told us involves her brother, who was an officer in the army, and the allegation that Anna made to us was that her brother had been involved in a spy ring, that he had been passing secrets to the Germans and that many of the factories he was involved in checking had subsequently been heavily bombed"*.

All previous versions and accounts reference Jack MOSSOP; this is the first reference to a brother or an army officer.

Una had two siblings, both girls, Eugenia Stella and Annette Rosannah Thirza. If this account were to be correct, then it would mean there was a step brother. Annette Rosannah Thirza married Jean Augustus Brandon GOODYEAR in 1924 and Eugenia Stella married Harold T LANE in 1936. The only other 'brother' would be Jack MOSSOP's brother Louis.

The programme then shows actors in a car following the BYFORD-JONES narrative where Bella is killed in the rear of the vehicle. Commentary over the clip is provided by John STALKER, who says, *"Anna later reveals how Bella became a threat to the three German spies"*.John STALKER concludes by asking, *"Is that how Bella ended up in the Wych Elm, assassinated on the orders of wartime intelligence?"*.

Jonathan LEAKE finishes by talking about one set of files that [they] have been unable to access, which contain full statements of everyone involved in the case, including people in Holland and Germany. He suspects quite strongly that there will be more secrets to come from these files, but doubts that they will ever be made available.

The Alison VALE version #6

On 22nd March 2013, journalist Alison VALE wrote an article in the Independent newspaper[233] titled, 'Is this the Bella in the wych elm? Unravelling the mystery of the skull found in a tree trunk'. She wrote that the mystery surrounding the wartime discovery of a human skull in a tree trunk may finally have been solved.

In her version, Alison references 'Anna' as alleging a connection between Bella, espionage, and the music hall in her letter to Quaestor in 1953. Furthermore, she states that 'Anna' claims that Bella had been murdered by a German spy ring involving a British Officer, a Dutchman, and a Music Hall Artist.

I was unable to find any letters from Anna to Quaestor to support this account.

The article then goes on to reference the (1999) declassified wartime MI5 files housed in the National Archive, an executed German spy called Josef JAKOBS, and a photograph of a woman that was in his possession at the time of his arrest.

Alison writes ...*the photograph was of a cabaret singer and German movie actress, called Clara BAUERLE.*

JAKOBS tells that Clara was his lover, that they had first met in Hamburg where she had been singing at the Café Dreyer with the Etté Orchestra. She was well connected with senior Nazis and had been recruited as a secret agent. She was due to parachute into the Midlands after he had established radio contact, but he claimed that since he had been captured before he could send word, this was now unlikely to happen.

---

[233] https://www.independent.co.uk/news/uk/home-news/is-this-the-bella-in-the-wych-elm-unravelling-the-mystery-of-the-skull-found-in-a-tree-trunk-8546497.html

This initial reference has been extracted from several reports and is a reasonable summary of MI5's findings. However, Alison then goes on to write; *...MI5 learnt that BAUERLE had been born in Stuttgart in 1906, making her 35. She was indeed a cabaret artist – in fact, she spent two years working the music halls of the West Midlands before the war and was said to speak English with a Birmingham accent.*

I was unable to find this reference within the documentation in the National Archive. However, some of the details do refer to an inquiry of a woman called **Klara Sofie BAUERLE**, who was born in Stuttgart in 1906. I was unable to substantiate the rest of the quote.

Finally, Alison notes that Clara BAUERLE's singing career appears to have come to an end around the same time as Donald McCORMICK's 'Clara' parachuted into England in March/April 1941. This is incorrect, as Clara recorded records as late as December 1941.

Whilst the whole interrogation and background to Josef JAKOBS is fascinating, for this chapter I have focused only on the Clara BAUERLE element and associated references.

Josef JAKOBS[234] was a German soldier and secret agent who was dropped by parachute over Ramsey[235] in Huntingdonshire, England on the evening of 31st January 1941.

He fractured his right ankle, either on leaving the aircraft[236] or when he landed, and was unable to walk. The following morning, at about 8.20 a.m., he fired his pistol and attracted the attention of two farm labourers, Charles BALDOCK and Harry COULSON, as they walked across Dovehouse Farm on their way to work, and he was captured. At first, Josef told the men he was a Frenchman and said, "Me sole flying… leg broke… me not in this war… from Luxembourg… made to come".

Prison photograph taken 2nd February at Camp 020

---

[234] His nickname was 'Langlich': KV2-24-1(1) Special Branch report 28.2.4.
[235] 500 yards bearing 135 degrees from Dovehouse Farm, map reference 778031. Also referenced as being two miles S.E. of Ramsey at Dogs Farm.
[236] JAKOBS claimed that it was broken while leaving the aeroplane, not on landing. He indicated that the wind hurled his foot against the plane whilst hanging out of the trapdoor. The doctor said the bones were splintered, caused by direct impact when hitting the ground. The dispatcher thought that (SNOW report) he had injured himself when leaving the aircraft.

Among his possessions was identity documentation in the name of James RYMER, plus the postcard previously mentioned, with a message on the back.

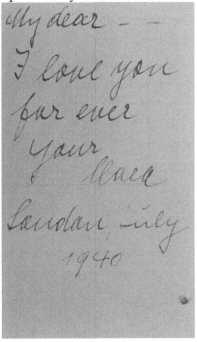

My dear _ _
I love you
for ever
  Your
    Clara
Landau. July
  1940

Researching the identity of Clara and her relationship with Josef, leads to another identified captured German secret agent called Karel RICHTER, whose account adds detail to the story. However, the principal narrative is generated by Josef.

Karel RICHTER was parachuted into Britain four months after Josef, on 12th May 1941, into London Colney, a village in Hertfordshire – two days later he was also captured.

Karel and Josef trained as spies together, and were able to provide their interrogators with information about each other and Clara.

Josef was first questioned by the Security Service (MI5) on 2nd February and specifically about the postcard on 10th February[237]. Initially, Josef's interrogators are not sure if the name on the reverse was Clara or Mara, and he is asked, "Who is Mara?". He tells them that she is Clara BAEURLE, a German from Ulm, a

---

[237] KV/24 21a

'singerin'[238] in the Bernard ETTÉ orchestra. She is a friend[239], who lives in Berlin, and does not speak English.

The interrogators call him a "damned liar... why has she written in English then?"

Josef confesses that she learnt English at the Berlitz School, but did not know how many lessons she had had because she went there before him. He also says that, although Clara lives in Berlin, she tours with the orchestra between Berlin, Hamburg, Koln, and Munich.

Like the name 'Mara', the interrogators are not sure about the word written before July 1940 on the rear of the postcard. They think it could be London. Josef confirms that the word is Landau[240].

At the same time, there were concerns that more parachutists may have landed, and it appeared that "a fearful flap has been caused" as a result of Josef's capture[241]. Unfortunately, despite a 'Stop Notice' to the press being issued by the Ministry of Information, and those involved in the capture being told to keep it secret, it became common knowledge. This is evidenced by the postal censorship that intercepted several letters detailing the event, and an incident involving the Home Guard Battalion Commander who is named as having given out details *in a loud voice, to a large number of people at a cocktail party*[242]. This would ultimately seal Josef's fate – any chance that MI5 could turn Josef into a double agent were prevented once news of his capture became known.

On 10th February, MI5 request that the Secret Intelligence Service (S.I.S.), also known as MI6, use their resources to investigate Clara.

---

[238] Finnish for singer.

[239] No mention is made of Clara being his mistress in this transcript. But, the 9a summary report by STEPHENS, SAMPSON & MEURIG EVANS indicates she was.

[240] A town 70 miles south of Frankfurt, Germany.

[241] 01/02/41 & 02/02/41 B.2a.

[242] Around 15th February.

They respond on the 12th indicating that they believe the postcard was printed in Germany because the space for the address on the back shows a thicker underlining under the penultimate line – a usual thing in continental countries. They also say that it was typical of hundreds of postcards you could buy in any shop in Germany, and that the writing is obviously that of a German and their expert considered the place name to be 'Landau'..

They say that they have no trace of the woman and that no one in their office recognises the photograph. They suggest that further enquiries be undertaken with persons connected with theatrical ventures. They then name four people worthy of contacting, but question their trustworthiness. MI5 appear to agree with that assessment, regarding them as 'slippery customers' and not being prepared to believe a 'no trace' return from them. Instead, they suggest a trusted Special Branch Inspector and his contacts be used to inquire. The same day, MI5 make a 'request for information' to the Home Office[243] for a Clara BAUERLE or BAUERLEIN, a German, aged between 20 and 30, who may now be in this country.

The Home Office respond on the 14th, stating: no trace in the Traffic Index, Central Aliens Register, or Home Office file.

Next, MI5 contact the Police Special Branch[244] on 26th February. They write: *I attach a photograph of a German cabaret singer whose name has been given to us as Clara BAEURLE or BAEURLEIN. There is no trace in the Traffic Index of a visit to this country by this woman, but we have reason to believe that she may, in fact, have been here.*

I imagine that there may be some of your officers who have reliable contacts in the theatrical world through whom some enquiries could be made. If so, I should be grateful for your assistance in the matter.

Special Branch respond on 17th April: *With reference to M.I.5. letter PF 55039/B.2. dated 26.2.41, requesting the enquiries be made to trace*

---

[243] KV 2/24: 12th February 1941 – MI5 request to Home Office.
[244] KV 2/24/40a: 26th February 1941 – MI5 request to Special Branch.

the whereabouts of Clara BAEURLE or BAEURLEIN, (copy photograph enclosed), a German cabaret singer, believed to have visited this country, but of whom there was no trace in Traffic Index:

The spelling of the German names given above is rather unusual, and is more likely to be BAUERLE or BAURLEIN. However, I have made exhaustive enquiries to ascertain whether she has ever visited this country, but without result. A further search in Home Office records revealed that one Klara Sofie BAUERLE, a German, born 29.6.06, registration certificate No. 453027, arrived in the U.K. on 20.10.30, and left Warwickshire for Germany, date unknown (Central Register of Aliens notified of departure on 21.6.32). The Central Register slip is attached herewith. No request for enquiries to identify this woman has been made to the Warwickshire Constabulary.

I communicated with the secretary of D.G. WHITE Esq., and learned that the original of the photograph was taken from a German parachutist captured in this country. When subsequently interrogated and asked who the woman in the photograph was he gave a name which was taken down phonetically as BAEURLE or BAEURLEIN.

My suggestion that the matter be referred back to M.I.5. pending a further interrogation of the prisoner – he is at present in hospital – was agreed to, and should an alternative spelling be obtained further enquiries will be made by me.

In response, MI5 request that Special Branch carry out further enquiries with respect to Klara Sofie BAUERLE.

Josef is interrogated for two hours on 25th April[245], during which time he is questioned again about Clara BAUERLE, but gives a different account to that given previously. The interview summary reads as follows:

JAKOBS began to take lessons in English at the Berlitz School in Hamburg in November/December. He had taken the lessons together with Clara BAUERLE. She was in Hamburg for the whole of October

---

[245] KV 2/25/68a: 25th April 1941 – MI5 Interrogation summary of Josef JAKOBS by Lt. SAMPSON.

and then went on tour for a short time and returned to Hamburg at the end of November. When JAKOBS left Hamburg, she was still there. Just before leaving Holland on the 21st January by aeroplane, he received a letter stating that she was very ill and had been sent to hospital. As far as he knew, she might be dead now. She was 33 years of age. When she came to Hamburg for the first time in October, she had had a private apartment in the Hansaplatz. He could not remember the number, but inadvertently mentioned the number 10, although he corrected himself afterwards. He believed that a lot of artists lived in this house in Hansaplatz. When she returned at the end of November, she lived with him at the Hotel Sorgenfrei. JAKOBS met her for the first time in October in the Café Dreyer where the "Etté" Band was playing. He was asked why she should write on a postcard to him, "Landau, July, 1940", if he only met her in October. He could not understand this, but she had been a very capricious woman and had given him picture postcards of herself with various dates. She knew JAKOBS' wife and knew about his work for the German Intelligence Service. She was anti-Nazi but did not belong to his society. She did not travel with him when he went to Berlin for the weekend.

Four days later, Josef is interviewed[246] again and adds some additional information:

Regarding Clara BAUERLE, JAKOBS said that this woman had been the mistress of the Medical Officer of a U-Boat flotilla at Kiel.

JAKOBS had introduced her to Dr. BEYER, who had arranged for her to get an engagement entertaining the troops; for her work with the Etté Orchestra at the Café Dreyer, BAUERLE received about 400 R.M[247]. and she naturally preferred the engagement with Dr. BEYER, as she earned more and was independent.

JAKOBS did not know what had happened to her, and although he knew that the Orchestra was in Hamburg in March 1941, he did not know

---

[246] KV 2/25/69b: 29th April 1941 – MI5 Interrogation Report of Josef JAKOBS by Lt. SAMPSON.
[247] German currency during WW2: Reichsmark.

whether she was appearing with the Orchestra. He did know that in December she had left Hamburg.

As BAUERLE knew many Officers and was not a Nazi, she had unwittingly given him information useful to his anti-Nazi organisation. She knew of his connection with the German Intelligence Service.

On 2nd May, Special Branch respond[248] to their enquiry into Klara Sofie BAUERLE:...*A further search in Home Office records revealed that one KLARA SOPHIE BAUERLE, German, born on 29.6.06, registration certificate No. 453027, arrived in the U.K. on 20.10.30, and left Warwickshire for Germany, date unknown (Central Register of Aliens was notified of departure on 21.6.32). The Central Register slip is attached herewith. No request for enquiries to identify this woman has been made to the Warwickshire Constabulary. I am calling for the Home Office Records relating to this woman and will let you know in due course whether anything further emerges about her.*

On 4th May MI5 inform Special Branch that the correct spelling of the woman's name is BAUERLE, and on 17th May they respond:

With reference to M.I.5 letter PF. 55039/B.2.c. of 4.5.41, regarding Clara BAUERLE, a German cabaret singer, who may have visited this country:- Exhaustive enquiries have been made among contacts in the theatrical world and elsewhere, but nothing has come to light to suggest that this woman has visited London.

On 15th and 19th May, Karel RICHTER is interrogated[249] and asked about Clara. He responds by saying that he had met Clara twice, once in November[250] at the Café Dreyer with Josef, but he did not speak to her, and he then saw her later in the street but again had not spoken to her. He says she was noticeable on account of her "*tallness*". Josef told him that she was a singer with the Etté orchestra, and that if he wanted to hear the orchestra, he would have to go to Berlin. Karel also says that Josef appeared to

---

[248] KV 2/25/75a: 2nd May 1941 – MI5 to Camp 020 re: Special Branch report.
[249] KV 2/30/4a & 15a: 16th May 1941 – Summary of Karel RICHTER statement.
[250] Later he would admit to being in Hamburg in October

be mainly interested in his affairs with women and describes Clara as *'a large, not very good-looking woman'*.

There is no indication that Karel was or was not shown the postcard to verify that Clara was the same woman/mistress he had seen with Josef. He also states that he met her in November, but Josef indicates it was October as Clara was touring in November. Furthermore, Josef will go on to say that Karel saw Clara perform, but Karel says otherwise, and that she was only introduced as a singer[251].

On 20th May, Josef is interrogated[252] and asked again about Clara:

At this time JAKOBS was still living at the Reichshof Hotel where he remained until October 26th, when he removed to the Sorgenfrei at the request of Clara BAUERLE. Clara BAUERLE was not, at the time, living at the Sorgenfrei but at another boarding house. Several of her friends from the Etté orchestra lived at the Sorgenfrei, so that this place was suitable for the meetings between JAKOBS and his mistress. On October 31st in the evening Clara BAUERLE left Hamburg with the Etté orchestra for a tour which included Leipzig, Dresden, Forst, East Prussia and Berlin. JAKOBS telephoned to Clara at Forst on November 7th to arrange a meeting in Berlin. She was with the Orchestra at Schöneberg, Berlin on the 18th, 19th and 20th November, and at the Neue Welt, Hasenheide, Berlin, on November 23rd and 24th. She returned to Hamburg on November 25th and lived with JAKOBS at the Sorgenfrei.

JAKOBS was asked whether it was not possible that RICHTER had seen Clara for the first time after November 25th when she came back to Hamburg. JAKOBS was quite positive that he had seen RICHTER twice at the Café Dreier[253] after their first meeting on October 22nd, before the

---

[251] Note: Kare's account of Clara and his recruitment, dates and places etc. changes constantly.
[252] KV 2/30/19b: 20th May 1941 – Interrogation report of Josef JAKOBS by Lt. SHORT & Lt. WINN.
[253] Elsewhere spelt Dreyer

end of the month, and that RICHTER had on these occasions heard Clara sing in the Etté Orchestra.

Finally, JAKOBS was questioned about the Klara Sofie BAUERLE who is recorded as having arrived in the United Kingdom on October 20th, 1930. He said the name of the woman he knew was always spelt with a "C" and that as far as he knew she had no second name. He was not certain when her birthday was, but that it might be July. It might, however, have been in June. The woman he knew was 35 years old last summer, and would, therefore, have been born in the year 1905. He was quite certain she had never been in England.

The same day MI5 make a 'request for information' to the Home Office[254] for *Klara Sofie BAUERLE, German, born 29.6.06: Home Office records have already revealed that Klara Sofie BAUERLE registration certificate No. 453027, arrived in the U.K. on 20.10.30 and left Warwickshire for Germany, date unknown (Central Register of Aliens was notified of departure on 21.6.32) but we are anxious to have any further details that may be procurable.*

The Home Office respond[255] on 22nd May, indicating that they have no additional information. They provide a copy of Klara's *Alien's Registration Card which indicates she was born 29.6.06 in Stuttgart, arrived U.K. 20/10/20 left U.K. 22/1/32 re-entered U.K. 22/2/32. Last Registration District, Warwickshire. Remarks: To Germany 21/6/32.*

This appears to be the part reference made in Alison's article; however, MI5, MI6, Special Branch, and the Home Office were unable to establish that Klara and Clara were the same person. I was also unable to find an occupation for Klara; therefore, her being a cabaret artist working the music halls of the West Midlands before the war and speaking English with a Birmingham accent appear to be assumptions.

---

[254] KV 2/25/83b: 20th May 1941 – MI5 request to Home Office, Klara Sofie BAUERLE.
[255] KV 2/25/83b.

MI5 finally close their inquiry into the postcard and Clara BAUERLE on 25th June in the following summary[256]:

While in Hamburg in October, 1940, JAKOBS met Clara BAUERLE, a singer in the Etté Orchestra, which was performing at the time in the Café Dreyer. During November the orchestra was touring other parts of Germany, but returned to Hamburg at the end of that month and Clara BAUERLE then went to live with JAKOBS at the Hotel Sorgenfrei. JAKOBS states that she had previously been the mistress of the medical officer of a U-Boat flotilla at Kiel. She knew many officers and was not a Nazi, and had unwittingly given him information useful to his anti-Nazi organization.

She knew of JAKOBS' connection with the Intelligence Service, and he had in fact introduced her to Dr. BEYER who had arranged for her to get an engagement entertaining the troops. Among JAKOBS' possessions was a picture postcard of Clara BAUERLE with an affectionate message in English, dated Landau, July, 1940 and signed Clara. He said the message was in English because they had taken English lessons together at the Berlitz School in Hamburg. He could not explain why the card was dated July, 1940 while he first met her in October, 1940, except that she was a very capricious woman who distributed photographs of herself generously. JAKOBS was introduced in October by a girl-friend of Clara to a man called von ROEDERN, who organized Fifth Column activity outside Germany. JAKOBS was on this occasion introduced as a member of the Intelligence Service. If JAKOBS' statements are true, it is curious that he was known to belong to the Intelligence Service not only to Clara BAUERLE, but also to her girl-friends and presumably therefore to a large number of other people.

So, who was Clara? She was born Hedwig Clara BAUERLE[257] on 27th August 1905, in Ulm, Baden-Württemberg, Germany and died on 16th December 1942, at the Königin-Elisabeth Hospital,

---

[256] KV 2/25/96: 25th June 1941 – Summary Report on Josef JAKOBS written by Lt. SAMPSON.
[257] Spelt Bäuerle.

Berlin, Germany[258]. Clara is credited with acting parts in two movies: the 1933 film Die Blume von Hawaii (The Flower of Hawaii) and the 1940 film Bal Paré. Clara was also a singer and between September and December 1940, she recorded[259] three songs with the Bernhard ETTÉ Orchestra. Between March and December 1941, Clara recorded eight more songs, some with the Bernhard ETTÉ and Juan LLOSSAS orchestras as an Orchesterbegleitung[260].

The question I ask myself, was JAKOBS telling the truth about Clara and himself? The files in the National Archive indicate what MI5 thought.

In Lt SAMPSON's 'Liquidation Report[261]' he says that[262] ...*there are a number of serious divergencies between JAKOBS' various statements, especially between the earlier ones made to the police on February 2nd, and later statements made in April after his final return from hospital. In spite of the fact that he was in considerable pain on February 1st and 2nd, his statements on these dates may be taken as being on the whole more reliable, as he had not had time to think out a complete story. These divergencies throw an interesting light on JAKOBS' true motives in coming over.'* He goes on to say that ...*JAKOBS is an unprincipled blackguard[263] with a criminal background, who now hopes to curry favour by a show of willingness to help us... a scrofulous Nazi.*

In another report[264] which references the information provided by RICHTER and JAKOBS. It says that [for RICHTER] ...on the whole I am inclined to believe that much of it is true[265]. JAKOBS, on the other

---

[258] Death certificate: Lung infection due to *Veronal* poisoning; living at No. 32 Bleibtreustrasse, Berlin.

[259] Recording dates

[260] Orchestra accompaniment.

[261] KV-2-25-1 p17 – p22

[262] KV-2-25-1 p19

[263] KV-2-25-1 p22

[264] B.L. Report dated 17.6.41

[265] Later, STEPHENS says that RICHTER's stories changed so much, that daily reports were necessary

hand is so anxious to please that he draws upon his imagination, and I therefore consider that much of what he says is false.

Major STEPHENS assessment[266] *of JAKOBS interrogation on the 14th June, was ..that he does not know very much. ...I regard JAKOBS as an unprincipled scoundrel with a good deal of low cunning, and I think all his statements should be taken with the utmost reserve, though occasional grains of truth may be extracted.*

The Jayne HARRIS version #7

One of the most recent versions is in the 2017 film documentary called The Untold Secrets – Who Put Bella In The Wych-Elm?, presented by Jayne HARRIS. In the film, Jayne discusses three of the spy theories: Una HAINSWORTH's (14.3) version, Donald McCORMICK's Clara DRONKERS' (14.13) version, and Alison VALE's Joseph JAKOBS and Clara BAUERLE (14.15) version. I have included Jayne's contribution because she introduces additional material that develops my previously described versions.

The spy theory section of the film starts with a truncated version of the BYFORD-JONES and Anna of Claverley introduction and the meeting with Una HAINSWORTH, although says *"...her 'true name' was MOSSOP...".*

The following are conflicting statements, or where I was unable to find any documentation to support them:

"Jack worked at a munitions factory" – I believe Jack worked in an assembly shop manufacturing aero engines for Bristol Hercules.

"....Jack apparently admitted to Una that Van RALT was a Nazi agent and he'd been selling him information about local industrial sites, which was in turn being sold to a female agent..."

"... the 'Dutch Piece' was Van RALT's girlfriend..."

---

[266] B.L.(a) 16.6.41 GS/FHL [KV-2-25-2(1)p33

"...Van RALT had ordered him to drive up the Clent Hills with his girlfriend in the car. By this point the argument had turned incredibly violent and apparently Van RALT had strangled the woman. MOSSOP and Van RALT then panicked and hid her in a tree..."

"...Una's husband was apparently so traumatised by the poor woman's death that he had a nervous breakdown tormented by horrific visions of a woman's skull in a tree and her ghost haunting him..."

"...Jack was institutionalised at Stafford Mental Hospital and in 1942 he died from an overdose..."

"...in the village of Claverley, Jack MOSSOP was well known for wearing an RAF uniform. However, we know from his police file that he was never a member of the RAF..." – This statement is similar to that made in a 2015 radio broadcast[267] that discussed the case.

"...MI5 got involved..."

Next, Jayne briefly discusses Donald McCORMICK's version and challenges *"...the validity of his supposed findings..."*, noting that he's been *"...highly criticised over the years..."* asking *"...did McCormick simply know how to write an interesting story?"*

Last, Jayne discusses Joseph JAKOBS and Clara BAUERLE, using the Alison VALE version as the base for the narrative, saying that, *"...Joseph names the woman in the postcard as his lover, had been a performer in the West Midlands and could speak with a Birmingham accent..."*, also, referencing Clara as being *"...born in Stuttgart in 1906..."*

The Canadian Links

On 3rd April 1956, the Birmingham Post published an article headed 'The Spy Caesar of Edgbaston'.

---

[267] Steve Punt (2015) Punt PI – broadcast 6th Aug, BBC Radio 4, Who Put Bella in the Wych Elm?

The article referenced a book called 'War of Wits'[268], and named a German Canadian, called Hans CAESAR, a man who had lived in Edgbaston, Birmingham, and who it alleged had been engaged in espionage during the war. It was suggested that he was now in an asylum but was merely simulating insanity in order to escape the consequences of his wartime activities.

On 19th May 1956, the Birmingham Post published an apology. It transpired that Hans CAESAR had lived in Edgbaston prior to the war as they had indicated, and was a well-known figure in the jewellery trade. However, he had spent most of the war in the German Infantry on the Russian front, where he was captured and was not repatriated by the Russians until 1949. He had never been in an asylum and was alive and well, living and working in Birmingham.

The apology read: *We desire to tender to Mr Hans Caesar our sincere apologies for having given circulation to these false and damaging statements concerning him and to express our deep regret for the inconvenience and distress which we recognise the article must have caused him.*

The previous reference is important, because the next Canada reference appears ten years later in Donald McCORMICK's 1969 book, 'Murder by Witchcraft'[269], where, alongside Clara DRONKERS, he discusses the German infiltration of the Midlands during the war and a mysterious spy. He names the spy as German Canadian Karl DICKENHOFF,[270] who lived in Edgbaston, Birmingham. He writes that Karl's real name was said to be Hans CAESAR, although he apparently had many aliases.

The next mention appeared in the Black Country Bugle in 1973, which reported on an anonymous letter with a Toronto

---

[268] (1954) Ladislas FARAGO, also a similar article in the Evening Despatch 13/6/45.

[269] p. 157 & p. 158. Also this chapter, 14.13.

[270] Book reference: (1946) Entlarvter Geheimdienst by T. BUSCH.

postmark[271]. The letter appears to draw its narrative from McCORMICK's book.

The next Canadian reference is in Joyce M. COLEY's 2007 book[272]. It recalls an incident involving Douglas OSBORNE, the Special Constable who guarded the tree on the evening of 19th April 1943. Joyce writes about a story told by Douglas to his son Peter Ernest Douglas OSBORNE.

Douglas had served in the RAF during the war, and at the end of hostilities he had been in Europe and was making his way back to England via Holland. En route, he made friends with a group of Canadians who had been inspecting the records of the German Secret Service. They were trying to find out what had happened to some of the British Special Operations Executive, also known as 'SOE' personnel. They were returning to Canada with documentation recovered from an office in The Hague. Douglas travelled back to the UK on the same boat, and they swapped stories. He told them about the unknown woman in the tree, and they told him about spies who had worked in the area around the Midlands. Apparently, amongst the documents they found the description of a woman that matched Bella – the same age, stature, colouring and dental formation. She had been dropped by parachute in 1941 from Holland. Two were captured, two others were sent by boat, and the other, a woman, failed to make contact. For a while, she had lived in the Midlands and she never revealed her identity. This account is almost identical to the spy story version #4 described in Chapter 14 and in the book 'Murder by Witchcraft'[273].

In Joyce's book, Peter also recalls that in the 1960s there was another outbreak of writings on the walls, and when he asked his father for details about the case, his father refused to talk about it and forbade him from mentioning the subject again. I was unable

---

[271] Full transcript chapter 19.1
[272] BELLA: An Unsolved Murder p. 16-p19.
[273] p. 111-p120.

to find any reference to wall markings produced or reported in the 1960s.

CHAPTER 15
VICTOR CRUMPTON

The next contact with the inquiry following the publication of the Quaestor articles was a letter sent on 23rd November 1953. It was addressed to Superintendent INIGHT and came from Fredrick Victor CRUMPTON, aged 44,[274] of 35 Harcourt Road, Old Hill, Halesowen. His reason for writing was because the article on 19th November had indicated that the police had been unable to identify who had made the chalk markings on the wall at Old Hill in 1944.

He starts by saying that the letter was prompted by the Express and Star article, and he introduces himself as having spent 25 years living with his family at St Kenelm Hall in Romsley[275] and that he had lived at Old Hill since 1940[276].

He recounts that a PC B HOLLOBIN, who had been stationed at Old Hill police station, told him that he had caught the man responsible for the chalk markings on the wall[277]. Victor was concerned that, despite the offender being caught, there had been no conviction or any record of the incident.

Victor then tells what he had been told by PC HOLLOBIN: *At about 4am one morning PC HOLLOBIN heard footsteps coming up the road from the direction of Halesowen and concealed himself with a commanding view of the wall. When the man halted and started to write with chalk on the wall the officer crossed the road and jumped on the culprit's back, causing him to faint with shock. The culprit apparently came from Halesowen and was going to Netherton via Bell Vale in time for 'early turn' at the Ironworks.*

---

[274] Born 4th April 1909, died July 1988.
[275] Approximately 2 miles east of Hagley Wood.
[276] 1911 Census: 2 High Street, Old Hill, 1939 Register OKAB6/3 St Kenelm Hall, helps father who was a grocer and farmer.
[277] Chapter 4, 27/03/1944.

I was unable to find any further documentation or reference to any inquiries resulting from this correspondence in the archive but this is not the end of Victor's involvement with the mystery. Two weeks later, at 7.50 a.m. on Monday 7th December, PC 59 DAVIS was on morning patrol on the High Street, Stourbridge, when he met Victor, who he knew from when he had lived in Romsley.

Victor told PC DAVIS how earlier that morning, at around 4 a.m. he had *'visited the scene of the Wych Elm murder in Hagley Wood for a "wager". Upon arriving at the scene, the emotional tension had made him 'excrete', and in attending to the wants of nature he had lost his wallet and contents near the scene...'*

He told the officer that he had *'...received a head injury during WWII service at a "Beach Landing" operation, and that at some stage he had been given electrical impulse shock treatment which had done him 'no good' owing to his 'strong personality'.*

PC DAVIS's meeting with Victor was immediately brought to the attention of Superintendent WILLIAMS, who met with Victor the same day, commenting in a memo that in his opinion *"he is slightly mental"*.

In a police report,[278] it appears that Victor was already known to the inquiry and *'the possibility that he could have committed the crime could not be ruled out'* – despite this observation in the report, Victor does not feature in the 2005 Closure Report under the Suspect heading. The report goes on to say that a few days prior to his early morning visit to Hagley Wood, Victor had helped with the 'laying out' of the body of a female neighbour, who had died of natural causes. It was noted that he had been emotionally upset since then, and also, that he had been a patient at Barnsley Hall Mental Hospital in Bromsgrove[279].

---

[278] Report: Stourbridge, 7th December 1953.
[279] Worcestershire Mental Hospital 1929–1947, Barnsley Hall Mental Hospital 1948 and Barnsley Hall Hospital for Nervous and Mental Diseases 1949–1966.

The report finishes by saying: *If he is eventually certified, it would be very interesting to know what his reactions will be under the modern science treatment given to subjects such as he with 'Truth Drug' injections, etc., as applied in Mental Institutions.*

The day after Victor met with Superintendent WILLIAMS, he wrote another letter, in which he provides the details of two Staff Nurses from the Romsley Sanatorium who he says are missing and who could possibly be Bella.

The first was a Miss WILLIAMS, about 5′ 3″, aged 36, Welsh, and a single mother with a son named Ronald. Victor says that she refused to marry him because she was still in love with the child's father who had to go to Canada.

The second was a Miss May NEVIN, age 32, 5′ 8 ½″, Irish, who had a child after she was sacked from the Sanatorium.

A week later, he wrote another brief letter[280]. It contains mostly pleasantries about Christmas cake and dancing, but indicates that he will be going into hospital for a few months from 1st January 1954. There is no reference to the inquiry, and he signs the letter *Fredrick Victor (Burgess) CRUMPTON.*

On 28th December, Superintendent WILLIAMS responds to the two previous letters from Victor. He discusses the two missing nurses and indicates that they were both too tall. He references that the one at 5′ 3″ (Miss WILLIAMS) was the nearest in height, but says that the victim was only 4′ 11″ in height when she was wearing shoes. He then questions why Victor used so many Christian names, particularly the one in brackets – Burgess – and wonders if it was after the council department, 'Burgesses of Rowley Regis', where he had once worked. Victor's birth name was Fredrick Victor and his mother's maiden name was BURGESS. Laura Gertrude BURGESS married Fredrick William CRUMPTON in December 1903.

---

[280] 15th December 1953.

Victor responded with his last letter on 13th January 1954. He was now on R Ward at the Barnsley Hall Hospital. The letter thanks Mr WILLIAMS for his response dated 28th December and explains that he was admitted on 4th January and is *'happy and contented'*. The letter contains no further references to the enquiry.

I was unable to find any record of a Miss WILLIAMS with a son called Ronald but Victor died age 79 in July 1988.and of note is that, like Wilfred BYFORD-JONES, Victor lived in proximity of the chalk markings in Old Hill and Halesowen.

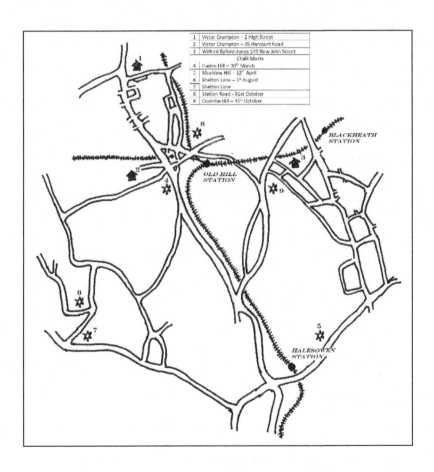

CHAPTER 16
THE CLAIRVOYANTS

Zita BOYDON (Part 1)

Zita Maria BOYDON, née NEWEY, was born on 30th October 1911, and spent her childhood at 107 Albert Road, Handsworth, Birmingham[281]. In 1932 she married William Norman BOYDON, a schoolteacher, and in 1939 they were living at 117 Merridale Road, Wolverhampton. Zita died on 19th January 1962. Her death certificate describes her as a 'widow' although William was still alive.

Within four days of the Quaestor's articles and the publication of the first 'Anna' letter, the police received a handwritten letter. It was dated 24th November 1953[282], was addressed to Chief Constable, Mr S INIGHT, Worcestershire, and was from a Mrs Zita BOYDON of 58A Compton Road, Wolverhampton:

Dear Sir,

Reading about "Lou Bella" in the Express & Star & the several suggestions put forward.

There are a number of things I know which might give you a lead.

If possible, also I would like to pay a visit to the tree in Hagley Wood?

Also is it possible for me to see the remains of clothing found on the skeleton?[283]

I would like to discuss these things. Can it be arranged?

Yours faithfully

(Mrs) Z. BOYDON

---

[281] 1911 Census, 1939 Register OQNJ45/21.
[282] Received 25th November 1953. Passed to D/Supt WILLIAMS 25/11/53.
[283] Possibly because this would aid Zita to make direct contact rather than to use a spirit guide.

Two days later, Zita sent another letter, and this time it was four pages long[284].

(page 1) I wrote to you a few days ago and have also visited Quaestor with the foregoing statements. Maybe I should explain that my delibera-tions are not imaginary but might prove to be facts. Proof that this is so might be obtained from Scotland Yard, Halifax police, Carmarthen police Richmond police etc., with details relating to several recent murders – towpath murder XXX Hackett murder t- The recent Harries murder – etc. etc. One might term it visionary – call it what you like – for this reason then I tell you the following which might relate to the "Lou Bella" affair. She was a country type, slower spoken – fresh coloured, brown hair. She worked in an institute or home – I believe a Catholic place as a general help. The man who put her body in the tree was tall, blonde, tanned, fresh skin. He wore a leather jacket with a sheepskin collar. He was, I believe, a Dutch Canadian[285]. ...

(page 2) XXX such as Franz or Franc (short for XXX) could be the Chris-tian name with the XXXXX of Christina or Kristina. In appearance – blue eyes rather fixed looking lightish hair, particularly fair around the back of the neck and more noticeable there on account of the tan. A straight nose with a tip to the end like a boxer. In private life maybe a traffic 'cop' – at any rate one who rode a motorcycle and was dressed in dark blue uniform with a badge. The woman's dress denotes handed-on institute clothes. I believe she waited on children also. The building she was in had good solid oak polished floors and was not completed. Maybe her own child, now about 12 years old might be in a home or institute – a body child resembling father. She wore also on her middle finger of right hand a ring with a round top – like many soldiers coming from the con-tinent I have seen  *wearing it might have been a ring with a saint in it, often worn by religious folks. She had small fat fingers with pointed ends. I believe "Bella" and I'd with*

[284] Dated 26th November 1953.
[285] German Canadian also appears in 14.16.

something wrong with her throat or maybe strangulation. She was hauled into the tree by means of a rope looped under the...

(page 3) ... XXXX. The rope was not tied with knots but expertly looped so that once the victim was released from being hauled the rope could easily be pulled away. A name which might help also is HIPKINS I say might. A song relating to "Bella" was popular then I believe called 'Bella Bambina[286]'. Also someone may have called her a "daft Loob Ella" which may have been where Lou Bella was derived. It might be difficult to probe Catholic homes and institutions for quite naturally they do not like notoriety. I believe the child to be solid, plump with straight hair, short, tied with a ribbon, broad, flattish nose, blue eyes. The reason why Bella's life was tormented was no doubt on account of not being married and wanted to be – perhaps the man was already married. Was a child abandoned during that period? Could that be ascertained? Why not try all homes round about the Midlands area?

(page 4) ...XXX almost convinced that there is a child in an institution of a religious type. I am so sure of the features that were I to see her I would know at once. I cannot give you material proof, but sometimes other sources are much better though not openly acknowledged (as I am well aware) by the police – or Army – proofs are the essentials – no matter how XXX.

   Yours faithfully (Mrs) Zita BOYDEN

Of note is that this letter was written prior to the first meeting[287] between Una HAYWORTH (Anna of Claverley), BYFORD-JONES (Quaestor) and the police. Zita confirms that she had already met with Quaestor, and in this letter (page 2) references 'Franz or Franc' – this is on 26th November 1953. The meeting between Una et al. took place on 4th December. It is then that the police follow up with an investigation to identify a 'Fruck, Frik or Frack', eventually identifying the act 'Frick and Frack'.

---

[286] Al BOWLLY, recorded (London) December 1939.
[287] Chapters 14.1, 14.2, 14.3, 14.4, 14.6.

171

Did BYFORD-JONES already know what Una was going to say to the police, did he share information with Zita, or is this proof of Zita's clairvoyant skills and therefore should more consideration be given to her letters?

Following this letter, the police visited Zita; their notes written on the last letter indicate that they visited on Sunday 29th November. We do know that PW HILL[288] was in attendance, and possibly Mr WILLIAMS. There are also some notes written on the rear, but no context is provided:

A sketch of the road junction in Wolverhampton joining Bath Road and Lord Street.
C. Annie WORTHINGTON 74 Lord Street[289]
Canadian Army ...uniform

Zita wrote again on 11th December, and this time provided impressions of 'Lou Bella', which she hoped would be helpful.
Herewith further "impressions" of "Lou Bella" which may help and which I believe applies to her. She pushed a cream coloured pram with black a navy-blue canopy. Old fashioned, low a XXX low build. When hood was up "Lou Bella" needed to look round the side of the pram as she pushed it being too short to look over the top. Also get the impression of a small end house not too far from a bridge of sorts.

(page2) Also get the impression of "Lou Bella" using an old-fashioned iron. At times the iron seems an ordinary size at others it seems a big and very deep one. She was quite a lively happy natured person – animal type. Watchful. Skin and check bones red, fine lines running from eyes over cheek bones. Smiling, merry laugh.

The letter also included a drawing:

[288] Involved in the FRICK and FRACK inquiry, Chapter 14.6.
[289] 1939 Register OQNN 290/1 74 Lord Street, born 10th July 1888.

On 16th December,[290] the police responded to her letter:

Dear Mrs BOYDON,

Thank you for your further letter of the 11th December 1953 which I have studied with interest.

I have not been able to come and see you, because of other important developments in this matter, but rest assured, I shall take the first opportunity of doing so, should the need arise.

The following month, on 11th January 1954, the Birmingham Gazette published an article about George ELWELL, which would prompt another letter from Zita.

George ELWELL

On 11th January 1954, the Birmingham Gazette published a story titled: Hypnotised Man Provides New Clues... 'BELLA': KILLER IS NAMED IN TRANCE. The man behind the story was Mr George Henry ELWELL (b.1906 d.1986), a British Railway official, who lived about three miles from Hagley Wood at 'Lansdowne', Meriden Avenue, Wollaston, Stourbridge with his wife[291] Jessie.

---

[290] TNW/FH.

[291] Married 1938, Jessie (née PAYNE) died in 1997, no children.

The 'Quaestor Seeker' article a few months earlier, and the subsequent 'Anna from Claverley' correspondence, had sparked his interest, and he recalled how he had been intrigued by the riddle of 'Bella'.

A week earlier, on Tuesday 2nd January, George told how he had walked alone through Hagley Wood, paused by the Wych Elm and stood there for ten minutes in the darkness, assimilating the "atmosphere". He then returned to his house and decided to carry out an experiment in the hope that he could help the police.

He e described himself as an inventor and he had built an instrument to help put himself into a trance. He used a blinking car headlamp and a mirror to lull himself into a hypnotic trance whilst forcing himself to concentrate on the murder.

As he fell into a trance, he recorded every word. Fifteen minutes later, he woke and played back the recording.

The Birmingham Gazette published part of the recording: *It is very cold… there's a horse neighing somewhere… raindrops on the trees… dark, very dark. A tree, yes… what's he got on his shoulder? Oh, God. Blood down her face on to her hair. Oh, she's dead, she's dead. Name, name, what is her name? BRADMAN – no. BRADLEY, that's it… Annie BRADLEY, of Leeds.*

Mr. Elwell listening to the recording last night.

The reporter, John WILCOX, also provided the inquiry with a transcript of the recording, which was made on 10th July and provided more details.

Concentrate. You will not wake until the alarm sounds on the clock. Do not awake until the alarm sounds on the clock. Concentrate. I want to know the name of the man. What is the name of the man? What is the name of the woman?

Where does she come from? Concentrate....

(Pause of about a minute)

Cold.... It is very cold. Hear a horse neighing somewhere....

It is cold very cold....

Rain dropping on the trees on the leaves.... Dark very dark...

Horse neighing again.

A tree, yes, a tree.... what has he got on his shoulder?

Oh, God!

Untying string...

Oh, my God!

Blood down her face onto her hair.

Oh, she is dead... she is dead.

Name, name, name. What is her name?

BRADMAN, no, no. BRADLEY... yes that's it. Annie BRADLEY, of Leeds.

Yes, the man.

Tall... moustache... five buttons down his jacket...narrow trousers.... Light blouse... funny sleeves... John CONNOR.... John CONNOR... C O N N O R

Tying it up. Got to get away...

In all, the recording lasted about 15 minutes.

Grettia BRADLEY

On 14th January 1954, Mrs Mary BRADLEY, Kilcully, Ballyjamesduff, Co. Cavan, Eire, wrote to Inspector WILLIAMS after reading the George ELWELL article.

Dear Sir

Reading the daily express a paper I get every day since it started to be sold here in Bally f duff I read about a murder that happened that the body of a woman was found in the trunk of a wych elm in Hagley Wood in 1943 of course it gives the name Annie BRADLEY of Leeds

I had a daughter Grettia BRADLEY who went to England about 16 or 17 years ago she worked for a time in Sheffield and she came home three times on holidays the last place I heard from her was from the National Hospital Queens Square London that would be about 14 years ago Since then I never heard any account of her I often wonder what has become of her I know she left the hospital about that time for I wrote to the matron she was a cook there

I wrote to a place in England to trace her they sent me a form and I was to fill it in and return to that place and XXXX but my husband died about that time with one thing after another the address and form got lost

I never sent it but I often think what has happened during all those years she never wrote

Yours truly Mary BRADLEY Kilcully Bally James Duff, Co Caven, Eire

Please she be about 40 years of age now if she is still living.

Inspector WILLIAMS responded on 18th January. He calls her Greta BRADLEY, not Grettia, and discusses that the name BRADLEY was provided by a man named ELWELL, stating that "I do not place much reliance on this information".

He also writes that the victim was barely five feet in height and was about 37 years of age in 1941, so 'therefore if you say that your daughter would now be about 40, if she is still alive it could not be her'.

This statement is confusing as Professor WEBSTER indicated that the victim was aged between 25 and 40, but was probably 35 years, plus or minus a few years. 37 years is at the top end of the estimate; with Grettia being about 27 in 1941, she would have been within the scope of the investigation.

The 1939 Register[292] shows her living at 23 Mornington Crescent, St Pancras, London with a four-month-old baby boy and her future husband, Abdul MADJID. They marry in 1941, and the 1959 Electoral Register entry shows them living at No. 158 Hampstead Rd. Grettia/Greta died in June 1973.

Zita BOYDON (Part 2)

Within a week of the Birmingham Gazette article about George ELWELL, Zita sent two more letters, both referencing George's subconscious revelations.

The first letter, dated 15th January[293] 1954, is helpful because it includes some information about what was possibly discussed at the meeting on 29th November 1953, or possibly at another

---

[292] ASBJ217/2. Born 08/10/1914.
[293] Police stamp 16 Jan 1954.

meeting that was not recorded. What follows is a full transcript, although some words (XXX) are illegible. I have reproduced this letter because many of the observations feature elsewhere.

Dear Mr WILLIAMS,

No sign of the <u>Leeds</u> in Bradley – only <u>the Lees</u>[294]. Perhaps Mr ELWELL's subconscious revealed his liking for 'Leeds United' – but I was interested in the tall soldier. Remember the one I mentioned as having come from Liverpool? <u>He</u> used to ride a motorcycle but no doubt you took notes, mentally unless it was overlooked, since you and Inspector INIGHT were too anxious to "cat & mouse" me for "ulterior motives".

I know my friend. I Know! My friend was with me – Jacques[295]. He laughed like mad coming home with me and said "Toujours la politesse."[296]

Have you by any chance seen the photograph of 'Annie's' daughter who was put away about 14 years ago[297] so much like Lou Bella – hair style, shaped face etc. you won't see it <u>now </u>anyway. It's in a box in the cupboard in wardrobe upstairs. I "see" where it is, but you can't!

Incidentally there is a village in Kent called LEEDS 4 miles from Maidstone.

Could the Liverpool police find out where John WORTHINGTON lived & what happened to his son Franc (Francis) & his daughters? Franc: came over this way. He was a <u>tall soldier</u> & he rode a <u>motorcycle.</u> He had shock through the war – on the bombing in Liverpool. Where did he die? Did he die insane? John WORTHINGTON had very forward projecting teeth – like Lou Bella's type. John is in America – Georgia may where all "Lilly's" are called Lillibella.

---

[294] Mary LEE inquiry Chapter 2.1.
[295] Possibly Zita's 'Spirit Guide'.
[296] Always polite.
[297] Jill Kyra MOSSOP/HAINSWORTH died March 1942, Chapter 14.10.

(page 2) If the names I have mentioned do not reveal some truth then surely there is something amiss for I never "see" or "hear" anything without quite a lot of truth in it.

Incidentally I 'saw' the dumb boy, David ANDERTON in a stream. Isn't it strange how sometimes the 'bereaved' become themselves? Why use black neckless gloves. Why a crooked stick? Why hide the face with black cloth? Why on Christmas Day? Why call him 'silly' the child was very sane. All life is pain – that little boy knew what was to happen & there are so many like him – Canals are useful too – & Christmas Day – a Christmas Eve makes a finer "holy" cover for un-holy deeds. Wasn't that Hitler's method?

Sometimes I think a lot about Father BORYNSKI[298] & when I "see" him now he has blood running from the corners of his eyes & he is pale & still.

Do not forget about the shoes of Lou Bella if you wish to try this method at any time it will be XXX – no need for 'sandy boots' & while on the subject & Sandy boots if possible think they ought to look a little wetter – how about you?

I expect you had my card after the 'phone call' – I couldn't wait – that's all!

Everything seems so slow.

Many good wishes also from DIXON yours sincerely Zita BOYDON.

A few days later, another letter, postmarked 18th January 1954[299] and addressed to Superintendent WILLIAMS, was received, commenting on Mr ELWELL's revelations. The letter said that *...You could interpret the clairvoyant message as follows: - Annie. Bradley – Leeds. Annie who comes from the Leeds (name of a street) in Bradley, Bilston.*

---

[298] A Roman Catholic priest called Henry BORYNSKI, who disappeared in mysterious circumstances in July 1953.
[299] Police stamp CID Hindlip Hall 18 Jan 1954.

Clairvoyant messages can be confusing & certain names can be of people, streets towns etc. So before jumping to conclusions dear sir, consult Madame Zed. Try – The LEADS Bradley Bilston.

This letter references a Madame Zed. I was only able to find two articles about a Madame Zed, and I was unable to establish a link between the Madame Zed in the newspaper articles and Zita or Wolverhampton. The first article[300], in 1927, indicates that Madam Zed's real name was Jeanne BRAZIER[301], who was married and living at 7 Claremont Road, Bishopston, Bristol. She was described as 'of French parentage' and a spiritualist who claimed to have certain psychic powers. The article reports that she was fined twenty shillings for breaching the Witchcraft Act 1735 and the Vagrancy Act 1824[302].

The second article[303], in 1930, references her as a Franco-British clairvoyant with a travelling carnival.

Two weeks later, Zita sends another letter dated 2nd February 1954: *'…On the subject of 'Lou Bella' and the seeing's which she had.'*

She feels a Catholic atmosphere in the background – a house in the village of Churchill, which is in West Hagley (4 miles from Hagley Wood). It has five oak staircases and was once used by monks.

She asks if the house was used as a reception centre during the war, and if it is possible that relatives of 'Lou Bella' refuse to come forward because they may be in receipt of hush money.

On 17th February, Zita writes – all in block capitals:

---

[300] Western Daily Press, Bristol, 4/11/1927.

[301] b. 1881 d. 1955, 1939 Register OAAF 113/2, 56 Alma Road Bristol.

[302] Vagrancy Act, 1824, express provision for the punishment of persons who fraudulently purport to act as spiritualistic mediums or to exercise powers of telepathy, clairvoyance or other similar powers.

[303] Western Daily Press, Bristol 10/7/30.

DEAR MR: WILLIAMS.
WILL HAARLEM FIND LUEBELLA?
N.B. I AM PRINTING TO STOP SOMEONE ELSE FROM
PUSHING MY PEN!
SAW YOUR NICE LITTLE "SCHOOLBOY" FACE IN THE
EXPRESS & STAR.
EVERY GOOD WISH & HAPPY HUNTING
YOURS VERY SINCERELY
Zita BOYDON

On 26th February, Zita writes:

Jacques tells you this:- 5' chestnut hair, straight and curly (permed) fresh or red complexion. Blue eyes, wide happy 'toothy' smile. Blue white stripes. Linen cupboard, many sheets, children's home an orphanage preferably for boys. See socks on the line... ...Not fat. Sorry – "By the Windmill" –

I've more – you have enough to go on

Toujours la politesse! Zita BOYDON

The next letter is a short note dated 4th March 1954:

58A
W'ton
March 4 54
Dear Mr WILLIAMS
I am told
1937 might prove
a "useful" date
Big iron, little
iron, many sheets
Z BOYDON

This appears to be a specific reference to the previous letter sent on 11th December 1953 (page 2), which places Bella in a domestic situation where she is ironing, surrounded by bed sheets. One interpretation of this letter is that this is when and where Bella was killed.

A final undated letter, which provides three descriptions: the first of Anna, the entrance to her home, and a gold ring she wears. The second description offers possible alternative names for Lou Bella – MELLOR, MILLER, and Louis MELLOR, as well as three drawings. It also queries whether Bella's child's father was a Dutch Canadian – Franc CHRISTENA? Or someone called HIPKINS?

It ends with a statement that reads 'Queen Juliana[304] When Quaestor Was known'. Also ...was man related to Anna – was he sent to woods for sticks? Did he hide in/up tree, leap out on Bella?

---

[304] Queen of the Netherlands 1948–1980.

The last letter in the file was sent several years after the previous one, and has a postmark on the envelope of 29th October 1957, but no police stamp. The three-page letter is addressed to Superintendent WILLIAMS and signed Zita BOYDON. Zita's postal address has changed to 21 Oaks Crescent, Wolverhampton.

The letter starts by telling how she is happy, and discusses a *'nice'* letter she received from a Roman Catholic priest. There follows a *'silly'* poem about a mermaid with a knot in her hair, which she hopes to include in a children's story. The letter closes with reference to the cat, then apologies for taking up *'your valuable time with so much nonsense'*. It finishes with two comments that could provide the reason for the correspondence. Zita asks ...*Oh, by the way did you say recently to someone that "you would be pleased to know the result of this experiment?"*

...*I had – through a well-known medium a message from Inspector INIGHT*[305] – *but I'll tell you of that later... All fond wishes, Super. Yours Sincerely Zita BOYDON.*

I note that the handwriting and signatures do not always appear to be from the same person.

24/11/53	*Z. Boydon.*
26/11/53	*Zita Boydon.*
18/01/54	*Zita Boydon.*
02/02/54	*Zita Boydon.*
17/02/54	*Zita Boydon.*
26/02/54	*Zita Boydon.*
1957	*Z Boydon.*

Alfred ARMITSTEAD

---

[305] Possibly a reference to Assistant Chief Constable Sidney William INIGHT who died on 3rd March 1955.

A letter addressed to the Worcestershire Chief Constable, and dated 26th November 1953[306], was received three days after the second 'Anna' article in the Express and Star newspaper was published. It was sent by Alfred ARMITSTEAD, of 1 Great Stanhope Street, Bath, Somerset, and contained what the 2005 Police Closure Report describes as a premonition[307].

Alfred references the Anna article, which '...*he read the same day*', and an article in the Sunday Pictorial from a year or so earlier, asking the general public for help and information concerning murders and missing persons. He provides a description of the murderer:

'*... a man tired someone who'd travelled for hundreds of miles more than one country someone who could get no rest.*'

He provides a sketch of the man who he believes had returned for a very brief time. The image he sees is a man resting one leg on a stile or stone wall and gazing at the tree, which is within a hundred yards or a mile.

Alfred also asks if Anna was the man's sister[308], and indicates that she wrote because she also had '*...no rest*'.

---

[306] Police stamp: Superintendent's Office C.I.D. Hindlip Hall 27 Nov 1953.
[307] Chapter 22, Obsessionalists and Theorists.
[308] Anna's brother also referenced in 14.14, STALKER's spy theory.

CHAPTER 17
PROFESSOR WEBSTER

Introduction

A significant milestone in the mystery occurred in October 1955, the year that Professor James Mathewson WEBSTER, known as the 'Prof', retired from his post as the Director of the Birmingham Forensic Laboratory. I feel it is significant because the Prof's formidable reputation as a forensic expert has meant that his findings at the crime scene have remained unchallenged. Furthermore, it is reported that when he retired, the exhibits, including the skeleton, were given to Birmingham University.

I wanted to understand how his reputation came about and if it was justified. I also wanted to follow 'the paper trail', in the hope that I could find out what happened to the exhibits. What I have discovered, like so many facts reported about this case, is that there is another version of the story to be told.

In Volume One[309], I looked at the Prof's career up until 1943 and the discovery of the skeleton. In this book, I provide the background to some cases of interest that helped to create the 'legend', an alternative version of the circumstances behind his retirement, and what happened afterwards. I will introduce other people and places that have relevance to the mystery not previously discussed. All this research helped me to uncover what really happened to the Hagley Wood murder exhibits.

The reason the Prof gave for becoming a Police Surgeon in 1929 was because of his experience in general practice. He felt the focus was more on cash generation than health care, resulting in *"sharp practices"*. He is quoted as saying that 'it was this experience that decided him to give up practice and try to get some honest work'.

---

[309] Volume 1 The Crime Scene Revisited p. 21-28.

He also made it clear that he distrusted the Metropolitan Police and felt that their forensic facility at Hendon was a 'flop' and not as good as his Birmingham Laboratory, despite considerable investment. He also described public water analysts as being as 'unreliable as handwriting experts.'

The Prof's reputation was already established when he took up his position as Director of the Birmingham laboratory in 1937. It was reported[310] ...*that the Home Secretary wishes to take advantage of Dr WEBSTER's outstanding qualifications and experience in connection with the development of forensic science over the country as a whole...*

Later, in 1943, on his appointment as Professor of Forensic Medicine at Birmingham University, he was described as[311] ...*a famous pathologist... for some years he has been waging a test-tube battle with crime and he has been a witness in many leading criminal trials.*

On receiving his CBE in 1951 he is described[312] as the *"Spilsbury of the Midlands"*, a reference to the celebrated London-based pathologist.

The Prof retired[313] as Director of the Birmingham laboratory in 1955, aged 57. According to newspaper reports at the time, the reason given for his retirement was 'advice on medical grounds'. It was reported that he had not been in good health for some time and had recently suffered heart attacks. He was also suffering from coronary thrombosis, auricular fibrillation and osteoarthritis of the spine. The decision to retire was apparently taken in June 1955 when his arthritis and heart condition worsened during the investigations into the death of Evelyn Pat HIGGINS, a ten-year-old school girl murdered by Charles HARDING. Evelyn was buried in a wood, and whilst on the case, the Prof was out all night

---

[310] Yorkshire Post & Leeds Intelligencer 22/01/1937.

[311] Dundee Courier 13/01/1943.

[312] Dundee Courier 07/06/1951.

[313] Succeeded in November by Ernest PEDLEY, former Senior Scientist at the North West laboratory.

in drenching rain, resulting in him spending the following week in bed.

His retirement valedictories in the newspapers were glowing. He was described[314] as *Best detective of them all...has probably helped to solve more murders than any other pathologist in Britain.* On a similar theme, ... *the greatest detective of them all, taking into retirement a thousand secrets that may never be told*[315]. *Also, a brilliant scientific investigator... one of the most brilliant pathologists in Britain today... has had few equals and which has drawn many high tributes from judges, barristers and police officers.* He was also described as...*kindly, a bustling little man in the scruffy raincoat whose evidence has sent more murderers to the scaffold than that of any other pathologist in Britain.*

The Prof apparently caricatured the popular image of a professor: absent-minded and paying little attention to his appearance, looking like he had spent the night in his clothes. He was a familiar sight, generally wearing baggy trousers with an old brown Harris Tweed jacket, and was even known to attend

---

[314] Yorkshire Post & Leeds Intelligencer 08/10/1955.
[315] Birmingham Mail 8/10/1955.

inquests in his carpet slippers[316] with his tie halfway round his neck. He would respond that he 'often looked untidy because his labours had forced him to sleep in his clothes'. But the outward appearance did not reflect his work. His case notes were immaculate, and his forensic skills were classed as unparalleled, although often disputed. He was sometimes referred to as 'the Home Office pathologist'; a title that he apparently enjoyed despite the fact the appointment did not exist at that time.

Reference is made to his travelling around 30,000 miles a year, often at considerable hardship, and how he had never had a holiday where he was not recalled back to work. He would also continue with his hobby, a smallholding, where he reared pigs and laying hens. He would eventually turn to gardening as increasing physical disability affected him.

Of note is that when he retired in 1955, I was unable to find reference to any exhibits from the Hagley Wood murder or any other of his cases being given to Birmingham University – this would be expected as they were not his property to gift.

Although he retired as Director of the Birmingham laboratory, he continued as the Professor of Forensic Medicine and Toxicology at Birmingham University until 1963, when, on retirement, he was given the title of Emeritus Professor. It was also reported that he would undertake limited pathology work, continued giving instruction to police trainees, and lectured at Birmingham University on forensic medicine and toxicology.

The Prof worked at the University alongside Ben DAVIS[317] who succeeded him as Head of Department in 1951. Ben's role involved close liaison with the forensic laboratory and its staff. From 1978 to 1983, Ben was Vice President and President of the Forensic Science Society, and it was during this period that he

---

[316] Rugby Advertiser 14/10/1955.
[317] b.1920 d.1998.

would become involved in the mystery with the Mr COGZELL shoe incident (Chapter 19). In 1973 he also wrote the Prof's obituary in the Birmingham University Gazette.

Benjamin Tillit DAVIS

What is significant is that in the Prof's obituary, Ben makes the statement: ...*upon his retirement from the University he gave his comprehensive collection of mounted specimens to the medical school, to be followed after his death with an extensive and unique collection of lantern slides of his cases.*

This is the only reference (made in 1973) that I could find that reports that the Prof gave anything (in 1963) to the University. However, despite the reference to '*after his death*', his will[318] makes no such provision but bequeaths his effects[319] to his wife Linda.

His obituary also references that ...*in later years, he earned a reputation amongst clinical management as being dogmatic and he apparently antagonised many of his professional colleagues with his outspoken views on cases which came to his attention.* I will shortly reference some of the conflicts he had with institutions and particularly with Sir Frank NEWSAM, the Permanent Under Secretary of State at the Home Office.

During his three years[320] at Chesterfield Royal Infirmary, the Prof undertook midwifery training and saw some very tragic cases. As

---

[318] Thomas WARMINGTON & CAVE: Ref: 3/2608/16/CR.
[319] Less diplomas and decorations to Sally WALKER (niece).
[320] 1924–1927.

a result, he became an advocate for outlawing the 'female pill' used to induce abortion, and for the prosecution of abortionists. When he took up his position in Birmingham, he became friends with Mervyn Phippen 'MP' PUGH, the Agent for the Director of Public Prosecutions[321]. 'MP' was also passionate about the same issue, and they worked together through the London Abortion Committee to change the law. At the time, doctors were too frightened to get involved with such prosecutions, but the Prof had no such reservations and was prepared to give evidence that the drug had caused, or may cause, abortion or would undoubtedly endanger the life of an expectant mother.

The two men shared concerns around the use of capital punishment, and one such case in 1951, when William WATKINS was hanged for murder, is discussed later. The relationship between 'MP' and the Prof is relevant because 'MP' would have made a decision on whether the police had obtained enough evidence to proceed with a prosecution in the Hagley Wood murder, and the Prof would have probably been aware of his decision as well as having knowledge of the police investigation.

Mervyn Phippen 'MP' PUGH

Without detracting from the main focus of this book, it is worth briefly referencing significant events and cases in the Prof's career.

---

[321] 1924–1958.

1944

The Prof made the news in 1944[322] when he gave evidence at the trial of Ernest Charles DIGBY, who murdered his three-week-old daughter, Dawn. He battered her to death in woods near Milborne Port, Bristol on 15th November 1943. He denied killing the child, saying that he *"only abandoned her in woods because his wife did not want her, and that someone would find her"*. The jury found him guilty of murder, and he was hanged on 16th March 1944.

1946 Principles of Forensic Laboratories

In 1946, the Home Office notified all the Directors of Forensic Science laboratories of guiding principles for future operation. The principles were laid out in a report written by Mr S.J. BAKER[323]. A full transcript is provided at the end of the book[324]. In brief, the report says that the forensic science laboratory system should work as one, and it would be wrong to allow an expert from one laboratory to appear for the prosecution, and an expert from another for the defence. It acknowledged this meant the defence might find it difficult to deal with expert evidence, but pointed out the laboratories are not the sole repositories of learning on forensic science.

This report is an important artefact, as the Prof would go against these principles on numerous occasions, providing evidence to the defence where he believed the expert for the prosecution was wrong. Ultimately, this would bring him into conflict with the Home Office and it seems likely to have contributed to his early retirement.

---

[322] National Archives – ASSI 26/56/4, MEPO 3/2264, Derby Daily Telegraph 28/01/1944, Aberdeen Journal 08/02/1944.
[323] Ref: 810062/93 dated 20/07/1946 & HO 287/1412.
[324] Document 2.

1947

In 1947, the Prof appeared for the defence in the famous case[325] known as the 'Porthole Murder'. Actress Eileen Isabella Ronnie 'Gay' GIBSON vanished on the liner, Durban Castle, whilst en route from South Africa to Southampton. A steward, James CAMB, claimed that they had consensual sex, but she had died of an apparent sudden illness, and he panicked and threw her body out of the porthole. Whilst he did acknowledge that pushing her through the porthole was *"a beastly thing to do"*, he always strenuously denied killing her, stating that she had choked or suffocated whilst they were in bed together. CAMB was however found guilty of her murder and sentenced to death, although the sentence was later reprieved.

Of note is that the Prof appeared for the defence in this case. The prosecution called Dr MONTGOMERY, a biologist from the Metropolitan Police Laboratory, and a pathologist called Dr TEARE[326]. The fact that the Prof gave evidence against an expert from another laboratory was in breach of the Home Office principles and would later become an issue[327].

1948-1950

The case that is often used to indicate the Prof's 'brilliance' involved the 'Moon Killer' murderer, Allan Dennis WITCOMB.

In October 1948, at Hingeston Street, Hockley, Birmingham, 67-year-old Harriet MILLS was found dead at home lying across her bed. At her inquest, the Prof gave evidence and ruled out the possibility of death by natural causes, concluding she had died of *"manual constriction of the neck"*.

---

[325] R. v. CAMB (917519/73).
[326] He was not officially connected with the Home Office or the laboratory service.
[327] NEWSAM report.

The inquest jury disagreed that she had been strangled and returned a verdict of *"accidental death"*.

Two years later, on 30th March 1950, the body of 57-year-old widow (and Harriet's neighbour), Elsie Ivy ASTON, was also discovered at home in her bedroom on Hingeston Street. Allan WITCOMB was arrested, and this time confessed to both murders. The Prosecutor was 'MP', and WITCOMB was found guilty but insane and sent to Broadmoor prison.

Another capital case involved William SHAUGHNESSY who was charged with murdering his wife, 46-year-old Marie Alexine, and daughter, 20-year-old Joyce, at 319 Arundel Street, Portsmouth on 18th and 19th December 1950[328]. SHAUGHNESSY was convicted of strangling his wife with a stocking and then hiding her body in a cupboard, but his daughter's murder was 'left on file'. He was found guilty and hanged at Winchester Prison on 9th May 1951.

Like the 1947 CAMB case, the Prof was called for the defence. The pathologist who gave evidence for the prosecution was the famous Dr Keith SIMPSON. Although, like Dr TEARE, Dr SIMPSON had no official connection with the Home Office or the laboratory service, the case would later also be used against the Prof[329].

1951

Following a two-day trial[330], William Arthur WATKINS[331] was hanged at Winson Green Prison, Birmingham on 3rd April 1951 for the murder of his newborn baby son. On 21st January 1951, WATKINS told his partner Florence WHITE that he was going to bathe their baby. A few minutes later, he told her that he had

---

[328] National Archives – HO 45/25674, PCOM 9/2066, Yorkshire. Evening Post 09/05/1951 & R. v. SHAUGHNESSY (POL 885/1/10).
[329] NEWSAM report.
[330] Before Mr. Justice FINNEMORE at Birmingham on 15th and 16th March 1951.
[331] Execution: One Man's Life and Death by J.M. PUGH, 2005.

slipped with the baby and the child had drowned. Neither of them reported the death, but it came to the attention of the police by neighbours who were concerned about the newborn. Police discovered the baby's body in a pillow case, and WATKINS offered no explanation to why he had not made any attempt to resuscitate the child or call for medical help.

At WATKINS' trial, Florence testified that he had told her, *"I have done it. The baby is dead."* His account was that the death was an unfortunate accident and he never admitted to murder.

This case is significant because the circumstances around the case and the fact that WATKINS was suffering with advancing congenital deafness meant that many people, including 'MP' and the Prof, were uncomfortable about the verdict, and the sentence of death by hanging. Representation was made to the Home Office for a reprieve on the grounds of diminished responsibility. WATKINS' fate was in the hands of Sir Frank NEWSAM, the Permanent Under Secretary of State at the Home Office; a man that neither 'MP' nor the Prof respected or liked. The unexpected denial of clemency that followed caused further concern for both men.

1951

In 1951 the Prof gave evidence in the trial of Herbert Leonard MILLS, hanged on 11th December 1951 in Lincoln Prison for the murder of Mabel TATTERSHAW, who he battered and strangled to death at Sherwood Vale, Nottingham on 3rd August 1951.

1952

On 16th July 1952, Leslie GREEN murdered Alice WILTSHAW. GREEN had been Alice's chauffeur and she had fired him a few months earlier for using her car for his personal use. He stabbed and battered her with a poker before stealing jewellery valued at £3,000[332]. He was hanged in Birmingham on 23rd December 1952.

1953

In 1953, the Prof gave 'damning' evidence at the inquest of Mrs Laura Maud STEPHENS[333] who had died whilst being a patient at Selly Oak Hospital. He reported that, at her time of death, Laura had a bladder infection, her heart was in poor shape, and she had been in a shocking state of constipation. She had received a leg fracture whilst being lifted into bed, which the Prof said was caused by bad nursing. He also said that the constipation should not have occurred, and that more should have been done about her bladder infection, both being the consequence of poor medical practices.

A verdict of death from natural causes was recorded by the coroner; however, the Prof then voiced strong criticism about *'bad doctoring and bad nursing at Selly Oak Hospital'* in a letter published in the Birmingham Post in November 1952. This resulted in a public inquiry[334] being held to investigate the allegations.

The next case is one that is often quoted. Louisa MERRIFIELD was executed at Strangeways prison, Manchester, on 18th September 1953, for the murder by poisoning of Sarah Ann RICKETTS at her bungalow at 339 Devonshire Road, Blackpool. At her trial, experts[335] from the Preston forensic laboratory gave evidence for the prosecution, and the Prof appeared as an expert witness for the defence. It was his opinion that Sarah had not died from poisoning, as the Preston laboratory had testified, but from necrosis of the liver. The jury didn't accept his evidence and she was convicted. It was this case that caused the Home Office to intervene and remind the Prof of the laboratory principles.

---

[332] Dundee Courier 19/07/1952, National Archives – ASSI 89/4.
[333] Née GREAVES, aged 57, formerly of Parkeston Crescent, Kingstanding.
[334] Chaired by A.F. BRADBEER: Hospital Management Committee.
[335] A Scientist Turns to Crime p. 131-152.

1954 Sir Frank NEWSAM

In February 1954, the Prof had a meeting with Sir Frank NEWSAM. The purpose of the meeting was to discuss the laboratory principles that had been published in 1946, referencing the Louisa MERRIFIELD case as an example.

This, and other correspondence, highlighted cases where the Prof had not been compliant. They include the previously mentioned cases of R. v. CAMB and R. v. MERRIFIELD, but in addition, a manslaughter case at Worcester (POL 885/1/45), R. v. STEWART (POL 885/1/62), and a Bootle case (POL 885/1/18).

The following is a transcript[336] of the meeting between Sir Frank NEWSAM and Professor WEBSTER on 1st February 1954.

Sir Frank NEWSAM yesterday saw Professor WEBSTER. Mr P. ALLEN was present. Sir Frank said that he wanted to make three points:-

(a) *The unfortunate experience in the Merryfield case, where two Home Office experts had been contradicting each other in the witness-box, had led him to the conclusion that he should now issue instructions which would ensure that whenever a representative of the Laboratories was called, whether ~~for~~ [by] the prosecution or the defence, the whole resources of the laboratory organisation should be behind that expert so that he could give the best possible assistance to the court, and that he would not be permitted for another expert from the laboratories to be called as a witness by the other side. [The function of the laboratories was to give expert and independent evidence & not to act as witnesses for the prosecution or defence]*

(b) *Professor WEBSTER had criticised the way in which the post-mortem had been carried out in the Merryfield case. Sir Frank was most anxious that the best and most thorough practices should prevail throughout the Laboratories and he would do all that he could to ensure that this was*

---

[336] HO287/1412.

done. [*He asked whether Prof. WEBSTER had any ideas how best to achieve this end*]

(c) *Professor WEBSTER had said that he was going to take an opportunity of airing his views about the Merryfield case. Sir Frank said that it had been for the jury to decide, on the evidence before it, whether the prisoners were guilty, subject to review by the Court of Criminal Appeal, and it was not proper for a Home Office official to make any public statement to the effect that in his view that the jury, and the Court of Criminal Appeal, had come to a wrong decision in the case of Mrs. Merryfield. [or that the case against her had not been proved] If Professor WEBSTER waited until he retired before expressing any such view, that was another matter, and if he [then] chose to run the risk of losing his pension, or of being prosecuted, that was his own affair.*

Sir Frank made it clear that he had not sent for Professor WEBSTER to reprimand him but to secure his help and to give him some advice. Professor WEBSTER said that of the three points raised by Sir Frank NEWSAM he was in entire agreement with the first and would welcome the implementation of this decision. As regards the second, he was in no sense in any position of authority over other pathologists in the service of the Laboratories; they had all had adequate training, and they all had a chance of getting plenty of experience. He did not think that it was for him to try and correct any ignorance or laziness which were displayed by other Home Office pathologists. On the third point he said that he understood the position. He had no intention of publishing or saying anything in public on this point until he retired, and he would then be prepared to run whatever risk there was.

In the course of a more general discussion, Professor WEBSTER said that he had no desire to bicker with other members of the Forensic Science Laboratories, but he said that it was his habit, if attacked by others, to defend himself with vigour.

3/2/54 [handwritten notes] Nat Archives Ref: HO287/1412

1954

James ROBINSON killed Mary Ann DODSLEY on 15th December 1954 at her home, 'The Hollies', in Skegby, Nottinghamshire. Ann had been raped and strangled. ROBINSON was convicted on a palm print[337] recovered from a broken window. He was hanged on 24th May 1955. There are many who feel this was a false conviction and it is often reported that the Prof gave evidence at this trial on the palm print – rather than a fingerprint expert.

1955

The last case I will reference is the murder of a ten-year-old Coventry school girl called Evelyn Patricia 'Pat' HIGGINS. Pat was sexually assaulted, suffocated, and stabbed in the throat, before being buried in a wood.

Ernest Charles HARDING was convicted of her murder and was executed in Birmingham on 9th August 1955.

It is this case that reports that the Prof was out all night in drenching rain, resulting in a worsening of his health and eventual retirement.

In February 1955[338], the magazine Tit-Bits interviewed the Prof in an article about the Hagley Wood murder. This provides clues to what happened to the skeleton and is discussed further in chapter 22.

---

[337] Fingerprint expert: Superintendent M RAY.
[338] Issue number 3615, centre page spread, by Mark PRIESTLEY

1956 TV Broadcast

On 22nd May 1956, a television interview was conducted with an unnamed pathologist, who was referred to as *"Professor"* but not introduced by name, apparently by order of the British Medical Council (BMC). The following day, the interview was reported in the newspaper under the heading: TV Revives the Wych Elm Mystery. The article reported that a 'famous pathologist' had reopened the 13-year-old mystery and quoted him as saying:

"I would particularly like to emphasise the fine work done by the Chief Superintendent of Worcestershire C.I.D".

"When the body was discovered I was given the task of piecing her together." "I determined she had red hair and rather prominent buck teeth and that the twin incisors crossed at the front." "I gave this information to the police, but unfortunately the description fitted nearly 200 women who had been reported missing in the last few years."

"But after extensive inquiries by the Superintendent, he was able to identify her. It was a classic piece of detection."

The paper noted that this was the first indication ever given that the name of the dead woman was known to the police. However, when the reporter contacted the Prof, he said, *"I know nothing about any broadcast. I have nothing to say about it at all"*. The reporter also tried to contact Superintendent Tom WILLIAMS, but he was not available.

The article then goes on to reference the BYFORD-JONES, 'Quaestor' version, but changes it to say that the Dutch woman was killed by a person who died insane in 1942. It also interviews 'Quaestor', who says that *"visits were paid to Holland and at least one important witness was questioned"*. I was unable to find any reports to support that statement.

The following day, the newspaper published another article. In it Tom WILLIAMS was asked about the pathologist's statement and responded by saying, *"I can't make any comment about it at the moment. The case is not closed. I don't think it would be advisable to make a comment at the present time"*. When pushed on the subject, he said, *"I would rather not make any comment on it except that her hair certainly was not red. All I can say is that I feel the description of the dead woman given during the earlier inquiries was a correct one"*.

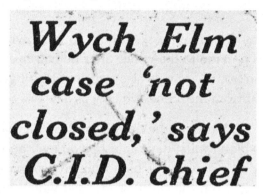

Wych Elm case 'not closed,' says C.I.D. chief

There is no confirmation that the mystery pathologist in the TV interview was the Prof.

In 1959, the Prof and his family moved to the south of the city to the district of Bromsgrove and he would remain at 37 Beacon Hill, Rubery until his death.

The Prof retired in 1955 and, apart from the 1956 TV broadcast, I found nothing about him in the newspapers until 1960 when he returned to work. He then continued to undertake pathology work until he finally stopped working in 1970, two years before he died.

To highlight some of the cases and incidents that happened after his retirement will add colour to another reference in his obituary: *...a reputation amongst clinical management as being dogmatic and he apparently antagonised many of his professional colleagues with his outspoken views on cases which came to his attention...*

1960

George RILEY, aged 21, was a butcher's assistant who was convicted of the murder of Adeline Mary SMITH, aged 62, at 47 Westland Road, Shrewsbury, on 8th October 1960. He was executed on 9th February 1961[339]. The official version is that he had been out drinking and spent the night sleeping on a sofa in the garage. When he awoke, he realised he had spent all his money so decided to rob Adeline SMITH who lived nearby. She woke up and disturbed him, so he hit and killed her.

RILEY was convicted almost entirely on his own confession, which had been made to the police after he had been in custody for some seven hours. He was also told that his fingerprints had been recovered from the scene, which was a lie.

The Prof gave evidence for the defence at RILEY's trial. He stated that Adeline's blood must have splashed all over and 'saturated' her killer. Indeed, a piece of bloodstained wallpaper that the police had taken from the staircase, against which the murderer had brushed against when leaving the murder scene, was not produced in evidence.

In contrast, the police found a tiny splash of unidentified blood on RILEY's trousers and a few spots of blood on his jacket. His defence was that this had resulted from a fight (which the police had been called to) at a dance hall that evening but although he withdrew his confession, the jury found him guilty.

1966-1970

Three events of interest occurred in 1966. Elsie May SHELDON,[340] from Netherton, died whilst being transferred between **Wordsley Hospital** and **Dudley's Guest Hospital**. A principal cause had been that the oxygen bottles on the vehicle were empty. It was the Prof's and the Coroner's recommendations that ensured all ambulances carried oxygen bottles as standard. The Prof was also critical of Stourbridge's **Corbett Hospital** after Annie SMITH[341]

---

[339] National Archives: DPP 2/3173, HO 291/250, PCOM 9/2166, HO 291/251, ASSI 6/210.
[340] Birmingham Daily Post 24/3/66 & Birmingham Daily Post 29/7/66.
[341] Birmingham Daily Post 8/11/66.

died following treatment on the wrong hip due to her x-ray plates being mislabelled. In that same year, the Prof was a member of the BMA Sutton Coldfield Branch's panel of experts[342] at the **Good Hope Hospital** medical inquiry into the Termination Of Pregnancy Bill.

In 1968, the Prof 'clashed' with a surgeon at **Wordsley Hospital** at the inquest into the death of Audrey Mary HAYDEN,[343] when he said that Audrey had not been fit to be operated on. She died whilst under anaesthetic prior to surgery. The verdict was death by misadventure. He was also critical of **Dudley Road Hospital** after a three-day-old baby suffocated in one of their cots, which he described as 'an abomination[344]'.

In 1969, he was critical[345] of a doctor at **Kidderminster Hospital** after a patient died from head injuries that were not detected. He was also critical of **The Royal Hospital** when Gerald Bernard BAKER[346] died after being given aspirin.

In essence the Prof was a man who believed implicitly in his own judgement and was unafraid to oppose views that differed from his own. Having formed his initial views in Bella's case, he was unlikely to change or retract them whether he was right or wrong.

---

[342] Birmingham Daily Post 8/12/66.
[343] Birmingham Post 10/2/68.
[344] Birmingham Daily Post 23/11/68.
[345] Birmingham Daily Post 16/08/69.
[346] Birmingham Daily Post 17/7/69.

CHAPTER 18
DONALD McCORMICK
'MURDER BY WITCHCRAFT'

McCORMICK circa 1959

George Donald King McCORMICK[347] became part of the story when he published his book, 'Murder by Witchcraft', in 1968 and introduced 'Clara' or Clarabella DRONKERS into the mystery. His version of the Hagley Wood murder is the one most often quoted and seen as an authoritative account of the mystery but it is in fact an embellished version of the BYFORD-JONES account.

McCormick was an author[348] and journalist[349] who wrote crime books under his own name, and 'spy' books under the pen name Richard DEACON. In 2004, the personal accounts of people who had worked with Donald were published and, overall, the assessment of his work was critical: *'...a fantasy historian...who falsified his way through thousands of pages of British and European history...'* In 'Hayek',[350] the assessment by several academics and specialists of Donald's writing career includes terms such as, *'fraudulent career', 'hoaxer' and 'liar'.* Also, his *'...reliance on an*

---

[347] b.11/12/1911 d.02/01/1998.
[348] He published 29 books.
[349] Sunday Times, Foreign (Desk) Manager 1963.
[350] Hayek: A Collaborative Biography Part III, Fraud, Fascism and Free Market Religion, Leeson, Robert (Ed.). @Howling Pixel. Casebook.org.

informal network of oral informants, and his eye for a good story, means
that it is often difficult to judge the reliability of his more controversial
claims.'

Although he wrote extensively about spies, he also wrote crime
books; one being the 1959 publication, 'The Identity of Jack The
Ripper'. This book has been criticised for its *'lies'* and *'fabrication*
of evidence'. It is not alone. Two books were published in 1970:
'Murder by Perfection' is described as *'containing many faked events*
and conversations', and 'The History of the British Secret Service'
apparently has *'too many inventions to list'*.

In 1979, McCormick claimed that a man called Rudolf PEIERLS
had been under investigation as a Soviet Agent. He was sued and
had to make an out-of-court settlement to avoid court
proceedings. He also claimed another man called Arthur PIGOU
was a Russian Agent, and that he had documentary evidence as
proof. However, the artefact was never produced.

After his death, his private papers were sold at auction and are
now part of the Ian SAYER Archive. I have made contact to see if
any details relating to the mystery are within the archive, but I
have been unable to gain access.

'Murder by Witchcraft' was publicised in the Birmingham Daily Post on 20th August 1968. The newspaper article included an image from the book described as *'The police reconstruction of the skeleton, 'Bella''*. This image is not contained within the archive material, nor was it previously published.

As far as shining light upon the Bella mystery is concerned the best that can be said of McCormick's work is that it is speculative and in no sense backed up by hard evidence.

CHAPTER 19
THE BLACK COUNTRY BUGLE

Introduction

The Halesowen-based Black Country Bugle newspaper was first published in April 1972. None of its published articles on the mystery resulted in any of the reported police inquiries or are included within the archive's 'press cuttings' folder. This is surprising as the newspaper, and a book published by the Bugle's editor, are the sources of some of the more popular elements to the story, such as screams heard in the wood around the time of the murder, a parachutist on Clent, and the sighting of an airman with a woman in a car on Hagley Wood Lane. They also provided the only 'statement' given by one of the boys who discovered the skeleton, which has never been reported elsewhere.

It seems what was originally reported by the Bugle, like so many other stories, has been adapted and altered, not only by the principal author[351], but by other contributors, who often do not acknowledge the source material. By returning to the original sources, I have discovered some amazing photographs of the tree, that have not been widely published – reproduced here with the kind permission of the Black Country Bugle. This chapter revisits the original articles that were published prior to the release of the police files, and with the added benefit of time and additional research, hopefully add value to the Bugle's contribution and provides some new revelations on the way.

The 1973 Bugle Article

The first is a melodramatic article that appeared in the Bugle on 18th September 1973, and is titled: Who Put Bella in The Wych-Elm. It starts by saying "...*The Wych-elm is still there, in Hagley*

---

[351] There are differences between the facts reported in the 1973 and 1978 articles and in the 1987 book, all written by Harry TAYLOR.

Woods. It bubbles like an obscene growth from the underbrush of its hillside location, rotten and gnarling, still keeping the sinister secret which has troubled Midlands criminologists for 30 years..."

The article indicates it was 'written & researched by the Bugle Crime Consultant'. This was, in fact, Harry TAYLOR,[352] the Bugle's founder and editor, who also went under the pen name Aristotle TUMP.

Harry grew up in Halesowen and tells that he had seen one of the Bella chalk messages[353]. He had been enthralled and intrigued by the case, and in 1973 had the opportunity to fulfil his schoolboy ambition and investigate. He was limited to the number of words he could write in the newspaper column but in 1987 he provided a fuller (and sometimes contradictory) account of his research and investigation in a book titled 'Black Country Ghosts & Mysteries'.

The Tree

Not only does the Bugle article indicate the tree was still there in 1973, it also provides a photograph of a Mr Dave PARTRIDGE, described as a site-clearance contractor who, at the time, was employed felling trees in the 'Bella' section of Hagley Wood. Dave is pictured standing next to the tree and pointing to the cavity where the skeleton was discovered. This picture helps to support what happened during the crime scene recovery phase of the investigation, which tells that only "a large wedge-shaped hole was cut into the side of the tree" to gain access and remove the skeletal remains. The tree was apparently not nearly destroyed during the initial investigation as is often stated in other publications. Also, having Dave pictured standing next to the tree helps confirm its reported scale and dimensions.

---

[352] b. 1932 d. 2003.
[353] Probably 30th March, Haden Hill Old Hill, Halesowen message, as he went to Barrs Road School.

Richard SKERRATT Interview

The article reports that they interviewed retired Police Inspector Richard 'Dick' SKERRATT[354], who provides three interesting facts.

First, he tells that PC Jack POUND[355] held the view that the offender was a serviceman who had been in North Africa.[356] Jack was quoted as saying, *"I reckon as the chap we'm lookin' for is now helping to drive Rommel out of North Africa."*[357]

I found nothing in the police files to support this assumption.

Then, he says that Inspector Tommy WILLIAMS had, in 1943, *"traced all six pairs of shoes sold at a Black Country market"* (Chapter 1). A reference does exist to six pairs of shoes being sold to C. A. ALLEN Ltd., who had shops in Bilston, Wednesbury, and West Bromwich but Inspector WILLIAMS' police reports do not say

---

[354] He was then living in Moors Cottage in Clent.
[355] Arthur John POUND b. 14/03/1895 d. 04/03/1954.
[356] Reference to the 8th Army Campaign, 10th June 1940–13th May 1943.
[357] Black Country Ghost Mysteries p. 101–103.

that he had traced all the shoes. To complicate things further, in his book Harry Taylor says that Tom WILLIAMS, with the close cooperation of the shoemaker firm, managed to trace all but six pairs of the batch. Those he couldn't account for had been sold at a Black Country market with no clues as to the identity of the purchasers[358].

Screams in the Night

Finally, Dick tells that "... *he had been called to Hagley Wood about 18 months before the discovery of the skeleton, by a local man who heard screams in the vicinity of the Wych-elm, during the night. Along with PC Jack POUND he had made a thorough search of the area without result. Jack considered that the sound had been the scream of a vixen which is often mistaken for a human voice. Also, that there had been reports of noisy quarrels amongst gypsies camped in the area at about the same period. The gypsies were traced but nothing came of that line of inquiry...*" It is not clear to which gypsy group Dick is referring.

Other versions indicated that in July 1941 two men – a businessman and a teacher – reported screams.[359] I note that Dick indicates "*a local man*" not two, nor is profession given in the articles and book for the supposed witnesses.

A month later, on 16th October, the Bugle reported that the previous article had resulted in letters, phone calls, and visits to their office in a follow-up article titled: 'Bella' Story Revives Some Fascinating Speculation On the Hagley Woods Skeleton!

Witchcraft and Parachutists

A Mr Geoffrey C GROVE[360] of Grove House, Two Gates, wrote that he had been an NCO in the Home Guard at Cradley in 1941.

---

[358] Murder by Witchcraft p107; refres to four pairs sold on Wednesbury market
[359] Murder Casebook, No.71, p. 2539; A SPARKE 2016 p. 11.
[360] 1939 register living at 9 Foxcote Lane, Halesowen. b. July 1925 d. Nov 1994. He would have been 16/17 years old in 1941.

He provided two facts; firstly that Witches' Sabbaths[361] were held in Hagley Wood and that this was common knowledge in the area and secondly that two of his colleagues had found two German silk parachutes by Colman Hill Flats. They had removed the parachutes from their harnesses, which they concealed under some bushes, and had taken the parachutes home to make into clothing, but they had been discovered by the police.

He finishes by stating that it was said the harnesses were old and unsafe for use but it was his contention that two unknown agents did land and escape together; one of them being Bella.

It is worth noting that many parachutes were recovered during the Birmingham Blitz, as they were attached to the German *A-type Luftmines* that were dropped in great numbers, as well as being attached to signal flares used to direct bombing raids.

At the same time as Geoffrey contacted the Bugle, another former Home Guard soldier named Mr Harry BASTERFIELD[362], of Longmoor Road, Halesowen, went in person to the Bugle Office and told his story.

Mr Harry BASTERFIELD

[361] A meeting of those who practise witchcraft and other rites, sometimes also called a coven, which usually refers to a group or gathering of witches.
[362] 1911 Census living at 59 Islington Road, Halesowen: 1939 Register living at 28 New Road, Halesowen (QJFX44/: Worked at Halesowen Steel Works, as a forging smith: b. Jan 1905 d. March 1979.)

Couple in the Car

Harry Basterfield reported that around the time of the murder he was attached to the local Home Guard with their HQ in the Drill Hall, Halesowen. He recalled that after receiving information that parachutists had landed in the vicinity of Clent, he led a four-man patrol with instructions to clear the hills of any persons who were found there, after first establishing their identity.

The patrol set off in the late evening with orders to report back to HQ at 1 a.m. They encountered several courting couples during their tour of duty, in parked cars and on foot, and checked their identities before ordering them to leave the area. It was past midnight when the patrol parked near the mouth of Hagley Wood Lane and "fell out" for a well-earned smoke before reporting back to HQ.

He says that it was a clear moonlit night and as they chatted at the roadside, the sound of a motor-horn, coming from the direction of the lane, disturbed their conversation. After a few seconds, several urgent "bleeps" on the horn were heard, and the patrol scrambled aboard their vehicles, bent on investigating what they thought to be an SOS call, when the distant car horn sounded again.

After driving a few hundred yards up Hagley Wood Lane, they came across a car parked on the grass verge, near to the woods on the right-hand side. They approached the vehicle and found that an RAF Sergeant was sitting in the driver's seat and that a woman, largely covered by a trench coat, was huddled beside him. When challenged, the man took a service identity card from his pocket and pressed it against the window. He did not speak nor wind the window down. Harry then asked one of his colleagues to go around to the other side of the car and "check the woman out". She had remained perfectly still, and the coat effectively covered her face. Harry's colleague declined the task of questioning the lady as she appeared anxious to remain hidden, and they concluded that she was a local woman who was trying to avoid being caught in an embarrassing situation. They decided not to pursue the matter but merely warned the RAF Sergeant that a clearance order was in effect and told him to move off. They then returned to their vehicles and drove back to Halesowen for the 1 a.m. rendezvous at HQ.

About half an hour later, the patrol motored back to Hagley Wood Lane to ascertain that the vehicle had left the spot as ordered. It had, and the patrol continued its routine duties.

Harry left Halesowen several months later and was not around when the body was discovered, and not being in the locality, it was not until he read the article that he coupled the incident in his mind.

The Bugle article notes that the car was parked only a couple of hundred yards from where Bella's tree stands.

It seems that two different Home Guard parachute accounts have merged into one, specifically when discussed alongside the different spy theories; mostly that the parachutes (the numbers vary, sometimes as many as four) were found on Clent Hill. Another version is that the patrol was not sent to look for parachutists but to visit a secret Radar station on a site close to the stone circle, also known as 'The Four Stones' on Clent Hill.

Letter from Canada

The article goes on to discuss an anonymous letter, which it says introduces a "Bulldog Drummond"[363] ingredient into the mystery – hinting at a Nazi espionage network and a "Secret Service" assassination. It says it has reproduced the letter in its entirety:

"Who put Bella in the Wych Elm? Hasn't the answer been known to those who matter for many years?

Didn't she die a year before she was found?

---

[363] 1920s' famous fictional character.

When the answer was discovered [found] wasn't it allowed to rest out of kindness to those, dead and alive, who were involved for the most part unwillingly in a situation which was not of their making?

Aren't these the questions you should ask?

What was the connection between Hagley Wood, Germany, Canada and Holland?

Who were the pro-Nazi sympathisers in Birmingham, Wolverhampton and Stourbridge before the war?

Who knew the Dutch girl living under the name of DRONKERS in Birmingham before the war?

Who was the Dutch girl's manfriend in Stourbridge?

Was the Dutch girl known as Clara?

Did Clara work for Abwehr III?

Did Clara drop in on her old friends in April, 1941?

Did Clara visit anyone in Stourbridge?

Who died insane in 1942?

Was Karl DICKENHOFF really Canadian?

What did he do while living in Edgbaston?

What happened to the dead woman's child and who was the father?

There are those on both sides of the Atlantic and in both hemispheres who you could ask these questions, but why?

There is an eternal justice beyond earthly law"

Despite the obvious fact that the letter appears to draw its narrative from McCORMICK's book (see Chapter 14), the newspaper does not reference this connection and it would be another four years before the Black Country Bugle would publish its next phase of the story.

The 1978 Bugle Article

On 13th June 1978, the Black Country Bugle ran a front-page article titled, 'BELLA IN THE WYCH ELM CASE REVIVED'. The article references that they had previously reported the case in 1974. This is in error; the only other articles were those discussed previously from 1973.

The principal subject of the article is Leonard COGZELL, but it also contains a reconstruction of the crime scene using a skeleton borrowed from Halesowen Fire Station and revisits the interviews with Dick SKERRATT and the Home Guard search in 1941 of Hagley Wood Lane.

Skeleton borrowed from Halesowen Fire Station

Leonard COGZELL was born on 24th January 1905[364], the oldest of three brothers – Fredrick Arthur (b. 1906) and Wilfred Albert (b. 1908). He spent his childhood at the family home of 2 Brighton Terrace, Hill Street, Stourbridge,[365] with his father Leonard, a general dealer, his mother Florence, and his brothers.

Leonard married Elizabeth Nora née WILD in 1933, and they had a son, Robin, in 1936. Records also show that between 1935 and 1939[366], the family were living at 117 Bell Holloway, Northfield, and Leonard owned a boot and shoe repair business, half a mile from the family home, on Chatham Road in Northfield[367]. Sometime around 1945, the family moved a short distance and were living at 70 Farren Road in Northfield.

---

[364] Died 24th March 1980.
[365] 1911 Census.
[366] 1935 Electoral Register.
[367] 1936 p. 123, 1937 p. 1461, 1939 p. 1606 Birmingham Trade Directories.

Leonard contacted the Black Country Bugle because he believed he knew something about the shoes recovered from the crime scene. Leonard recalled watching a television programme, screened in late 1969 or early 1970,[368] which hosted Professor WEBSTER[369] discussing the Hagley Wood murder and displaying the shoes recovered from the crime scene. He had observed that the left shoe had a cut on the instep about two inches long, which had been hand repaired. He recognised the damage to the shoe and the stitch work as that of his old friend, Bill FIELD.

Concerning the damage to the shoe, Leonard tells that it was common for workers' shoes to be cut in this way by the sharp edges of sheet metal that were strewn around factory floors. He specifically references the women employed at a works called 'Philip ROUND and Stephen THORNOLD' in Lye, that made buckets and baths out of sheet iron.

Mr William 'Bill' FIELD was a boot and shoe repairer who worked from his business premises at Dudley Road in Lye. Leonard had known him in around 1933, when he himself had a business in Ashford Street, Lye. Bill's distinctive repair method involved the use of wax thread, with a stitching style so unique that it was virtually the same as if he had written his own signature. The method involved going over the stitch in the centre a second time in a certain manner, that no other cobbler used.

Leonard explained that the long delay in coming forward was because his wife Nora[370] had been ill at the time the show aired, and she had asked that he *"not make any fuss"*. He said, *"I complied with the wishes and it was not long afterwards that Professor WEBSTER himself died*[371]*. I know without any shadow of doubt that the shoes he showed on television were ones that Billy FIELD repaired at Lye in 1933.*

---

[368] The Bugle was unable to locate the film clip via the BBC or ATV archives.

[369] 17.2 references a 1956 TV Broadcast. Obituary does reference *'personal television series of programmes'*.

[370] Nora died aged 62 in March 1970.

[371] 17/11/1973.

I am now retired, and I was recently reading an old copy of the Bugle when I came across the Bella case again. I decided that at long last I would do something about the matter."

Prior to contacting the Bugle, Leonard had tried to track down the shoes himself. First, he visited the Police Headquarters in Birmingham and was directed to go to the authorities in Worcester where it was thought the shoes were kept. He then contacted Hindlip Hall[372] and they told him that the shoes were no longer there. At this point, he contacted the Black Country Bugle, which prompted the June article.

In August, the Bugle published another article, reporting that 'information obtained from West Midlands Forensic Laboratory led them to believe that Bella's complete skeleton, together with her shoes and all other items found at the scene of the crime in 1943 were in the possession of Dr B.T. DAVIES at Birmingham University's Medical School'. I believe this to be Dr Ben DAVIS, previously discussed in Chapter 14, but will use the Bugle's spelling of his surname in this chapter.

The Bugle contacted Dr DAVIES, who denied having possession of any 'Wych Elm Case' exhibits except for the shoes, which had been passed on to him by his predecessor, Professor WEBSTER. Leonard went to the university to view the shoes, which were labelled with the catalogue number 220 and apparently matched the description 'Wych Elm Shoes' in Professor WEBSTER's records. However, the shoes presented to Leonard did not have the cut or the repair on the uppers as he had remembered, and he declared, *"These are not the shoes which Professor WEBSTER showed on television in 1970".*

The article includes an image with the caption 'Mr COGZELL looks disapprovingly at those controversial shoes'. The shoes that Leonard is holding in the photograph do however appear to be

---

[372] Worcestershire Constabulary Headquarters.

the same as those photographed and published in 1943 and discussed in Chapter 1.

Leonard was also certain that the repair by Billy FIELD took place in 1933, which was ten years before the skeleton was discovered. Furthermore, the shoe manufacturer indicated that the shoes had been made between April and June 1940

The article includes an image with the caption 'Mr COGZELL looks disapprovingly at those controversial shoes'. The shoes that Leonard is holding in the photograph do however appear to be the same as those photographed and published in 1943 and discussed in Chapter 1.

Leonard was also certain that the repair by Billy FIELD took place in 1933, which was ten years before the skeleton was discovered. Furthermore, the shoe manufacturer indicated that the shoes had been made between April and June 1940.

As well as the error in the year that the previous article was published, the new article also makes a change to the previous narrative, specifically to the Clent parachutist reference.

1973 version "…after receiving information that parachutists had landed in the vicinity of Clent, he led a four-man patrol with instructions to clear the hills of any persons who were found there, after first establishing their identity".

1978 version "…in 1940 a Home Guard patrol made a search of Hagley Wood Lane following reports that four parachutes had landed in the vicinity".

1987 book version "…night in 1940… information was received that parachutists had landed in the vicinity of Clent and he was ordered to lead a four-man motor patrol with instructions to clear the hills of any persons found there, after first establishing their identities".

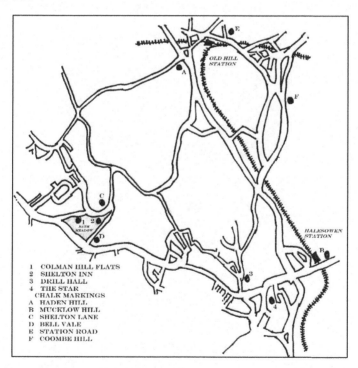

Letter from Devon

In August, the Bugle published another article, principally following-up on the COGZELL story, but it also reporting another anonymous letter, by the same author as the 1973 Canadian-postmarked letter, this time with a Devon postmark. It read:

Bella was 'raised' in 1973 not 1974. It was 25 September 1973 when my letter was mailed to you from Toronto. Her death was not self-inflicted. The broken bone in her neck proved the way she died.

The owners of the parachutes found in the Bath Meadow[373] by the man who looked after Mr HOLDEN's horses in 1941. Knew all the answers.

Please let it rest. The authorities did.

Black Country Ghosts & Mysteries

In 1978 Harry TAYLOR published a book titled Black Country Ghosts & Mysteries under the pen name Aristotle TUMP.

Harry TAYLOR, pictured in 1973 during the reconstruction of the crime scene with the model skeleton loaned from the Halesowen Fire Brigade

---

[373] Adjacent to Colman Hill Flats, also in close proximity to chalk markings, Shelton Lane 03/08/44.

As well as the Home Guard and Mr COGZELL stories, the book provides a transcript of a signed statement given on 1st July 1978 by Bob FARMER, who lived in Bald's Lane, Lye at the time of the discovery. He tells what happened with him and his three pals who lived in Wollescote: Bob HART of Pearson Street, Tom WILLETTS of Park Street, and Fred PAYNE of Stocking Street.

As usual, on that Sunday morning, we set out with our dogs – Trix and [N][374], two lurchers both capable of catching a slower rabbit – and Jock a crossbreed Fox Terrier and a great 'bush dog'. The route was the same as we invariably took – over Oldnall Road down through Lutley, turning off right by Lutley bridge into the woods which ended near the main Birmingham to Kidderminster road.

Crossing the road, we entered Hagley woods and set the dogs to work. The slow rabbits turned out to be fast ones we had no luck in the chase.

Continuing our walk up and over the Clent Hills and on to Walton Hills we realised, once again, that this particular part of English countryside is more suited to the quarry than to the hunters.

By then, it was about midday, so we decided to return home by retracing our steps while concentrating more on finding nests than hunting game.

We re-entered Hagley Wood and approached a line of trees containing some of the Wych Elm variety.

A startled Blackbird left the foliage of one of the Elms and on investigating, we found the Nest contained four eggs. Bob HART was a few yards to our right and shouted… "have a look at that other Elm – it's similar to this one". After a few more seconds of searching, Bob called out again… "come over and see what this is?" We join him and saw a hole in the top of the tree about 18 inches in diameter. Peering in to where Bob HART pointed, we saw a

---

[374] Offensive sounding name for the black coloured dog.

grinning skull, lying on its side in the bole of the tree. There was also what appeared to be another bone, a shoe and a green bottle.

The skull was just out of hand reaching distance, so I snapped a branch off the tree and after several thrusts, managed to hook the branch into the orifice in the base of the skull and pulled it out to examine it.

There was a small patch of rotting flesh on the forehead with lank hair adhering to it and the two front teeth were crossed. We studied at the skull for some minutes and then replaced it in its original position. We then stuck three branches into the soil near the tree forming a tripod to enable a quick identification of the location should we wish to return.

We then continued on our journey home and were nearing Oldnall Pits when we met Donald PAYNE (the elder brother of Fred). We told him of our find and he seemed very sceptical, so to prove it, I suggested that he go back with me to the Wych Elm and he agreed. I remove the skull from a tree again and he was convinced. Upon returning home we naturally, all told our parents. Mr. Harry WILLETTS (Tom's father) reported it to the police

CHAPTER 20
THE STALKER CASEFILE

The former Deputy Chief Constable of Greater Manchester Police, John STALKER,[375] hosted a television show called Crimestalker Casebook, which in 1994[376] featured the Bella In The Wych Elm mystery. I have referred to this specific TV programme because it is mentioned several times in the 2005 Closure Report.

Within the 'Witnesses' section of the report it states that ...*Over the passage of time no other witnesses have been identified despite the factor that the death was broadcast nationally in an investigative style programme by John STALKER.*

Within the 'Under the Media Appeals/ Communications Strategy' section it states that ...*The prospect of receiving information, which would move the enquiry forward following a general media appeal, is minimal. Indeed, the prospect is that the appeal would generate considerable interest from the perspective of obsessionalists, theorists[377] and individuals as archived in the rear of the folder. The opportunity of working with an investigative journalist who seeks to undertake a program or a part program concerning the case is rather more appealing. This would potentially facilitate a mechanism of re awakening the public awareness, and those having genuine knowledge prompted to be in touch. That said, the case was subject to a television programme produced by John STALKER, broadcast nationally, which resulted in no additional material being forthcoming.*

To me, this implied that the police in 2005 considered the John STALKER programme to have been an investigative style media event of value. I wanted to explore if it was worthy of such praise. What I found was that the programme, which contains inaccuracies throughout, only presents four elements of the

---

[375] d. 15/02/2019.

[376] ITV Central Broadcasting, Birmingham. Transmitted 14th September 1994. Nine minutes and thirty seconds run-time.

[377] Chapter 22.

mystery: the discovery of the skeleton, the witchcraft, one of the many spy theories, and the chalk markings. What I found strange was that it does not contain any interviews or statements from the police.

The Discovery of the Skeleton

The show starts with an incorrect reconstruction of when the skeleton was discovered, and includes interviews with two of the boys, Bob FARMER and Bob HART.

Bob FARMER tells how, after they discovered the skull, he removed it from the hollow tree. *"I broke a branch off the tree and poked at it until I got purchase in the orifice at the base of the skull, then we identified it for what it was"*.

Bob HART explains why they did not immediately report the find. He says, *"if you want the true story, we decided not to report it in case we got summoned for trespassing"*. Bob FARMER confirms *"that's correct"*.

Later, John STALKER references that the police theory was as follows: *"Fabric found in the mouth of the skull suggested that the victim had been choked with her own clothing in a crime of passion."*

I have been unable to find any reference in the police files to their belief that it was a crime of passion.

Bob FARMER is asked about the cloth in the mouth,[378] and he says that when he was *"jabbing at it"* and *"poking around ...that was when the cloth probably went into that orifice at the base of the skull"*.

Witchcraft Theory

Next, John STALKER presents, standing next to a hollowed-out tree[379]. His delivery indicates that he is next to the actual tree and he points to it and declares, *"inside the tree they found most of the*

---

[378] A skull has no mouth, Volume 1 p. 5&6.
[379] The general belief is that the tree and film location were in Wychbury Wood.

skeleton, and the rest of it including a severed hand[380] was found some distance away, giving rise to a dark and ominous theory".

There is then a discussion about 'Devil Worship' and an interview with Terry WARDLE[381] who discusses witchcraft rituals.

Spy Theory

There is then an interview with an Express and Star journalist, Jonathan LEAKE, who discusses the spy theory, which introduces a Dutch woman and Anna's brother, the Army Officer, previously referenced in Chapter 14, The John STALKER Version #5.

Chalk Markings

Standing next to the Wychbury obelisk, John STALKER introduces how the name 'Bella' came about. He says that the graffiti (WHO PUT BELLA IN THE WITCH ELM) appeared at the same time as the 1944 chalk marking. This is incorrect[382].

Of note is that the (chalk) lettering applied the previous year is 'faded' and the production enhances the lettering to show the text. The graffiti that can be seen today appears to have been painted directly over the original lettering.

John STALKER rules out the 'crime of passion' theory and indicates an occult execution as being possible but unlikely.

---

[380] Discussed in Chapter 13.
[381] Editor, Bygone Birmingham.
[382] Chapter 4.

CHAPTER 21
THE MISSING SKELETON

Although there must be several bones and a couple of teeth still in Hagley Wood, the focus has to be to locate the missing skeleton.

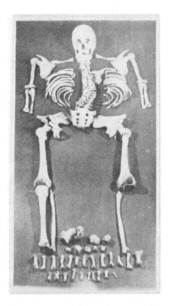

Photograph HW/46, from booklet File No. 16/158 dated 3/5/43.

The contemporary photograph above shows the missing Tibia bone but the display is not laid out anatomically correctly so it would be wrong to assume it is the left Tibia.

The 2005 Closure Report says: *The final resting place of the bones has yet to be ascertained. In such cases, the remains were buried in a 'paupers' grave. Enquiries with the cemeteries within Stourbridge and surrounding West Midlands area have failed to identify the resting place of the deceased...*

The location of the skeleton has also been referenced as being elsewhere. In Joyce Coley's book,[383] at the time of the COGZELL event

---

[383] J M COLEY, (2006) Bella an unsolved murder, p. 13-p14.

it was with a Dr GRIFFITHS[384] at the Forensic Department at Birmingham University, and Andrew SPARKE[385], Alison VALE[386], Jayne HARRIS[387], and Steve PUNT[388] all indicate that it was in the Birmingham University Medical School.

The Prof's obituary indicates that *...Upon his retirement from the University he gave his comprehensive museum collection of mounted specimens to the Medical School, to be followed after his death with an extensive and unique collection of lantern slides of his cases...*

In October 1955, the Prof retired from his post as the Director of the Birmingham Forensic Laboratory. The retirement mentioned in his obituary[389] occurred in 1963, when he retired as the Professor of Forensic Medicine and Toxicology at Birmingham University. I believe the collection this refers to was his lecture material, and it is my belief that the skeleton remained within the forensic laboratory when he left in 1955.

This assumption is supported, in part, by a newspaper article within the archive folders. Within a wallet labelled 'press cuttings' is an article from the February 1955[390] edition of 'Tit-Bits' magazine. It contains a story – 'Wych-Elm Mystery of the Suffocated Corpse'. This article contains a possible clue to the whereabouts and condition of the skeleton. It also reports to have interviewed the Prof just prior to his retirement in 1955.

...In the museum of the Midlands Forensic Laboratory, amid the bloodstained knives of murderers and the knotted ropes of suicides, there hangs a skeleton bleached by the acids of crime detection. It is small and pitifully anonymous, the skeleton of a woman which figured in a murder mystery

[384] The Prof's replacement was Mr E PEDLEY.
[385] A SPARKE, (2014) Bella In The Wych Elm p. 24.
[386] 22nd March 2013, journalist Alison VALE wrote an article in the Independent newspaper.
[387] Jayne HARRIS (2017) The Untold Secrets, Documentary. ~41mins.
[388] Steve PUNT (6th Aug 2015) Punt PI ~7mins.
[389] Written in 1973.
[390] Issue number 3615, centre page spread, by Mark PRIESTLEY.

now nearly twelve years old. The scientists call the relic "Bella" though no one knows the real name.

Sometimes young police trainees study "Bella" as a grim reminder that, no matter how great the resources of crime fighting, a murderer may still escape scot-free.

"One of my failures," says Professor James Webster, the head of this Home Office detection laboratory. Amid the gruesome crime relics, the skeleton creaks and swings at a touch. It was this grisly exhibit that frightened two schoolboys as they hunted birds' nests in Hagley Wood...

The museum that the skeleton of Bella was first displayed in was on the first floor of the forensic laboratory in Newton Street, where officers from all around the Midlands visited to learn about forensic science.

Museum of the Birmingham Forensic Science laboratory circa 1955

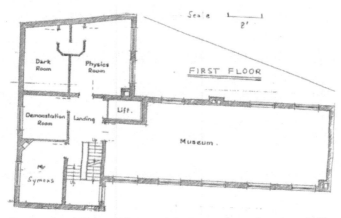

Birmingham Forensic Science laboratory floor plan circa 1955

The Newton Street laboratory closed in 1968, and it moved across the city to larger premises on Gooch Street North. However, the museum and its contents moved to the West Midlands Training Facility at Tally Ho in Birmingham. Exactly when the museum arrived in Tally Ho is not known; however. The facility opened on 11th March 1964[391], and in a newspaper report in 1966[392], there is no mention of there being a "black museum". It is therefore feasible that Bella and the museum contents came under the custodianship of West Midlands police around 1968 but we cannot be sure.

I submitted a Freedom of Information (FOI) request to the West Midlands police for any information relating to skeletal remains or artefacts held within their museums since 1943, their current status, and any information relating to disposal and/or destruction. West Midlands police informed me[393] that searches had been conducted by the Police Museum volunteers, and they have confirmed that they hold no exhibits and can find no documentation that may relate to this case, at either of the West Midlands Police

---

[391] Birmingham Mail March 12th, 1964.
[392] Birmingham Daily Post 17/9/66.

[393] FOI Request Reference: 7535/17.

Museums at Coventry[394] or Sparkhill[395]._Additionally, searches were carried out by the Force Records Team, who confirmed that there is no relevant documentation held with the Major Investigation Team or in external storage.

THE HAGLEY WOOD MYSTERY.

IN THE SPRING OF 1943 THE SKELETAL REMAINS OF A BODY WERE FOUND BY TWO BOYS WHO WERE COLLECTING BIRDS' EGGS IN HAGLEY WOOD. IT HAD BEEN HIDDEN INSIDE THE HOLLOW TRUNK OF A WYCH ELM TREE. FORENSIC INVESTIGATION INDICATED THAT THE VICTIM HAD BEEN FEMALE, AGED ABOUT THIRTY FIVE, FIVE FEET TALL, WITH BROWN HAIR. SHE HAD BEEN DRESSED IN CHEAP CLOTHING, AND HAD WORN A CHAIN STORE WEDDING RING. SHE HAD BEEN SUFFOCATED WITH A SCARF, AND WAS PROBABLY ALREADY DEAD WHEN HER BODY WAS DEPOSITED INSIDE THE TREE. AT THE TIME OF DISCOVERY SHE HAD BEEN DEAD ABOUT EIGHTEEN MONTHS.

IN SPITE OF A FULL INVESTIGATION, THE IDENTITY OF THE VICTIM, AND THAT OF HER KILLER, REMAINED A COMPLETE MYSTERY. FURTHER DEVELOPMENTS, HOWEVER, DID APPEAR TWO YEARS LATER, WHEN CHALKED COMMENTS APPARENTLY RELATING TO THE CRIME APPEARED ON WALLS AND FENCES IN VARIOUS PLACES IN THE WEST MIDLANDS, FUELLING POPULAR SPECULATION ABOUT WITCHCRAFT AND THE BLACK ARTS. AS BEFORE, POLICE INVESTIGATION YIELDED NO RESULTS.

THE ITEMS DISPLAYED HERE INDICATE THE COMPLEXITY OF THE INVESTIGATION INTO THE CRIME, BOTH TO ESTABLISH THE IDENTITY OF THE VICTIM, AND TO IDENTIFY A SUSPECT. ALONGSIDE THE FORENSIC REPORTS AND THE MASS OF PAPERS GATHERED AS ALL LEADS WERE FOLLOWED, CAN BE SEEN THE CONTACTS FROM THE CRANKS, THE PSYCHICS, AND MORE PATHETICALLY, THE FAMILIES OF MISSING PERSONS.

Display card amongst 'loose items' within the archive bundle

Another consideration is that the skeleton remained, along with the other exhibits, with the forensic science laboratory when it moved to Gooch Street North. The Birmingham laboratory later became part of a national agency called the Forensic Science Service (FSS), which the government closed in March 2012. However, the government formed a company called Forensic Archive Ltd (FAL) to retain and manage casefiles from historical cases, and all

---

[394] West Midlands Police Museum, Coventry opened in 1959.
[395] The site at Sparkhill has been operating since 1995 when it moved there from Tally Ho.

investigation work previously undertaken by the FFS. Their website indicates that *'material, some of which dates back to the 1930s, includes millions of casefiles, frozen material (such as DNA extracts) and retained items including microscope slides, fibre tapings and recovered hairs. All are valuable items when used in current cases, cold cases and potentially, future appeals...'*

I made two FOI Requests to FAL,[396] asking if they held any case files of exhibits in the case, and if they had been in correspondence with anyone regarding the case. They responded saying that they were unable to identify the case referred to in their records, and could not even be sure if the FSS were involved.

There is no indication in the archive files or within the 2005 Closure Report that the police considered either of these lines of enquiry.

I have discovered that it was not unusual for forensic exhibits to find their way into police museums like those in Birmingham and the famous Black Museum at Scotland Yard. Some even found their way into private collections and they often appear today for sale at auction. For example, at the November 2017 auction at Humbert & Ellis Ltd., there were several lots sold that had provenance as being former crime scene 'exhibits' or related paraphernalia. Of note was Lot 1007, the coat hook that murderer Harry DOBKIN hung his coat on whilst digging his wife's grave during the 1941 London Blitz. Also, within the same auction was a Webley Sports starting pistol used in extortion and racketeering in the East London in the 1960s by the gangster Ronnie KRAY, and a glass laboratory syringe used by the famous pathologist, Sir Bernard SPILSBURY.

---

[396] 14th March and 11th May 2017.

CHAPTER 22
OBSESSIONALISTS AND THEORISTS

In Chapter 20, I referenced a paragraph in the 2005 Closure Report[397], which mentions that a media appeal would generate considerable interest from the perspective of obsessionalists, theorists and individuals, as archived in the rear of the folder.

It is not clear which individuals *'archived in the rear of the folder'* the Closure Report is discussing. My best guess is that they are documents and reports referenced between 199 and 214 within the Closure Report's index; however, within this collection are the letters from Anna (208), which are mentioned in the Closure Report itself.

199	Letter re premonition	Chapter 16.4
200	Ramblings of J.G. BOWERS in letter	Discussed below
201	The thoughts of Zita BOYDON	Chapter 16.1
202	Letter re Greta BRADLEY	Chapter 16.3
203	Letters of Victor CRUMPTON	Chapter 15
204	Letters re EDGINTON	Chapter 4
205	Billy GIBSON	Chapter 12
206	Misc. docs without author or background	Discussed below
207	Mr ELWELL	Chapter 16.2
208	Letters from Anna	Chapter 14
209	John JONES	Chapter 5
210	Kenneth Francis PATTEN	Chapter 10
211	Edward SHERWOOD	Chapter 2.6
212	Gypsy Family SMITH	Chapter 2.4
213	John SWINDON	Chapter 9
214	Mr WOOD	Chapter 4

Extract from the 2005 Police Closure Report Index

Most of these artefacts I have previously discussed, apart from two folders, which are captured in this chapter.

---

[397] Within the 'Under the Media Appeals/Communications Strategy' section.

Of further note is index reference number 199: 'Letter re premonition'. This is a letter from Mr Alfred ARMITSTEAD, which is discussed in Chapter 16. It is not clear why he has not been credited like all the other references.

Index No. 200 – J.G. BOWERS

The index references number 200 as the Ramblings of J.G. BOWERS. This folder contains a five-page letter critiquing either the 1968 article by Donald McCORMICK, published in the Birmingham Post[398], or his book, 'Murder by Witchcraft'.

The letter from Mr J.G. BOWERS, of 25 Peel Street, Tipton, Staffordshire, was written on 26th October 1968, and was addressed to Superintendent WILLIAMS. He makes several observations as discussed below.

Mr BOWERS questions the ID card found near the Wych Elm tree in Hagley Wood[399], observing that if it was there at the same time as the body, then why had the owner not realised it was missing? Why had it not degraded into pulp? Had it been planted there or was it stolen? Was the woman lying? Had she been having an affair and lost it whilst in the wood? Did the same person who planted the card also do the chalk writings? He was critical of the police: '...I think you should have paid more attention to this'... he wrote.

He describes the Anna of Claverley story as 'Cock and Bull' and that she is a 'liar and an imposter'.

He references '...the gypsies camped near Hagley Wood at the time[400]', and that 'Luebella would be a name derived from the Bluebell and most likely a gypsy name. That they would know the tree. That she was a gypsy or lived with them' ... and that she was '...not known outside the gypsy environment, hence no one has come forward.'

---

[398] 20th August 1968: Murder by Witchcraft: Chapter 18.
[399] Murder by Witchcraft, p. 65.
[400] Murder by Witchcraft, p. 67.

He notes that four pairs of the shoes sold on Wednesbury Market were never traced. However, of one pair that was traced, the woman owner said that she had given them to a woman who called at the door, which pointed to that person being a gypsy.

That gypsies who were probably not connected to the crime, but recognised Luebella from the clothing, were responsible for the chalk markings, and they peddled their wares in the locations of the markings.

He notes that McCORMICK '...*so carefully left out the true words that were written on the walls. Omitting that she was a prostitute*[401]'.

Finally, he notes that the screams the two men heard could well have been Bella[402] and that she was dressed for fine weather.

The police acknowledged receipt of his letter on 29th October 1968:

Dear Sir

I am directed by the Chief Constable to acknowledge receipt of your letter which we received on 28th October, the contents of which have been noted.

I searched for a Mr J.G. BOWERS and discovered that, living at 25 Peel Street, Tipton in 1939[403] until his death in 1976[404], was a John Joseph BOWES, an electric crane driver who would have been 52 years old in 1968.

Index No. 206

Index number 206 is described as 'Misc. docs without author or background' and is a six-page note, with no identifying marks, stamps or envelope. The anonymous author indicates that they had met with Quaestor, possibly with Anna of Claverley, and had visited Hagley Wood. The letter reads as follows:

---

[401] Murder by Witchcraft, p. 67.
[402] Murder by Witchcraft p. 66.
[403] OSFH 129/2 b. 26/05/1916 d. 1976.
[404] National Probate Index.

Owing to the hunch of a regular army reserve officer, who hides behind the nom de plume of "Quaestor", I was given a vital clue on the Wych Elm case which has enabled the 11 year old mystery to be cleaned up at this late date.

This is very satisfying since we have in the course of investigating this, one of the most baffling mysteries of modern times, travelled many hundreds of miles, interviewed and read letters of thousands of people and followed many clues. "Quaestor" was frustrated by one aspect of this case – the aspect cannot be divulged since 1 solution of the crime opens up a wider and more important investigation + he collected as many facts as possible, had long interviews with 1 assistant chief constable, and later met me on two occasions. I also showed him the clues. He obviously was anxious to help me.

After visiting Hagley Wood & unveiling out his deductions Quaestor was able to hand to me an anonymous letter from a person who claimed to know who committed the crime: & later he was [scribbled out are the words – 'unable to be'] *present when I actually met the person & obtained certain facts.*

I carefully listened to 1 story & later made investigations & I can now say that the following represents the explanation of the remains found in wych elm tree in April 1942.

Further inquiries being made into another aspect of the matter was not possible to give name & address.

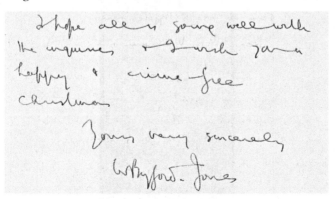

Extract from BYFORD-JONES letter

Of note is another handwritten letter in the archive, from Wilfred BYFORD-JONES to Mr WILLIAMS, dated 'Sat Dec 1953' with remarkably similar handwriting to this anonymous letter.

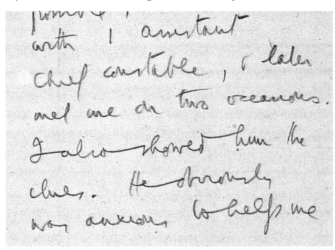

Extract from page three of anonymous letter

Also, within the documentation, but not specifically referenced in the index, is a photograph. The only information associated with the photograph is a name – Ethel PROSSER.

Without any context as to why Ethel is in the file, I can only assume she was reported as a missing woman, although her name
does not appear in the missing person inquiry in Chapter 3.

I could only find two local women of that name in the 1939 Register. One was living at 93 Dudley Road, Lye, near Stourbridge[405],
and the other was living at 28 Hill Street in Stourbridge[406].

---

[405] OJQY 2/2 b. 10/07/98 d. 1978.
[406] QJQI 153/2 b. 29/02/96 d. 1969.

CHAPTER 23
2005 POLICE CLOSURE REPORT

Detective Chief Superintendent Trevor ALBUTT[407] commissioned Detective Chief Inspector 'Sam' NICHOLLS 'to review the alleged Murder at Hagley Wood, deceased unknown, on 19th April 1943'.

On 13th July 2005, Sam NICHOLLS submitted his report, recommending that the case be identified as being closed, and that the documentation be archived in the Worcestershire Records Office as a historic document.

On 28th July, Trevor ALBUTT responded. He said that he agreed with the conclusions in the report, and he also noted that the lack of a grave site and investigative possibilities had influenced his decision to support the closure of the case.

Sam NICHOLLS' 13th July report is also known as the 2005 Police Closure Report, and is reproduced at the rear of the book (Document 1). In line with the recommendations, the original police documentation was archived at Worcestershire Archives and Archaeology – 'The Hive' – and is stored under reference number 010:18, account number 14908, and listed as police files relating to the Hagley Wood murder.

The Closure Report, along with two indexed A4 lever arched files that complement the report and contain copies of the original documentation, is also in the archive.

I had expected an accurate and well written report, but was disappointed as I feel it does not give a thorough account of what happened or present fairly the facts chronicled within the official documentation. Furthermore, there are many factual errors and omissions, and the chronological order of events have been misrepresented.

---

[407] Retired September 2013.

I have referenced these observations within the relevant chapters as I have gone along, but in summary:

The report indicates that the first issue, which took considerable effort, was the series of chalked messages (Chapter 4). This is incorrect. Prior to the messages, there were investigations into the shoes (Chapter 1), a gypsy called Mary LEE (Chapter 2), and missing persons (Chapter 3). By far the most intensive inquiry, which took considerable police effort, and lasted for seven months prior to the chalk markings was the Mary LEE and related gypsy inquiries.

With reference to the Mary WENMAN/LEE/BEAVER inquiry, there are several errors. The name HEYWOOD is spelt wrong; it should read as HAYWOOD. The protagonist was a man called Bill FLETCHER and not HAYWOOD as indicated. In fact, he had never even met Mary LEE. Furthermore, as previously mentioned, the search for Mary LEE was not as brief as indicated and the 'guise' mentioned was discovered within weeks, yet the search resumed.

The chalk markings provided the inquiry with several possible victims. One, named Bella TONKS (Chapter 6), is mentioned in the report; however, it then goes on to say that she was identified as living under her maiden name in Heath Hays – this is incorrect and relates to another inquiry into a woman called Bella SHEWELL (Chapter 6), who is not even referenced in the report.

Una HAINSWORTH/MOSSOP (Chapter 14) and her son are identified in the report as suspects but there is no indication as to why. There are also four errors within this part of the report: the period her son Julian stayed with her, her marital status – she and Jack MOSSOP did not divorce, her concerns about the association with witchcraft and assumptions made about the Lyttleton Arms in Hagley rather than the public house of the same name in Halesowen.

The John STALKER programme is referenced several times in the report and is seen as an investigative style media event of value. I challenge that assumption, as it contained many inaccuracies throughout (Chapter 20), and only presents four elements of the mystery: the discovery of the skeleton, the witchcraft, one of the many spy theories (Chapter 14, Spy Stories #5), and the chalk markings. The show also did not contain any interviews or statements from the police.

The lack of a grave site is specifically referenced as an influencing factor in closing the case. The report only makes reference to a *'pauper's'* grave and enquiries with cemeteries. There is reference within the archive documentation that offers another possibility, which is not discussed (Chapter 21).

There is no explanation as to why some people are discussed within the body of the report, such as some missing women, and not others, like Billy GIBSON (Chapter 12) or Bella SHEWELL (Chapter 6). Further, Victor CRUMPTON (Chapter 15) is identified as a possible suspect, and the police's engagement with clairvoyants (Chapter 26) is not referenced.

I discussed the report's forensic strategy in Volume 1: The Crime Scene Revisited, and highlight that this area would benefit significantly from a review, including several forensic practitioners and disciplines not listed in the report. I believe that the use of modern archaeological techniques, including the use of specialist light sources equipment, offers a real possibility of locating and recovering from Hagley Wood the missing bones and teeth[408].

I have sought clarity and transparency on decisions made in the report through numerous Freedom of Information Requests to Warwickshire Police & West Mercia Police's Information Compliance Unit (Reference No. 8269). Every request has been responded to; however, they were unable to provide any information. As a result, you find no reference to my requests if you were to undertake a search, as their procedure is not to

---

[408] Volume 1, p. 45.

publish on the force website when no information is held in relation to a request.

The report references the National Crime Recording Standards (revised April 2004), specifically the 'Balance of Probability' test; however, the government website indicates that 'This publication was withdrawn on 10 September 2015 and is no longer current'. It does not say what method of forensic recording has replaced it.

This leads me to wonder whether if the case had been reported in a different way it would not have been closed.

CHAPTER 24
LOOKING FORWARD

When I wrote Volume One, I collected what I thought at the time was all the available information on the crime scene and the initial investigation. If the additional information that became available after my book was published is anything to go by, then there will be much more of the mystery yet to be told, and I hope that, like the tree, the shoes, and the chalk markings, more people will come forward and share their stories and pictures.

When I look ahead to what I hope will help unravel the mystery, the first obvious area that has not had as much exposure is the Romany Gypsy element of the inquiry. I believe that there is definitely more information about what happened to Mary LEE, her family (Chapter 2), and their 'disappearance'. Most important has to be the missing family group (Chapter 2) that camped on Hagley Wood Lane. Their existence is not disputed, yet either they were not investigated, or their file has been lost or withheld.

Did the police know all about Bella, who she is, and who killed her? These questions may be easier to answer than expected, as the decision not to progress with a prosecution at the time would not have been made solely by the police. They would have taken 'the file', with all the information they had on the investigation, to 'MP' PUGH, the Prosecuting Solicitor for Birmingham City Police (Chapter 17) for his advice and a decision. Mr PUGH cherished his relationship with the police and fiercely guarded their and his reputation for successful prosecutions[409]. He was known for ensuring that only cases that would perceivably result in a conviction were brought before the court. If this case did not have enough evidence or a lack of witnesses, he would have told the police to go away until it had.

---

[409] Execution: p. 10–11; The Prosecutor: pp. 161–162.

What I find exciting is that Mr PUGH kept a record of his decisions. These files are stored in the National Archive[410], under reference DPP 3 1884–1956 Director of Public Prosecutions: Registers of Cases. They are listed as: *Registers of applications for advice on action and of other communications addressed to the Director of Public Prosecutions by chief constables, town clerks and others.* There are also separate registers of miscellaneous papers between 1899 and 1946.

Each volume of the register of applications has an index of applicants, accused, and offences, e.g. abortion, arson, bigamy, communism, forgery, indecent behaviour, incest, infanticide, murder, and perjury. It also indicates that action was frequently not taken.

There are two important files that cover the 1943 period. The first file[411] was opened this year and then closed again until January 2044. The reasons given were health and safety and personal information where the applicant is a third party. The second file, which covers the later part of 1943 and was at a period in the investigation where an approach to 'MP' was most likely, is due for release in 2020; however, I suspect it will also be reclosed.

Amongst other official sources of valuable information that will be helpful is the 1939 Register (Chapter 2.8), which will certainly reveal more information as more of the closed entries become available.

Also, on the subject of Professor WEBSTER (Chapter 17), the 'Prof' has no living relatives and the whereabouts of his personal case files, not just for this investigation but for all the other cases throughout his career, remain unknown. Hopefully, they are in someone's private collection and will one day become available. His official case files should have been retained in the Forensic

---

[410] http://nationalarchives.gov.uk
[411] DPP3/111: Jan–Aug 1943.

Archive when the Forensic Science Service closed in 2012 (Chapter 21) but they were not.

The two main contributors, who have modelled the modern narrative of the Bella story, are Wilfred BYFORD-JONES and Donald McCORMICK. Wilfred must be forever known as the architect of the basic outline story, introducing witchcraft (the hand of glory) and the first of the spy theories. His association with almost every element of the mystery, the people, and places mean that I suspect this will not be the last we hear of Wilfred BYFORD-JONES (Chapter 13). Neither will the contribution made by Donald McCORMICK (Chapter 18), who embellished the story further and introduced yet another spy theory. Who knows what revelations will be found in his private papers, which are now in the Ian SAYER archive?

Whilst there is still the possibility that the missing skeleton (Chapter 21) or the skull may still be found, there is also the possibility that the missing bone and teeth that are still in Hagley Wood could also be recovered if permission from the land owner were to be given. The use of modern (non-destructive) forensic archaeological methods provides an opportunity to survey and collect evidence without damage to the land or environment.

I do not feel confident that the police will review the Closure Report or revise their decision to close the case until something significant happens, such as the recovery of Bella's remains. Even then, if the quality and rigour given to the undertaking in 2005 is anything to go by, people like me will be writing about the mystery for a long time to come...

ACKNOWLEDGEMENTS & FOI REQUESTS

The National Archives

Worcestershire Archives and Archaeology - Ref: 010:18 Acc No. 14908; Police files relating to the Hagley Wood

The Library of Birmingham; Archive and Collection - Ref: MS4724, Home Office: Forensic Science Laboratory, Birmingham

Warwickshire & West Mercia Police FOI No: 8269

West Midlands Police FOI No: 2653/17 & 7535/17

Home Office FOI No. 45997

British Medical Council FOI No. F17/9192/SW

G U Williams LLB, HM Senior Coroner for Worcestershire

SATRA Technology – shoe enquiry

Liverpool University Press, Liverpool L69 7ZU#

The Journal Of the Gypsy Lore Society

Forensic Archive Ltd

SPECIAL THANKS

To; Ann Swabey, Rik Rawlings, Robin Fallows and the 'Top Team', Shellie Marlowe, Gigi Jakobs, Richard Lund, Liz Cormell, Joyce Coley, Andrew Sparke and especially my father.

REFERENCE BOOKS/MEDIA

1. J. Harvey Bloom (1930) Folk Lore, Old Customs and Superstitions in Shakespeare-land.
2. William Boyd (1932) A Text-Book of Pathology.
3. Books by Quaestor/Wilfred BYFORD-JONES
   Both Sides of the Severn (1932)
   Midlands Leaves (1934)
   Vagabonding Through the Midlands (1935)
   Death By Order (1935)
   The Shropshire Haunts of Mary Webb (1937)
   I Met Them in the Midlands (1937)
   Midland Murders, Hauntings and Odd Characters (1937)

Earl Baldwin's Country (1939)

Berlin Twilight (1947)

Adventures with Two Passports (1956)

Acceptable – Oil on Troubled Waters (1957)

Forbidden Frontiers (1958)

Grivas and the Story of EOKA (1959)

Quest in The Holy Land (1961)

Uncensored Eyewitnesses (1961)

Africa: Journey out of Darkness (1962)

Four Faces of Peru (1967)

The Lightning War (1968)

Severn Valley Stories (1968)

4. Mountford J. G. (1944) Halesowen Home Guard.

5. Arthur Ward (1948) Stuff and Silk.

6. Robert Fabian (1950) Fabian of the Yard.

7. Keith Simpson (1952) Forensic Medicine 2nd Ed.

8. Ladislas Farago (1954) War Of Wits.

9. Percy Sillitoe (1955) Cloak Without Dagger.

10. J.B. Firth (1960) A Scientist Turns To Crime.

11. Rupert Furneaux (1962) Famous Criminal Cases *7*.

12. Kenneth Ullyett (1963) Crime Out Of Hand.

13. William Kimber (1963) My First One Hundred Years.

14. Allen Andrews (1968) The Prosecutor.

15. Donald McCormick (1969) Murder by Witchcraft a Study of the Lower Quinton and Hagley Wood Murders.

16. A.K. Mant (1973) 'A survey of forensic pathology in England since 1945', Journal of the Forensic Science Society.

17. DG Browne & T Tullett (1981) Bernard Spilsbury, His Life And Cases.

18. Norman Vincent Ambage (1987) The Origins and Development of the Home Office Forensic Science Service, 1931-1967.

19. Aristotle Tump (1978) Black Country Ghosts & Mysteries.
20. E. Giles & P.H. Vallandigham (1991) Height Estimation from Foot and Shoe Print Length, Journal of Forensic Sciences, Vol. 36, No. 4, July 1991, pp. 1134-1151.
21. Jennifer Ward (1993) Origins and development of forensic medicine and forensic science in England 1823-1946.
22. Bernard Knight (1993) Simpson's Forensic Medicine 10Ed.
23. Bob Pooler (2002) from Fruit Trees To Furnaces: A history of the Worcestershire Constabulary.
24. Brian Lane (2004) Chronicle of murder: a dark and bloody history of our age.
25. Matthew Gull (2005) Inside Out, BBC West Midlands, broadcasted 9th September 2005 – Murder Mystery.
26. John Mervyn Pugh (2005) Execution, One Man's Life And Death.
27. Joyce M Coley (2007) Bella: An Unsolved Murder.
28. Anne Bradford (2008) Foul Deeds & Suspicious Deaths around Worcester.
29. Nicola Sly (2009) Worcestershire Murders.
30. Paul Newman (2009) Under The Shadow of Meon Hill.
31. Michael Posner (2009) Bristol Murders.
32. K Layborn & D Taylor (2011) Policing in England and Wales, 1918-39: The Fed, Flying Squads and Forensics.
33. S.P. Jitender, C.M. Mahesh, R. Y, K.S. Girish (2013) Stature Estimation from the Dimensions of Foot in Females Antrocom Online Journal of Anthropology 2013, vol. 9, pp 237-241.
34. Andrew Sparke (2014) Bella in the Wych Elm: In Search of a Wartime Mystery
35. Andy Williams (2014) Forensic Criminology

36. Steve Punt (2015) Punt PI – broadcasted 6th Aug, BBC Radio 4 Who Put Bella in The Wych Elm?
37. Jayne Harris (2017) The Untold Secrets, Documentary.
38. Alex Merrill (2018) Who Put Belle In The Wych Elm? Volume 1 The Crime Scene Revisited
39. Nellie Cole (2018) Bella
40. Giselle Jakobs (2019) The Spy In The Tower

NEWSPAPERS

Aberdeen Journal
Aberdeen Evening Express
Banbury Guardian
Birmingham Daily Gazette
Birmingham Daily Post
Birmingham Evening Dispatch
Birmingham Mail
Birmingham Post & Journal
Courier and Advertiser
Coventry Evening Telegraph
Coventry Herald
Derby Daily Telegraph
Dundee Courier
Express and Star
Glasgow Times
Gloucestershire Echo
Independent
Kensington Post
Lincolnshire Echo
Liverpool Echo
Mid Ulster Mail

Rugby Advertiser
Shropshire Star
Shropshire Journal
South Wales Echo
St. Andrews Citizen
Staffordshire Advertiser
Staffordshire Chronicle
The Scotsman
The Sphere
The Stage
The Whig
The Sunday Pictorial
University of Birmingham Gazette
Western Daily Press & Bristol Mirror
Western Mail
Wolverhampton Express & Star
Worchester Times
Yorkshire Post & Leeds Intelligencer

Document 1
2005 Police Closure Report

Regarding Alleged Murder at Hagley Wood, deceased unknown: 19th April 1943

Commissioned by: Detective Chief Superintendent T. Albutt
Author: Detective Chief Inspector I Nicholls
Report Date: 13 July 2005   Version One

Introduction

The purpose of this document is to record the review of the above file which pertains to the investigation surrounding the recovery of the remains of a female from within the naturally hollowed out trunk of an elm tree located within Hagley Wood adjacent to the main Birmingham to Kidderminster Road. This road is now designated as this A456. The remains were first reported on 19th April 1943. It was estimated that the body had been so located for a period of not less than eighteen months.

When recovered the skeleton was disarticulated and certain bones were missing. The nature of the bones missing would induce a presumption that the absence was as a result of wildlife intervention rather than being removed at the time of or immediately after death. It was assessed that the individual has entered the cavity feet first, and the probability of this occurring willingly or intentionally was remote thus it was determined that this matter was an offence of murder.

It is, I contend, most certainty an unexplained death however in the absence of a specific cause of death or indeed any identified injuries which indicate the individual was subjected to trauma, that to make the leap to a murder is questionable. However, in line with the current standards contained within the National Crime Recording Standards (Revised April 2004) specifically the 'Balance of Probability' test, the balance is that the individual was subjected to unlawful actions, which lead directly or indirectly to her death.

Executive Summary

- Incident occurred at the height of Axis bombing of the West Midlands conurbation
- The deceased has yet to be identified
- Investigation centred on the identification of the diseased
- Final resting-place still unknown
- Investigation skewed by false reports
- No further witnesses identified
- Forensic opportunities examined however no advantages identified
- Two potential suspects were identified as a result of information in 1953, one of whom was dead, the other remains untraced.

Investigation

The investigation of the offence centred primarily on the identification of the deceased, and through that process identifying any person who may have been involved in the death.

The identification phase centred upon the shoes retrieved from the scene, circulations appertaining to the deceased, and examination of missing person or persons allegedly missing.

To contextualise the event occurred at a time when considerable bombing by Axis forces was occurring within the Birmingham/Wolverhampton/Coventry conurbation, and thus it was considerably more common for persons to be transient and obviously death without record was a more frequent occurrence.

During the course of the investigation a number of factors caused a skewing of the resources involved.

The first issue, which took up considerable effort, was the series of chalked messages upon walls throughout the West Midlands conurbation from Wolverhampton, into the 'Black Country' and also into the city centre of Birmingham. The chalkings were undertaken over a protracted period of time. The reason for and also the authors of the chalking's were not established despite considerable investment.

Additionally considerable effort was expended attempting to identify the whereabouts of a Mary WENMAN@LEE@BEAVER, a traveller who at one time resided close to the location where the cadaver was recovered. A soldier HEYWOOD, who formerly having a relationship with the woman and sought to re-establish the relationship, initiated this. By a number of guises he used the Police to initiate an investigation to ascertain her whereabouts. The reality of the situation came to light and HEYWOOD subsequently admitted the details.

Bella TONKS was raised as a possibility following a media circulation. The name 'Bella' was seemingly derived from the chalk writings on the walls throughout the West Midlands conurbation, and as such the link to the enquiry was questionable. That said, the individual Bella TONKS was identified as living under her maiden name in Heath Hays.

Ann FORREST a traveller, was identified as having lived close to the deposition site, and was raised as potentially the deceased as a result of this. Enquiries traced FORREST in April 1944 as being alive and well.

Bella BEECH was draw to the inquiry's attention following her disappearance from bombed premises in West Ealing London. She had left the bombed premises to live in the Birmingham area, and contact had ceased. Enquiries traced this woman to a hospital in the London area where she was working as a nurse.

Bella LUER was a woman who moved from London to undertake factory work. The contact chain with persons in London was broken and thus she was raised as a possibility as being the deceased. Again the major factor was the term 'Bella'. Enquiries traced a Bella LUER as being a resident at Goring on Thames, however this individual was not definitely linked to the Bella

LUER who was formerly resident in the Stamford Hill area of London.

Violet GOODE was a female who had been invoked in a relationship with Thomas Henry TRUMAN resulting in his relationship with his wife Gladys TRUMAN failing.

Subsequently TRUMAN returned to his wife and a spurious assertion was made that GOODE had been killed to make way for this return. GOODE was identified as being alive and well, working and living in Stourbridge.

Lines of Enquiry unfinalised

Dinah CURLEY@O'GRADY

This line of enquiry commenced with the report of the above named person being missing by a woman, the recorded details of whom were Mrs M Lavin 56 Stanley Street, Manchester. This report prompted enquiries to trace both CURLEY and the reporter LAVIN. The thrust of the latter was following a labourer called Jack (John Edward) LAVIN.

Document 112 outlines page two of details of a number of persons reported missing for the time appropriate to the belived death, provides a number of persons albeit there is no reference to investigation into the circumstances of their disappearance.

From the information supplied there is insufficient to identify whether CURLEY@ O'Grady in fact existed. Enquiries to trace the person M LAVIN failed to do so however there were a number of coincidences with the labourer Jack LAVIN. His wife was Mrs Mary LAVIN nee DOWLING. Their home was 40 Lawrence Street, Stockport, Manchester. The reporter of the missing person allegedly resided at 56 Stanley Street, Cheetham, Manchester however she moved in about 1941 to an address in 32 Robert Street, Cheetham Manchester with a family called Lynch. The LYNCH family subsequently removed to an address in Haverfordwest. Jack Lavin was employed on a contract in the St. David's area of west Wales, residing at an address on the

Fishguard to Haverfordwest Road. Whilst there he was joined by his wife Mary.

Enquiries in the Haverfordwest area for the reporter LAVIN identified an address of 73 Belle Vue Terrace Haverfordwest until 30th March 1943 from where she removed to an address of 9 Claremont, Ripon, Yorkshire. The LYNCH family removed six months earlier to an address in Kettering, Northamptonshire Jack LAVIN was sought for non-payment at fines in Northamptonshire.

In respect of Ripon, to where Mrs M Lavin allegedly moved following leaving Haverfordwest coincidentally a Mr John Edward LAVIN resided at 9, Claremont, Ripon from 9th March 1943. The latter's previous address was recorded as being 40 Lawrence Street, Stockport.

Thus with all the co-incidences it is highly probable that the reporter for the missing person was Mrs Mary LAVIN, the wife of Jack (John Edward) LAVIN, despite denials by him of any knowledge and links to the 56 Stanley Street address. There is nothing on the file to indicate that Mary LAVIN was interviewed and challenged about these issues.

The reasons for the denial and the report being made remain unclear, however it is probable that it was personal gain, and that the alleged missing person CURLEY@O'Grady was a fictitious individual.

There are on file a number of communications which, it would seem prudent not to follow as the basis for the content is at best questionable.

Suspects

During 1953, his former wife, UNA HAINSWORTH, identified JACK MOSSOP as a potential suspect following a submission. MOSSOP, in later life, was suffering from mental illness and died in a mental institution in 1942. In 1932 the relationship of MOSSOP and the now HAINSWORTH produced a son, Julian

MOSSOP, who remained with his mother unit 1949, when he went to London and there became involved in criminality. At the time of the discovery of the deceased, Julian MOSSOP was eleven years of age, living in Kenilworth and as such can be discounted as a suspect

Mrs HAINSWORTH seemingly had some history, as it would appear that the removal from the Kenilworth address left behind considerable debts.

Following their divorce and in the later part of his life Hainsworth and Mossop met where he alleged he was losing his mind, suffering from mental images of a woman in a tree leering at him. At this stage HAINSWORTH was obviously not aware of the Hagley body as it was yet to be discovered, and thought it was a delaying tactic for resolving issues.

With the discovery of the body and subsequent media attention in a pictorial, HAINSWORTH wrote a letter signing it 'Anna'. At that stage some assertions with regard to witchcraft had been made and she wished not to be associated with it.

The story she outlined was that a Dutch male called Van RALT (term also includes the spelling Van RAALT hereafter) came to her home in 1940. He was seemingly without regular employment albeit he had considerable funds. HAINSWORTH made an aside that Van RALT may have been a spy. This aside seems to be the basis for later conjecture that the death involved spies.

In March or April 1941, MOSSOP arrived home noticeably having had drank alcohol, and in an agitated state when he allegedly stated that he had been to the Lyttleton Arms with Van RALT and the 'Dutch piece' (Presumably this meant a female either Dutch in nationality or associated with the Dutchman Van RALT). MOSSOP allegedly stated that the female had become awkward then passed out. Van RALT directed MOSSOP to drive to a nearby wood where the former stuck her into a hollow tree and left her there. It was allegedly stated that she would come to her senses the following day and the men returned to Kenilworth.

There was and still remains a public house in Hagley called the Lyttleton Arms, which was located on the main Kidderminster to Birmingham Road. More latterly with road enhancements, the public house now sits on a side road.

The logical route back towards Kenilworth from the public house would have been through Clent, to Bromsgrove, and thence into Warwickshire. This route is the opposite direction to the wooded area on the main Birmingham Road where the deceased was recovered.

It would appear that there was a link between Van RALT and an act appearing at the Coventry Hippodrome in 1938, the performers being known as 'Frick and Frack' however the grounds for such a link is undefined.

Checks of the nationality database subsequent to 1948 (probably in 1953 following the disclosure by Mrs HAINSWORTH) identify two Van RALT nominals.

The first is Pieter Van RAALT who landed in 1948, and had an address in London SE25, the second was a female who held a permanent address in London but occupied a teaching position in Nottingham. Significantly, the female, Laura Frances Ryllis Van RAALTE had on 17th August 1940, vacationed in Malvern staying at the Beauchamp Hotel, and thus has arguably some relationship with Worcestershire.

There is nothing on the file to indicate whether it was possible in 1954 to establish whether Ms Van RAALTE was still alive, however there is a report concerning the individual using the present tense which would seem to indicate that in 1954 she was still surviving. If one is to take the post mortem report of Professor WEBSTER as being precise, then in 1940, Ms Van RAALTE was over forty years of age and would just about fall outside the requisite parameters for the deceased.

Lines of Enquiry

Nomination of Suspects

Following the disclosure by HAINSWORTH, Jack MOSSOP and Van RAALTE appear to be worthy of review. If taken at face value, there are a number of factors, which would key in with the information known. Unfortunately it is now extremely difficult to clearly identify the degree of information which was released into the public arena which would allow for the story to be sewn together by HAINSWORTH.

In relation to the area of Hagley, HAINSWORTH may have had a degree of knowledge. When making the disclosure she was resident in Claverly, a small Shropshire village lying just outside the Wolverhampton conurbation. Hagley in those days would lie on a route between the Warwick, Shrewley areas and Claverly. It would appear that the Public House was quite well known and was a point to where persons would travel for a day out. It was a waypoint in the general area of Hagley and Stourbridge used as a means of direction or a marker for directions.

Review of Status of Crime

The status of the crime as an unsolved murder is based considerably on the post mortem report of Professor Webster, in his field, Professor Webster was regarded as being pre-eminent, however with the passage of time, the Identification of new concepts, and the modification of previously held beliefs may result in a differing perspective being placed upon the cause of death. Exploration of this concept has been undertaken and there is no advantage taking this forward.

Witnesses

Whilst the only identified witnesses survive, these individuals can only proffer information surrounding the discovery of the remains, some substantial time following the death. Over the passage of time no other witnesses have been identified despite the factor that the death was broadcast nationally in an investigative style programme by John STALKER. The prospect of locating witnesses at this juncture is remote.

Media Appeals/ Communications Strategy

The prospect of receiving information, which would move the enquiry forward following a general media appeal, is minimal. Indeed the prospect is that the appeal would generate considerable interest from the perspective of obsessionalist, theorists and individuals as archived in the rear of the folder. The opportunity of working with an investigative journalist who seeks to undertake a program or a part program concerning the case is rather more appealing. This would potentially facilitate a mechanism of re awakening the public awareness, and those having genuine knowledge prompted to be in touch. That said, the case was subject to a television programme produced by John STALKER, broadcast nationally, which resulted in no additional material being forthcoming.

Arrest Strategy

The passage of time, the demise of MOSSOP and the hitherto non-identification of Van RAALTE who would now be in the latter phase of this life, if indeed he has not predeceased this report. At this time there are no other potential offenders identified, thus an arrest is not envisaged.

Search Strategy

The passage of time has rendered impractical a search otherwise than in the event of the identification of a potential offender. It is highly likely that even after the passage of time, that the offender would maintain either media reporting or similar, and thus would be the subject of the search.

Interview Strategy

The interview strategy at this stage cannot be defined, but in the unlikely event of a suspect coming to notice this would be developed.

Identification Strategy

Identification of the deceased after this passage of time is somewhat difficult. There may well be opportunities to be explored in respect of DNA profiling and thereby gain a lineage match. Extensive enquiries to identify the resting-place of the remains have thus far failed.

An interment would have taken place, however it is unclear as to where the remains would be buried, and where the ownership of the remains lies.

Forensic Strategy

Consideration has been afforded to the use of the expertise of a Forensic Archaeologist, Forensic Anthropologist, Forensic Environmentalist, Palaeontologist and an Odontologist. Additionally the advances in DNA techniques have been researched.

The Forensic Archaeologist may have been able to assist had there been any photographs of the scone recorded. At this stage I am unable to identify whether this was the case. Most certainly there is no record of such on the file. The scene has decayed over the passage of time as indeed has the tree, and thus no scene worthy of calling such remains.

The identification of the deceased has a potential to move the enquiry forward. This can potentially be achieved by virtue of DNA analysis of the remains, and extraction of the mitochondrial DNA. Furthermore the origins of the deceased could potentially be ascertained through analysis of the bone constituents thereby providing supportive structure to the assertions of HAINSWORTH.

The final resting-place of the bones has yet to be ascertained. In such cases, the remains were buried in a 'paupers' grave. Enquiries with the cemeteries within the Stourbridge and surrounding West Midlands's area have failed to identify the resting-place of the deceased. Thus without source material such forensic initiatives are flawed.

Conclusion

At this stage with the passage of time, there are no clear investigative leads. If the location of the remains were established, development of the DNA processes has not afforded investigative opportunities. Any person involved, if surviving, would be in excess of eighty years of age and the prospect of a prosecution would at best be remote.

I therefore make the following recommendations:

• The case is identified as being closed,

• Consideration should be afforded to placing the documentation in the Worcestershire Records Office as an historic document.

13th July 2005
I Nicholls
Detective Chief Inspector

Addendum

As per attached e mail communication between DCI NICHOLLS and DCS ALBUTT on 28th July 2005, this file has now been declared closed and is not for henceforward to be regarded as a live investigation.

28th July 2005 I Nicholls Detective Chief Inspector

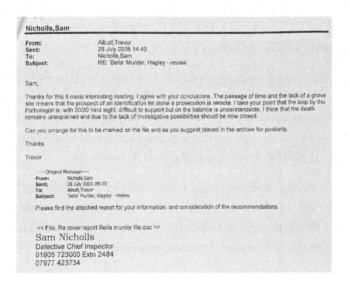

Nicholls,Sam

From:	Albutt,Trevor
Sent:	28 July 2005 14:40
To:	Nicholls,Sam
Subject:	RE: 'Bella' Murder, Hagley - review

Sam,

Thanks for this it made interesting reading. I agree with your conclusions. The passage of time and the lack of a grave site means that the prospect of an identification let alone a prosecution is remote. I take your point that the leap by the Pathologist is, with 20/20 hind sight, difficult to support but on the balance is understandable. I think that the death remains unexplained and due to the lack of investigative possibilities should be now closed.

Can you arrange for this to be marked on the file and as you suggest placed in the archive for posterity.

Thanks

Trevor

-----Original Message-----
From:	Nicholls,Sam
Sent:	28 July 2005 09:30
To:	Albutt,Trevor
Subject:	'Bella' Murder, Hagley - review

Please find the attached report for your information, and consideration of the recommendations

<< File: Re cover report Bella murder file.doc >>
Sam Nicholls
Detective Chief Inspector
01905 723000 Extn 2484
07977 423734

Document 2

Mr. S.J. Baker's Minute of 20/07/1946
Ref: 810062/93 & HO 287/1412

The whole principle of and the forensic science laboratory system is that it should work as a whole with the object of placing before the court the best expert evidence available; in the normal case the local laboratory can do all that is required, but it for any particular case questions arise which call for the services of a more highly skilled specialists than the laboratory possesses, it is the duty of the laboratory to call in that specialist from another laboratory, or in the last resort to advise the police to go outside the laboratory system. In hand writing cases, for example Dr. Harrison and is usually called in whenever the case occurs.

It would, however, be entirely wrong to allow an expert from one laboratory to appear for the prosecution, and an expert from another for the defence. The right doctrine on the subject is that enunciated in paragraph 433 of the report of the Committee on Detective Work and Procedure, namely that it is the duty of the staff of the laboratory, as it is the duty of the police, to present to the court all the material facts and that if the results of a laboratory examination made on behalf

of the police is not merely negative, but reveals information which may be of advantage to the defence, the result of the examination, if the prosecution proceeds, should be brought before the court by the police, or should be communicated to the defence with a view to their calling the evidence if they wish to do so.

It is true that the defence may find it difficult to deal with expert evidence unless they are themselves have the assistance of an expert so that council for the defence may be given such advice as he needs and may be able to cross-examine effectively.

It Is, however, difficult to see how the laboratories can assist in this way. All that can be expected of them is that they should report fairly and fully what they find and that their report should be available to the defence. The laboratories are not the only repositories of learning on forensic science; it is always open to the defence to obtain their own expert, and very often than they do so; where this is done, it is accepted practice that the laboratory gives this expert access to the material.

NON-FICTION FROM APS BOOKS
(www.andrewsparke.com)

Aramoana (Andrew Sparke)
Bella In The Wych-Elm (Andrew Sparke)
Croc Curry & Texas Tea: Surviving Nigeria (Paul Dickinson)
Istanbul: The Visitor Essentials (Andrew Sparke)
Magna Carta Wars Of Lincoln Cathedral (Andrew Sparke)
More Swings Than Roundabouts (John Wright)
Piggery Jokery In Tonga (Andrew Sparke)
Rear Gunner (Andrew Sparke)
Stutthof (Andrew Sparke)
The Devil's Cauldron (Pete Merrill)
The Strange Free-Fall Of Fred Ryland (Helen Pitt)
The Ways Of Mevagissey (Andrew Sparke)
War Shadows (Andrew Sparke)
What I Think About When I Think about Aikido (Mark Peckett)
Who Put Bella In The Wych Elm? Vol.1 The Crime Scene Revisited (Alex Merrill)